FOR DUMMIES
BESTSELLING
BOOK SERIES

Homeschooling For Dummies

P9-DOB-341

Cheat Sheet

Invaluable Web Sites

Hopping onto the Web is always more useful when you know where you're going and what you expect to find after you get there. These sites all offer solid educational material — some contain great articles worth reading, while others offer online lesson plans or other educational helps.

Site Name	Site Address	Why You Care
AOL@School	http://school.aol.com	K–12 lesson plans and resources
A to Z Home's Cool	www.gomilpitas.com/homeschooling	great resource site
EduPuppy	www.edupuppy.com	resources for Pre-K to 2nd grade
Eduscapes	www.eduscapes.com	in-depth, topical Web links for many subjects
Gateway to Educational Materials	www.thegateway.org	lesson plans; all subjects
HomeEducator.com	www.homeeducator.com	fantastic articles for homeschoolers
National Home Education Network	www.nhen.org	huge support group lists
Teach-nology	www.teach-nology.com	in-depth, science-oriented lesson helps

Calculating Grades

To determine a grade point average:

1. **Assign a point value to the final grade.**

   Generally A = 4, B = 3, C = 2, D = 1, and F = 0.

2. **Multiply the grade value by the amount of credit for that particular course.**

   This gives you the number of grade points for the course in question. (Course credits, also known as Carnegie Units, are covered in Chapter 9.) To make it easy for everyone, most courses equal one unit. This gives a one-semester course that was worth one credit a final point value of 4 (assuming your stellar student got an *A*.)

3. **Add all the grade points for the semester, year, or four years, depending on the span of time you want the grade average to reflect.**

   This gives you a total number of grade points. If our mythical stellar student takes two courses and gets an *A* and a *B*, the total grade points would be 7.

4. **Divide the grade point total by the total number of classes.**

   This gives you a grade-point average, otherwise known as a GPA. Your stellar student receives a GPA of 3.5 because 7 (the total grade points) divided by 2 (the number of classes taken) equals 3.5.

Homeschool Resource People

Use this section to record the names and phone numbers of local support group leaders, helpful people at your state homeschool association, or anyone else associated with homeschooling that you need to contact.

Name	Phone Number or E-mail Address	Position

Homeschooling For Dummies®

Cheat Sheet

Invaluable Newsletters and Magazines

When you want to read a homeschooling or educational periodical, where do you turn? These titles are a good example of the breadth available. Find a title that intrigues you and send away for a sample copy or hunt up the current issue at your local bookstore. Each of these titles caters to a slightly different clientele so you may need to peruse one or two before you find the one that suits your taste. Some of the periodicals listed here are designed specifically for homeschoolers, while others are written for children who aren't necessarily homeschooled but whose publishers and content embrace homeschooling.

Title	Readership	Address and/or Phone	Web Site
Al-Madrasah Al-Ula	Muslim Homeschoolers	MHSNR, P.O. Box 803, Attleboro, MA 02703; 508-226-1638	
AppleSeeds	Grade 2–4 history, social studies	800-821-0115	www.cobblestonepub.com
Ask	Grade 2–4 science, technology	800-821-0115	www.cobblestonepub.com
Boys Quest	Boys age 6–12	800-358-4732	www.boysquest.com
Calliope	Age 9–14 world history	800-821-0115	www.cobblestonepub.com;
The Catholic Home Educator	Catholic homeschoolers	P. O. Box 787, Montrose, AL 36559-0787	www.nache.org/che.html
Classical Homeschooling Magazine	Classical homeschoolers		www.classicalhomeschooling.com
Cobblestone	Age 9–14 American history	800-821-0115	www.cobblestonepub.com
Explore!	Ages 9–14 science/discovery	877-817-4395	www.exploremagazine.com
Faces	Age 9–14 world culture	800-821-0115	www.cobblestonepub.com
Footsteps	Age 9–14 African American history	800-821-0115	www.cobblestonepub.com
Growing Without Schooling	unschoolers	888-925-9235	www.holtgws.com/gws.htm
Home Education Magazine	inclusive homeschooling		www.home-ed-magazine.com
Homeschooling Today	Christian homeschoolers		www.homeschooltoday.com
Hopscotch	Girls age 6–12	800-358-4732	www.hopscotchmagazine.com
Jewish Home Educators Network	Jewish homeschoolers	2122 Houser, Holly, MI 48442	http://snj.com/jhen
Muse	Age 8–14 science, technology	800-821-0115	www.cobblestonepub.com
Odyssey	Age 9–14 science	800-821-0115	www.cobblestonepub.com

Copyright © 2002 Hungry Minds, Inc. All rights reserved.

Cheat Sheet $2.95 value. Item 0888-1.

For more information about Hungry Minds, call 1-800-762-2974.

For Dummies: Bestselling Book Series for Beginners

Homeschooling
FOR
DUMMIES®

Homeschooling FOR DUMMIES®

by Jennifer Kaufeld

Hungry Minds™

Best-Selling Books • Digital Downloads • e-Books • Answer Networks • e-Newsletters • Branded Web Sites • e-Learning

New York, NY ◆ Cleveland, OH ◆ Indianapolis, IN

Homeschooling For Dummies®

Published by:
Hungry Minds, Inc.
909 Third Avenue
New York, NY 10022
www.hungryminds.com
www.dummies.com

Library of Congress Control Number: 2001118279

ISBN: 0-7645-0888-1

Printed in the United States of America

10 9 8 7 6 5 4 3 2

1O/SY/RR/QR/IN

Distributed in the United States by Hungry Minds, Inc.

Distributed by CDG Books Canada Inc. for Canada; by Transworld Publishers Limited in the United Kingdom; by IDG Norge Books for Norway; by IDG Sweden Books for Sweden; by IDG Books Australia Publishing Corporation Pty. Ltd. for Australia and New Zealand; by TransQuest Publishers Pte Ltd. for Singapore, Malaysia, Thailand, Indonesia, and Hong Kong; by Gotop Information Inc. for Taiwan; by ICG Muse, Inc. for Japan; by Intersoft for South Africa; by Eyrolles for France; by International Thomson Publishing for Germany, Austria and Switzerland; by Distribuidora Cuspide for Argentina; by LR International for Brazil; by Galileo Libros for Chile; by Ediciones ZETA S.C.R. Ltda. for Peru; by WS Computer Publishing Corporation, Inc., for the Philippines; by Contemporanea de Ediciones for Venezuela; by Express Computer Distributors for the Caribbean and West Indies; by Micronesia Media Distributor, Inc. for Micronesia; by Chips Computadoras S.A. de C.V. for Mexico; by Editorial Norma de Panama S.A. for Panama; by American Bookshops for Finland.

For general information on Hungry Minds' products and services please contact our Customer Care department; within the U.S. at 800-762-2974, outside the U.S. at 317-572-3993 or fax 317-572-4002.

For sales inquiries and resellers information, including discounts, premium and bulk quantity sales and foreign language translations please contact our Customer Care department at 800-434-3422, fax 317-572-4002 or write to Hungry Minds, Inc., Attn: Customer Care department, 10475 Crosspoint Boulevard, Indianapolis, IN 46256.

For information on licensing foreign or domestic rights, please contact our Sub-Rights Customer Care department at 212-884-5000.

For information on using Hungry Minds' products and services in the classroom or for ordering examination copies, please contact our Educational Sales department at 800-434-2086 or fax 317-572-4005.

Please contact our Public Relations department at 212-884-5163 for press review copies or 212-884-5000 for author interviews and other publicity information or fax 212-884-5400.

For authorization to photocopy items for corporate, personal, or educational use, please contact Copyright Clearance Center, 222 Rosewood Drive, Danvers, MA 01923, or fax 978-750-4470.

Hungry Minds™ is a trademark of Hungry Minds, Inc.

About the Author

Between homeschooling the Kaufeld brood of two, reviewing educational software and technology for homeschoolers, and trying to catch up on much-missed sleep, Jennifer Kaufeld keeps plenty busy. She also spends many hours suggesting curriculum options to new homeschoolers who don't know where to look or who teach special-needs children.

Quiet days find her working on the never-ending, family-photo scrapbooks or showing one of the children how to fashion tissue-paper flowers. You may even find her playing a board game with the children. Between speaking engagements where she talks about technology and education, and crafting articles for *Homeschooling Today,* a national home education magazine, as well as other local and regional publications, Jennifer doesn't see many quiet days.

Jennifer's other books for Hungry Minds include *America Online For Dummies Quick Reference,* 6th Edition, and *Your Official America Online Guide To Internet Living.*

Jennifer lives in Fort Wayne, Indiana, with her husband, two children, and Sea Monkeys — the only pet she's found that doesn't die in the tank or mess the carpets. You can reach her on America Online, where she goes by the screen name *Homeschooler* (homeschooler@aol.com).

Dedication

To all those families throughout the United States and the world, both past and present, who courageously took whatever steps they needed to strengthen their families and show love to their children. I salute you, as do all those who currently homeschool in hopes of achieving that same end. You paved the way.

Author's Acknowledgments

After the book is safely off my desk, I get to finish the fun parts, like the acknowledgments. This is where I thank all those people who work together to pull a project like this off. While my name may appear on the cover, a special note of thanks goes to all the people whose names grace the Publisher's Acknowledgements page, without them this book would still be in my computer.

First and foremost, my project editor, Tonya Maddox, deserves both chocolate and kudos — unless a nice, long vacation sounds better. Tonya kept an eye on the book and guided it into being — no small task in itself. When we got down to the wire and found ourselves over page count (fancy that?) she stretched the limits of creativity to make as many words fit as possible. Thanks, Tonya! Working with you on my first noncomputer book was a pleasure.

Special thanks goes to Craig Young, my tireless editor at *Homeschooling Today* (and fellow homeschooler), who also agreed to act as the technical reviewer for this book. Little did he know what he signed up for! You've been a joy to work with for several years, and this project was no different. Thank you.

Thanks also to acquisitions editor Roxane Cerda who found herself with this project halfway through, yet still burned the midnight oil to ensure that everything was in place for a smooth launch.

Finally, a hearty thank you to my husband, John, who tirelessly manned the grill for several weeks so I could finish the book on time, gave encouragement when I most needed it, and even took over the end-of-the-year homeschooling duties. And of course, a big thanks to Joey and Becky, the research subjects who gave rise to the experiences that pepper these pages. Time for another lunch at Chuck E. Cheese, guys! (Unless, of course, one of Daddy's grilled steaks sounds more appetizing.)

Publisher's Acknowledgments

We're proud of this book; please register your comments through our IDG Books Worldwide Online Registration Form located at http://my2cents.dummies.com.

Some of the people who helped bring this book to market include the following:

Acquisitions, Editorial, and Media Development

Project Editor: Tonya Maddox

Acquisitions Editors: Roxane Cerda, Susan L. Decker

Copy Editors: Corey Dalton, Esmeralda St. Clair

Technical Editor: Craig Young

Editorial Manager: Jennifer Ehrlich

Media Development Manager: Laura VanWinkle

Editorial Assistant: Melissa Bennett

Cover Photos: © FPG/Getty Images

Production

Project Coordinator: Maridee Ennis

Layout and Graphics: LeAndra Johnson, Jackie Nicholas, Brent Savage, Jacque Schneider, Betty Schulte, Julie Trippetti, Erin Zeltner

Proofreaders: Valery Bourke, Susan Moritz, Angel Perez

Indexer: TECHBOOKS Production Services

Hungry Minds Consumer Reference Group

Business: Kathleen Nebenhaus, Vice President and Publisher; Kevin Thornton, Acquisitions Manager

Cooking/Gardening: Jennifer Feldman, Associate Vice President and Publisher; Anne Ficklen, Executive Editor; Kristi Hart, Managing Editor

Education/Reference: Diane Graves Steele, Vice President and Publisher

Lifestyles: Kathleen Nebenhaus, Vice President and Publisher; Tracy Boggier, Managing Editor

Pets: Kathleen Nebenhaus, Vice President and Publisher; Tracy Boggier, Managing Editor

Travel: Michael Spring, Vice President and Publisher; Brice Gosnell, Publishing Director; Suzanne Jannetta, Editorial Director

Hungry Minds Consumer Editorial Services: Kathleen Nebenhaus, Vice President and Publisher; Kristin A. Cocks, Editorial Director; Cindy Kitchel, Editorial Director

Hungry Minds Consumer Production: Debbie Stailey, Production Director

Contents at a Glance

Cartoons at a Glance

By Rich Tennant

"I think what you mean, dear, is a 'magnetic' storm."

page 7

page 295

"Okay - mommy's going off now to build a Boeing B-29 Superfortress. You kids behave or I'll bring my rivet gun home with me."

page 311

page 181

page 251

"I SUPPOSE THIS ALL HAS SOMETHING TO DO WITH THE NEW MATH."

page 107

"...and remember, no more German tongue twisters until you know the language better."

page 51

Cartoon Information:
Fax: 978-546-7747
E-Mail: richtennant@the5thwave.com
World Wide Web: www.the5thwave.com

Table of Contents

Introduction

Welcome to the adventure called homeschooling!

Teaching your children at home is a rewarding and engaging way to spend your time. You relearn cutting and pasting skills if you teach kindergarten, and you review algebra facts right along with your high school student. No matter what age your student happens to be, you find yourself learning and relearning right along with your child. If you tutor your children all the way through high school, you look up one day to realize that you just relived the academic portion of your high school years — doing it one-on-one makes school time less stressful for everybody.

About This Book

Whether you're just about to embark on the home education journey, you already have a few years under your belt, or you're interested in learning about this home teaching thing that your family member or friend pursues, *Homeschooling For Dummies* is your hands-on guide. These pages explain the intricacies of homeschooling in plain English and show you that you can do it too, if you decide that homeschooling meets your family's needs.

Knowing you picked up this book tells me who you are. You, of course, knew who you were all along. I'm the one who has to figure it out, and this is what I came up with so far:

- ✔ This phenomenon called *homeschooling* interests you and you want to find out more about it.

- ✔ You are thinking about teaching your children at home, you already teach your children at home, or you may know someone who does.

- ✔ This book is the answer to your search for an understandable guide that you can hand to concerned-but-loving grandparents, siblings, and friends because you already homeschool.

- ✔ You may have a computer at home with Internet access (because most homeschoolers around the country do). Or you may not. Either way, you can use this book because it was written with you in mind.

- ✔ Words such as *unschooling, classical education,* and *portfolio* reverberate in your mind like a half-understood foreign language.

If any of this strikes a familiar chord, then this book is for you.

Conventions Used in This Book

For the most part, this book reads exactly like any other: Words progress from left to right, sentences begin with capital letters, and so on. No surprises there, thank goodness. You may want to be aware of a couple additional features, however, as you read. They're designed to help you get the most out of this book.

Many pages contain an icon in the margin that points to important information. Icons save you the time and energy it takes to use your handy underlining pen. The following section about icons shows you the individual icons and tells you what they mean.

In other sections of the book, you may find words *in italics* or **in bold type**. These words tell you what to type into an Internet search engine if you want to find certain homeschooling information on the Web. For example, using **homeschool magazine** as a search term should give you most (if not all) the homeschool newsletters and magazines that maintain their own Web sites, plus a few miscellaneous discussions about the pros and cons of homeschooling magazines in general. (Don't you love the Internet?)

How This Book Is Organized

This book is divided into a number of sections. Each part concentrates on a specific segment of homeschooling. You can read the sections in order, if you want, or simply read the part that applies to your needs and questions right now and save the rest for later.

Part 1: Heading to Homeschooling

This section answers the questions that most people new to homeschooling ask, such as: Is it legal? How do I get started? And of course, the biggie: What about socialization? This is the place to start if you stand on the verge of homeschooling your own children or if the concept of parents teaching their kids at home is a new one to you.

Part II: Tackling Kids of Any Age

Certain ages require different handling. Just as you wouldn't hand your high schooler a pacifier, you also don't give your kindergartner a science textbook and ask her to regurgitate facts ad nauseam. This part discusses homeschooling from various age points — taking into consideration the growth that children show as they move from stage to stage.

Part III: Choosing Your Cornerstone: Basic Curriculum Options

Every parent who teaches a child at home chooses a particular teaching philosophy, whether she knows it or not. This section explains most of the teaching options available today and those terms that you may have heard floating around on homeschool day at the local library. Dip in here when you find your ideas about education changing, and you'll probably find a theory to hang your hat on.

Part IV: Nailing Down the Details

Homeschooling requires attention to plenty of individual elements. From ideas that help you keep a lid on your costs to organization in your homeschool, this section addresses the concerns that nag at you until you discover an answer. If you already homeschool, but you find that your books are everywhere and feel like a lone ranger in a hostile world, this is a section for you.

Part V: Making Your Year Sing with Extras

Step outside the educational boundaries of math, language arts, science, and social studies and have some fun! When you add in the extras, such as music, art, museums, and television shows, you create a whole learning environment for your child that reaches beyond the boundaries of books. Pick the ones that appeal to you (no one tries to do them *all*) and incorporate them into your school days as a change of pace or to introduce a whole different way of learning.

Part VI: The Part of Tens

What would a *For Dummies* book be without the Part of Tens? This section gives you the heads up on the most common objections you're likely to hear and the fears that assail us all. When you want a quick list of useful computer programs or ideas for general resources for your homeschool, this is the place to turn.

Part VII: Appendixes

This set of appendixes hold the information that wouldn't fit anywhere else. Here you find a glossary of educational terms that you may run up against as a homeschooler (but that I didn't talk about anywhere else in the book). Also, look here for a list of homeschool organizations by state and a quick glance through available resources for home education.

The Cast of Icons

Throughout the book, you see a collection of handy icons in the margins. While they manage to make the pages look cool as you flip through, they also perform a useful function. They mark information that you want to note for one reason or another.

Beginning homeschoolers need to know more than the basics. They want to see a working example of how homeschooling looks in real life. This icon gives you a glimpse into the daily life of a homeschooler, usually me. Browse through the paragraphs attached to these icons when you need a reminder that teaching your kids at home isn't always a bowl of chocolate ice cream (although whatever the current crisis, you usually find yourself laughing about it later). These icons mark real life in action: the frustrating parts as well as the huggable ones.

This icon saves you from tying strings around your fingers to help you recall information as you read. This icon sits next to a paragraph that you may need later, and it makes the section a little easier to find the next time you need it.

This icon makes your life easier. It may mark a handy resource you should be aware of, a shortcut that saves you time, or a tidbit of knowledge born of experience. These icons mark the places you may want to highlight so you can find them later.

Think: Danger, Will Robinson! When you see this icon, tread carefully. While nothing in this book causes your computer hard drive to crash or the dog to eat your brand new science textbook, these icons do remind you to pay attention. Some icons point out information that the general public doesn't know, but you need to be aware of. Other icons mark information that can change depending on which state you live in.

Jump In — the Water's Fine!

Because *Homeschooling For Dummies,* like all *For Dummies* books, is divided into easily managed sections, you don't actually have to start reading at Chapter 1 if you don't want to. Diving into the middle of the book is great — especially if it contains the information that you need right now. How you read the book is up to you. Read it from front to back, back to front (a little more difficult, but still manageable), or start in the middle and go from there. This decision, like almost every other one in homeschooling, is entirely up to you.

No matter how you decide to digest the book, dive right in — a wealth of information, ideas, and other tidbits await you.

Part I

Heading to Homeschooling

The 5th Wave   By Rich Tennant

"I think what you mean, dear, is a 'magnetic' storm."

In this part . . .

Sometimes you know where you're going when you begin a journey. You're headed to the store down the road to pick up a jar of that snazzy, new, peanut butter that promises all the taste with none of the calories. (Get me a jar too, would you?)

Other trips start out with more of an experience in mind than a final destination. Maybe you know that you want to retrace the steps of the soldiers that fought in the American Revolution, and you have three weeks to do it. Your adventure then encompasses a fluid destination plan that changes with the weather (especially because standing on the village green in the rain qualifies as a *no fun* activity). You know where you want to begin, you have a particular time limit in mind, and you know where you need to end up. How you get there and the amount of time that you take per attraction, however, is pretty much up to you.

Homeschooling is more like a revolutionary vacation than a trip to the local grocery store. You begin at a certain point (which may or may not correspond to a particular grade level), and you progress from there. Your final goal may be spring of the fifth-grade year, the beginning of ninth grade, or even high school graduation. How you reach this destination is up to you.

This part starts you out on the journey. It tackles the beginning questions and those steps that take you from the first realization that you want to teach your children yourself to finding your state law and its take on home education. It also touches on beginning to homeschool and the much-anticipated socialization aspect along the way.

Grab your map and sunglasses. The time to head to the homeschool frontier is now.

Chapter 1

Answering the Big Questions

. . . .

In This Chapter

▶ Thinking about homeschooling

▶ Knowing it all — or not?

▶ Affording the adventure

▶ Schooling as long as you like

. . . .

*P*erhaps you just found out that your best friend intends to homeschool his children next year, and you want to know more. Maybe you're thinking of pulling your children out of the local school and want to know about your options. You may be a veteran homeschooler who always taught from the textbooks and now want to add different subjects or unique learning opportunities into your day. Maybe you've heard one particular term over and over, such as "unschooling," and want to know more about it.

Whatever your reasons for picking up this book, start here if you want to begin at the beginning. This chapter answers those big questions that are uppermost in almost every new homeschooler's mind. (The other big question, socialization, gets a chapter of its own later in Part I.) Find a comfortable chair, settle in, and begin your journey into the world of home education.

Getting to This Point

Stunned, you look up one morning over your cup of coffee. How did you get from a perfectly happy public or private school parent to someone contemplating homeschooling? When did the feeling begin to dawn on you that you weren't ready to send your bundle of preschool joy out into the school world, and you also aren't entirely sure he's ready to go, either?

You may be tired of spending four hours on homework after your child returns from a full day at school. After all, they have to be learning *something* after spending all day in that building! Re-teaching the skills at night to a child who passed the daytime hours at school is exhausting and frustrating for both you and your child. You're both tired, you want to get the work done and out of the way, and you may even quietly resent the intrusion into what used to be your family time.

Maybe the escalated violence in elementary, middle, and high schools worries you. You hear reports of guns and knives in school, police patrolling the halls, and you want to ensure (as best as you can) that your children remain safe. Or violence may have already touched your community, and you feel the need to react in a positive way while you still have time.

Perhaps you see your family values, traditions, and religious beliefs lessening as your child spends more and more time in an institutional setting, and this bothers you. Children function best from a strong foundation, which is hard to build when they spend six to eight hours per day outside a parent's care while they're still young. Parents see amazing changes even after bringing high school students who clash with their family's values into homeschooling, but building the foundation when they're young is easiest. In this case, home-schooling builds (or rebuilds) strong families, which in turn provides balanced adults for society.

Although, a few years ago, faith-based families couldn't always find home-school materials designed to augment their teaching, today, Christian, Jewish, and Muslim homeschoolers, as well as homeschoolers of other faiths can locate tradition-specific homeschooling materials through their own faith communities or on the Internet.

Your child's lack of academic progress may concern you. As every parent knows, each child develops in her own time and in her own way. School materials are designed for the mythical middle-of-the-road child who learns certain skills at certain times. If your child fits outside the mold, she may fall behind in classes or show signs of stress. Pulling this child out of public or private school and teaching her at home takes the pressure off and allows you to spend as much time as necessary working through specific subjects or skills.

Perhaps family work or activity schedules clash irreparably with school schedules. Although not the most common reason for homeschooling, this is certainly as valid as any of the others. If one parent travels several months of the year or a family business or passion, such as stage or athletic performing skews your weekly schedule, then homeschooling may prove to be the optimal solution for your family. It allows you to be together, do what you need to do, and still meet your state's educational requirements.

No matter what your reasons are for wishing to homeschool your children, if they center around what's best for your family right now, then your reasons are valid and worth pursuing. Home education is all about meeting your child's needs. If the school no longer meets those needs, and you're willing to take the plunge and give it a try, then you may find homeschooling a perfect fit.

Knowing Not to Know It All

No one knows it all, not even the teachers in the schools. Many schools assign teachers to lead classes on subjects they were never even trained to teach. At the beginning of a school year, these teachers, scrambling as much as anyone else, read the teacher's manuals to determine what in the world fifth-grade science is all about.

You don't need to know it all. You come to homeschooling with certain strengths and specialties. The topics you love and those things you do well become natural subjects in your homeschool. If you love to cook, for example, home economics class becomes an effortless and fun way to spend close teaching time with your children in the kitchen while passing on something that excites you. There's a good chance that they'll learn to cook well, too, as they catch your excitement and internalize it.

In the beginning, until you develop a support network of other families with specialties of their own, you teach what you know and use teacher's manuals or library books for the rest. If your children are older, you can even turn them loose in the library to research a subject that you know nothing about and then ask your students to report back to you after they learn about it. This way, you both learn something new.

With a good textbook in your hand or a sound idea of what you want to teach or learn and access to a decent public library (almost every community has a good library these days), a homeschool parent learns alongside the student. Most homeschoolers, after three or so years teaching the kids at their houses, say, "I had no idea I'd learn so much along with them!"

After you meet a group of homeschool families who have children roughly the ages of yours, a natural networking begins to take place. You may offer to teach cooking to a group of kids (boys as well as girls) whose parents think that the family can opener is a prized possession. In return, if you don't know a bass clef from a quarter note, another homeschool parent may be willing to hold an introductory music class for the group. By joining together and sharing skills, nobody needs to know it all. You spend less time fussing over the teacher's manual, and you still get it all done.

Affording It

The truth doesn't always make good news stories. News media relies on the sensational and the bizarre, while normal, run-of-the-mill life generally doesn't qualify as news. Recent homeschool media stories that tout homeschooling as expensive, elitist, and only for the wealthy are simply not true. The truth, which is that anyone can homeschool for nearly free if they need to, doesn't make splashy headlines.

Many people manage to homeschool their children for about $300 per child, per year on the average or less. Some swing it on $300 per family. A few manage to teach for nearly free, but they're the truly dedicated bargain shoppers. Three hundred dollars per child, per year is a good round figure for estimation because you can get a good number of books, supplies, and even a few extra goodies for that amount. Now, opting for a $300 budget means that your child won't be using the coolest, newest whizbang textbooks for every subject, but it also means that you can provide a more-than-adequate education.

Set a budget for homeschooling supplies at the beginning of the year, but remember that you're bound to pick up some fun stuff along the way. So include that in your estimates. Setting up a reasonable budget can give you realistic boundaries while also letting you know that you can do this. Keep in mind that preschool and kindergarten are relatively cheap educational years. After you stockpile construction paper, glue, crayons, kiddy scissors, and some read aloud books, you're most of the way there.

As you rise through the ranks, however, books get more and more expensive, until you reach the high school level where a new science book may cost you $60 or more. With more than one child, however, your costs go down every time the next child in line uses that $60 book. Planning a $60 purchase when three children can use the book in turn gives you a sturdy text for $20 per child in the long run.

When you think about pulling your child out of a private or public school system, don't forget to consider all the items that you currently pay for that will become irrelevant, such as

- ✔ Book rentals
- ✔ Club fees
- ✔ School lunches
- ✔ Tuition (for private school)

You can apply that money to the extra costs that you now have, such as textbooks and lunches at home. Parents are often amazed at the amount of extra money they pour into the "free" school system when they sit down to total the funds they send for this project or that one. Even clothing costs take a dive when you realize that you can homeschool in your sweats and no longer need school-appropriate clothes for each day of the week.

If you opt for low-cost or almost free homeschooling, you find yourself trading time and energy for the money you'd normally spend on curriculum. Trips to the library take time; you may spend hours writing math practice sheets for your first grader or searching for them on the Web so you can print them out. Buying the books you need for the whole year saves you time and gas, but it means you need to fork over the money to pay for the books yourself *and* find a place to store them in your home. Chapter 19 covers cost-cutting measures in depth.

On the other hand, families can spend as much as they like on homeschooling. I know at least one family that considers homeschooling as their major spending hobby, and they have plenty of money to spend. Such a family may drop $2,000 per child, per year on homeschooling, but to do that you need to work really hard and purchase the most expensive curriculums that you can find.

Look for curriculum ideas and resources throughout this book. Also glance through Appendix A for more options. Although I could fill a 700-page book with nothing but recommendations for books and kits that you can use to teach with, I don't have that many pages. As I mention various teaching methods, age groups, and so on, I also try to throw in a few products or books that you may want to look at if you want to pursue that particular topic.

If you purchase everything mentioned in this book, you'll easily top the $2,000-per-child marker. No homeschool family does all this. For one thing, people only have 24 hours per day, and trying to follow all these systems and add-ons would take many times that.

Hanging In There

When you first jump into homeschooling, the question nags at you: How long can I keep this up? Another question that sometimes rankles is: How long will the educational establishment allow me to do this? Because these are two different questions, they need varying answers.

Signing up for the long haul

When your child spends her days in a home where she's loved, cared for, and guided to knowledge, she's in the best possible place. If you truly have her best interests at heart (and what parent doesn't?) then you'll ensure that she learns to read and add. Even more importantly than that, through day-in-day-out contact with you, she'll pick up on your values and priorities. No longer at the whim of this year's teacher, you have the freedom to teach your homeschooler the values that you want her to carry through life her.

Even if you miss something along the way, your child will grow to be a productive, useful adult. He can always pick up a community college course in the subject later if it proves to be extremely important to daily life. I know it's hard to believe, but many balanced, rational people came from educational systems that offered no weekly art class. (If you love art, and your child loves art, then structure it as a course in your homeschool. Your child will survive, however, if he learns everything but art appreciation.)

With the energy and assurance that comes from knowing that you're doing what's best for your family, you can homeschool until and even through college. Although many parents are ready for their children to spread their wings and fly a bit after high school and encourage their fledglings to seek schooling or work outside the nest, some situations encourage you to home-school even through college. I have a little 8-year-old friend who will probably be ready for college courses by the time she's 11 or 12. In a case such as this, college at home is the best possible solution — after all, she needs to pursue some type of schooling until age 16 (according to her state's education law), and where do you go after completing calculus when you're 12?

Just because you *can* homeschool through high school, of course, doesn't mean that you *have* to. Many families pull their children out of school for one or two years to help them over a tough academic or social spot. Then, after the problem is corrected and the student reads at grade level again or the sticky social situation irons out, they send their child back to school. The bottom line is doing what's best for your student. If he only needs a year away from the school routine to catch up, and you're comfortable sending him back after that year is over, send him! You may find, however, that after a year or two at home, he really doesn't want to return, and you don't want him to go. That's okay, too.

Most families take teaching one year at a time even after they homeschool several years. Those who find that homeschooling enhances family life and family schedules tend to stick with it the longest. We spent several years homeschooling during a time that the kids' dad traveled much of the time with his job. Because of our flexibility, we could periodically pack the schoolbooks in the middle of the fall, winter, or spring and go with Daddy to a conference. After we arrived in the conference city, I would cover school in the hotel room during the early mornings, and we would take advantage of local museums, parks, city fountains, and pools for the rest of the day.

Staying at home forever

The United States allows you to teach at home as many or as few years as you want to, no matter what state you live in. Although each of the 50 states publishes its own requirements for homeschoolers, none of them says that you can only teach between this year and that one. You can begin homeschooling in preschool and continue through college if you want to, although most home-schoolers begin homeschooling after their child has been in public or private school or place their children in public or private school after their child has been in homeschool. Parents often pull their children out of a public or private school because something isn't working. Or, if they begin homeschooling in the preschool years, they may opt to send their children to public or private high school. Few families homeschool all the way through the first four years of college.

Look for chapters that cover various homeschooling ages in Part II.

Breaking the News to Mom

The parents in your life, whether they are actually your parents, favorite aunts and uncles, or close friends who function in a guiding role for you, *always* have something to say when you announce a major lifestyle change. Sometimes they're for the change; other occasions tend to spark less-than-positive responses. Although they usually mean it in love, negative reactions from those around you tend to derail you if you aren't ready for them. Be prepared — when you announce that you're thinking of homeschooling your children, someone will probably give you flack.

Before you respond, take a moment to consider whether a person is having a knee-jerk reaction because you threaten to go against time-honored United States culture (at least for the past hundred years or so) or does this person voice well-grounded objections? If you truly believe this is the best course for your family members today, you need to proceed forward in the face of negative reactions.

Part of the reason for the confused looks you see may be that the people around you have no experience with homeschooling. If you're the first person they know who suggests it, they have no other information to draw on except what they read in the papers — which may or may not be complimentary or even true, depending on the article's author. Parents and the other role models in your life need good, solid information that assures them that you aren't off your rocker.

This book gives you the ammunition you need to discuss homeschooling rationally. In fact, you can even hand a copy to your mom, if you like. In a little less than 30 chapters, this book talks about all the major homeschooling movements, educational needs of children at various age levels, and even includes chapters on adding zing to your school days.

When you discuss your decision with your mom, tell her what you know. Homeschoolers do get into college if they choose to go, they aren't afraid to play outside or make friends, and today's homeschoolers have many, many activities to choose from in addition to time at home with the books. If you have already decided on a teaching approach (such as classical curriculum, unschooling, or operating as a satellite school, which are all discussed later in this book), tell her about it. Tell her why you chose this method over all the others. In short, share your enthusiasm and hope.

She may not agree with you at first, but time will probably prove your decision to be a sound one. When we began homeschooling I worked with a nonverbal, almost-3-year-old. Seven years later, he speaks his native language fluently (itself a huge accomplishment for him and for us, his parents), he reads insatiably, he knows how to operate a computer (as well as enter all the secret codes for the game Rogue Squadron), his handwriting is more than legible when he wants it to be, and he's completely at home with adults and children. So far, I'd say we're doing a pretty good job with homeschooling!

When we announced that we planned to homeschool, even our friends — not to mention our family members — thought we'd lost it. Ten years ago, home-schooling was much less common than it is today. (Some of the people who are close to us still think we're wackos, in spite of the evidence provided by two well-adjusted children. Oh well, there's no accounting for some people's opinions.)

Time and perseverance brought most people around. I don't talk much about what we do, although I do issue blanket invitations from time to time. Any family members or friends who want to see what a homeschool day is like are welcome to follow us around the house for a day or two to get a taste of it. I did that with a friend before I homeschooled, and it was a valuable experience that quelled quite a few of my own fears.

Of course, my homeschool day won't look like yours because I don't live with your family. However, there's value in seeing how anyone operates outside what our culture would call the mainstream. Seeing that we use textbooks for a few classes calmed several anxious hearts. I don't know why this was a big deal to them, but it was.

Chapter 2

Taking the Leap

So you're thinking about leaping into homeschooling. The excitement of a new life decision always brings some jitters with it. Although the idea of homeschooling intrigues you, a few questions may still nag at the back of your mind. For one thing, what exactly does an adventure like this involve? When is the best time to begin?

All these concerns work themselves out as you live home education day by day, but it's nice to receive some answers and reassurance before you begin. This chapter addresses the issues that may arise as you consider making the decision to homeschool — issues that range from why you want to homeschool in the first place to the pros and cons of homework. Look for information on more involved issues, such as specific curriculums, in Chapters 11 through 15 and where to locate a copy of your state law in Chapter 4.

Realizing That Anger Is Not Enough

Why do you want to homeschool? What propels you in this decision to alter your lifestyle so drastically from that of your neighbors? People have as many reasons to homeschool their children as there are homeschoolers. Sometimes more than one main reason makes you decide to take the plunge into home education.

Homeschooling needs to be your main educational option for the right reasons. Getting mad over what the teacher said to Sonny won't give you the inner strength that you need to continue teaching on those days when homeschooling lacks appeal. What will you do when you wake up and the anger is gone? Sending your child back to school proves that you removed him in anger. On the other hand, continuing with a program that you no longer believe in makes everybody miserable.

Ensuring educational excellence

Perhaps you aren't entirely sure that your child is getting what she needs at the local school. Maybe you watch her bring home page after page of review material that you know she mastered some time last year. She may tell tales of how boring school is, what little she learns, or the last time she corrected the teacher.

Does this mean your school system is awful? Nope. It simply means that your child happens to be beyond whatever the classroom is currently covering — even if her class is at her "correct" grade level. Look at it this way: Even the best introduction to a biology course bores someone with a doctorate in biology. It may be a good course, but the successful doctoral candidate took that class long ago and now thinks far beyond its introductory limitations.

Many parents decide to homeschool for educational excellence. They see a difference between the best private schools in their community and the public schools their children attend, and they bring their children home in an effort to bridge that gap. You can homeschool for much less than the $3,000 per year (a conservative figure) that a good private school costs, and the result can be much the same if you follow the classical curriculums most prep schools cover. (Read more about expenses in Chapter 19; see more about classical education in Chapter 12.)

Meeting your child's special needs

Sometimes the school system simply fails to meet your child's needs. If your child slips through the cracks and misses too much information, he falls farther and farther behind. Before you know it, the school wants him to undertake remedial work in an effort to make up lost time.

This situation is so frustrating for parents! You send them to school in the hope that the establishment will teach them what they need to know. By the time you find out there's a problem, though, it may be months after the issue reaches an almost critical stage.

Bringing a child like this home rescues him from the condemnation he feels at school. This alone often relieves enough stress so that your child can concentrate and make up the work with a patient parent sitting alongside. It's not unusual for a parent and student to wing through one to two years' worth of lessons in a school year and catch the student up to his current grade level.

If you rescue your child from an emotionally stressful or failure-ridden school year, he may need some time to unwind and get used to his new daily surroundings. Your best bet is to relax, take it slow, and give him some time. Think of it this way: If you bring him home in December and only get a couple months' of quality learning in before the end of the year, that's two more months than he was going to get in the classroom, right?

You can read about more specific special needs in Chapter 16.

Retaining religious convictions

If your child's new language and altered values horrify you, and you see them in direct opposition to what you carefully teach at home, you certainly aren't alone. Parents of all faiths are pulling their children out of the public schools to teach them at home, precisely because they want those early foundations to stay solid. It's hard to compete when your child stays away from you for six hours a day. Bringing them home to school allows you to gently reintroduce and reinforce those values and traditions that guide your life.

Homeschooling your child for religious reasons gives you several options. You can

- **Locate tradition-specific curriculum.** You may even be able to find a complete curriculum from science to history tailored to your particular belief system.

- **Incorporate religious instruction into your day as part of your class structure.** Use religious or secular materials for all subjects as you choose. If you select secular books, this means tacking an additional subject — religion — onto your day along with your state's requirements, but if you homeschool your children for religious reasons this won't be a big deal to you.

You may find that you need to alter adult materials or group curriculum, but as more people in your tradition begin to homeschool, your community will respond with materials written for you. I keep a shelf full of books that outline the theology, history, and events that I want my children to know. Because these are all written at an adult level, it will be some time before they read them, but I add a volume to my shelf as I locate it.

Accommodating family lifestyle

Sometimes lifestyle itself dictates a need to homeschool. If you work at odd times of the year and find yourself free and sitting at home alone while your children sit through classes wishing they were with you, you may find homeschool a great timesaver in the long run. It allows you to pursue family activities, such as vacations and hobbies, when work is light or concentrate your teaching time during off months and give the children a vacation while you're occupied.

Parents who follow other than nine-to-five jobs that incorporate much travel, public appearances, or endless conferences may want to look at homeschooling as an option. It gives you the chance to spend time with your children no matter where you are. When you travel, the children can go with you whenever you set out and take their schoolwork along — my kids think that hotel rooms come with desks specifically for them.

My children have a mom and dad who are both professional authors. Full-time writing creates a whole different lifestyle for those who pursue it. When we work, we work long and hard. On the other hand, when we have no deadlines, we're completely free to do whatever we want with no restrictions. We can travel, spend the day at the park during the week, or go sledding at the mention of the idea. Homeschooling works perfectly for us because it gives us the flexibility to take our vacations at odd times of the year between books, teach the children (who sit at a large table right outside our office door), and live life as a family instead of a group of humans doing (as opposed to humans being).

Determining What's Best For Your Family

This is *your* family. These are the people you live with. The ones you love best. When you look at all the educational options available, you need to consider your family's needs. Perhaps you'll find that homeschooling is truly the best solution for your family.

Perhaps the idea of working together appeals to you. You're willing to sacrifice where you need to so that the greater need is met. You want to take control of your children's education, to watch them learn and guide them into maturity. And even more importantly, this interests you enough that you're willing to make it a long-term goal whether "long-term" means this year or twelve years.

Okay, so you decide that homeschooling will be best for your family with child number one. What about child number two? Does it follow that you'll reach the same educational conclusions?

Not really. Even within a family, each child is completely different. What's best for one may not be best for all or even most. When you look at your family as a unit, you may find that the answers for each child differ. But that's okay.

You're looking for the optimal solution for your own family. Although it may seem strange, sometimes what's best actually means homeschooling one or two children and sending the rest to public or private school. That way, everybody's needs get met.

Most families who homeschool do teach all their children at home at once, but you aren't most families. You are you, with your family, your needs, and your strengths. If you look at educational options with your whole family in mind, it lowers your stress level in the long run. Then you don't have to wonder whether you made the right decision for this child or that one. You know.

Creating Solutions for Special Situations

Parents with special situations often feel trapped when they think about their children and education. Maybe you work full time and truly can't afford to quit. Perhaps you're a single parent. (If you are, I applaud your dedication and efforts!) Perchance your child is a special needs learner.

Special situations require some imagination and a little extra determination, but you can homeschool if you truly believe this is the best thing for your family. If you don't think this is best for your brood, why go through the effort? Keep things the way they are and watch for any signs of social, educational, or emotional deterioration in your children.

Working around your job

If you want to work homeschooling into your unusual situation, be aware that some of the solutions look rather unconventional. Some parents who work full time take their children with them to the office. Then everybody completes his or her tasks at the same time. The children do their schoolwork with your oversight, you do your office work, and everybody's happy. This functions especially well when the parent works out of the home.

Other parents schedule homeschooling in the evening instead of during the day. The children are usually up late, sleep in each morning, and have their free time while the parent is at work. Then the parent returns home and spends the two or so hours necessary to guide the students each evening, leaving them with any additional reading or projects to do the next day. This option really cuts into family evening free time, but parents make it happen when they want to.

If your family tends to function as night owls, you may find yourself teaching at night even if everyone stays home during the day. One of the perks of homeschooling is that you can usually teach whenever your children are most alert, so if they pay attention the best between the hours of 10 p.m. and midnight, pour yourself some extra-caffeinated coffee and go for it. (In rare instances, your state law might stipulate that you need to teach between the hours of such and such, but most states do not. See Appendix B for homeschool associations.)

Dealing with special learners

Parents of special needs students rarely settle into middle ground. Instead, they generally fall into two camps:

- ✔ Those who can't wait to bring their children home because they certainly couldn't do a worse job with their child's education.
- ✔ Those who worry that taking a special needs child from the school setting would deprive her of the extra resources she needs.

One on one

If you think you couldn't do any more educational harm, then you're already on the right track. Special education instructors mean well, and many of them certainly work hard at what they do, but no one can take the place of a child's parent. No one can care as much about that child as you do simply because no one loves her as much as you do.

Trying to teach a large group of special needs students — all of which usually have completely different physical and learning needs — is an educational nightmare. Mind you, it can be enjoyable, but meeting everybody's needs at the same time is difficult. Incorporate the special needs children into a regular classroom and the situation becomes even worse — now you have someone who was never trained to reach these children trying to teach them and 24 others at the same time.

Homeschooling brings education back to one-on-one tutoring, which is what special needs education was supposed to be in the first place. In a homeschool, you have your own children, who are used to dealing with each other, and you, who is used to working with them. You can schedule your day so you work with only one at a time, or if you have more than one child, you can arrange to work with two or more at once. It's completely up to you.

Continuing therapy

If you have a special needs learner, then you're already used to the specialist roundup. Physical therapist, occupational therapist, speech therapist, resource room teacher, medical specialists — sometimes they become almost like family because you see them so often. With time, you learn the jargon and even some of the solutions.

Getting special needs resources as a homeschooler often depends on the school system you belong to. Some systems provide therapists to home-schooled children as a matter of course; other systems provide the services if you fight for them. Still others deny all homeschool children special needs services even though portions of our taxes pay for those services.

One option when you homeschool is to continue whatever therapy sessions she previously attended on your own. Although speech therapy functions a little differently, physical and occupational therapists usually work on one goal for an extended period of time. Physical and occupational therapists use exercises specifically designed to reach that goal, whether it's flexibility, relaxation, or muscle toning. If you know your therapists already, they may feel comfortable working with you on a consulting basis. You work on the exercises during the week or two between consultations, and check in with them to tell them how it's going. They then redirect your exercise cycle if you need it.

Teaching a special needs learner requires creativity on your part. Whatever the need is, your job as a homeschooler is to present information so your child can understand it. Because this is *your* child, you're much more interested in stretching his mind than anyone else would be. And he usually responds better to you than he would to anyone else because he knows that you love him.

Chapter 16 discusses homeschooling students with special needs.

Beginning the Journey

Some parents agonize over the right time to start homeschooling their children. Actually, there really is no wrong time. Like most other things in homeschooling, it's totally up to you. Most families make their final decision to homeschool sometime in the late spring or early summer, when the thought of going through another year of public or private school makes them uneasy. (To get to the uneasy part, you've actually been thinking through situations and options for quite some time, although you may not realize it.)

They then spend the summer deciding on curriculum, detoxing from the school year, and reading up on homeschooling. Maybe they find other home-schoolers they know and talk to them about their decision. When August or September comes, these families begin school at home instead of sending their children on the bus. After mentally preparing themselves all summer and sketching a game plan in their minds, they're ready for the adventure.

Choosing the perfect time of year

A good number of new homeschoolers begin in January after winter break. It gives the children two weeks away from school, and they simply don't return. If a school situation deteriorates rapidly from September to December, these children usually benefit from the release of emotional stress they feel by staying home to school.

One little guy I know had an awful second-grade year. He failed every reading comprehension test the teacher gave him. The teacher then told his mother that he couldn't read and would have to repeat second grade. His distraught mother then called me. I asked, "What are you reading to him at home?" She replied that he really enjoys *The Lord of the Rings*. This was a child who didn't answer the comprehension questions at school because he found them boring! Now homeschooled, he does just fine.

In an extreme situation, such as a child who becomes physically ill at the thought of getting on the bus or going to school in the morning, parents sometimes take their children out that week. They then spend a few weeks allowing the child to relax and get used to being at home all day, and then gently begin working school subjects into the schedule. The child would spend that time home ill anyway; his parents simply use it productively to help him adjust to a rather abrupt change in schedule. The down time allows the frazzled parent time to gather thoughts together, research curriculum, and deal with her own emotions of anger and frustration.

Deciding at what age to begin

Many parents start homeschooling their children in kindergarten, but it's not unusual for a family to begin homeschooling a ninth grader. Some parents begin with an idea of homeschooling long before the first child arrives on the scene. They research the idea, talk to other parents, find out what materials are currently available, and make the decision before they even have children. Then, when their family becomes bigger, they raise the toddlers and preschoolers with an expectation that they'll be homeschooled until further notice.

Not all parents are this focused, however, and many begin to think of teaching their own children when they look into that sweet 5-year-old face and think of it being away from home all day. Perhaps kindergarten left a bad taste in your mouth and you want to look into other options. You suddenly realize you taught your child almost everything he knows to this point, so you may be qualified to continue the trend. Good for you!

Some families find out further along the line that public or private school doesn't work for their children. You may be one of these parents. Perhaps your child comes home bored each day because she isn't challenged. Maybe social or educational issues arise that make it difficult for your child to learn. Or perhaps your child learns things in the classroom and from other children that shock you.

When situations such as these arise, and you feel like homeschooling is the best option for your family, you can start whenever you like. Even tenth and eleventh graders come home to school if social pressures and threats of violence become overwhelming.

No one should have to learn in a place that they don't feel is safe. If you were concerned that someone may attack you at work when you left the house each day, would you go? If you worked in a place where your co-workers and perhaps even your boss called you stupid and lazy, would you go? Then why do we as parents send our little ones if they experience these things?

Assigning Homework

One of the main complaints parents voice about the local school system is the amount of homework. Although some repetition may be good and even necessary, four or more hours of homework each night seems a little excessive for second and third graders. As those of us who spent any time in the corporate world know, all work and no play leads to burnout.

Witnessing your child's progress

Remember those first toddler steps? Your child stood, wavered, and then plunk! Down he went. But he stood up again, wobbled a little, and took one step, and then another. You were so excited that you could cheer! Maybe you did (and soon after found yourself cuddling a crying toddler who was startled at that great big noise).

Homeschooling is like that. When you teach your child at home, you see the thrill in your child's eyes when she learns to add for the very first time. You hear the first words your child learns to read. You get to explain the wonders of the stars to wide, fascinated eyes.

And farther along, you unfold other mysteries of life to your learner. What is an atom? How do you solve this math problem for n, and why does anyone care what n might be in the first place? What happens when you forget to add salt to that bread loaf that you just made? (Oops. Saltless bread loaves aren't very tasty.)

Watching a child learn is a bit addictive, and with homeschooling, you have the opportunity to see it all (even the frustrating I-wish-I-could-throw-my-pencil parts). No matter how old your students might be, the sparkle still comes into their eyes when they master a new skill just like it did during those first steps. One of the greatest joys of homeschooling is getting to see the children learn for the first time over and over.

Homeschooling looks at education from a different perspective. You don't need to prove that your child is learning by assigning homework for her to do after hours. You're the parent, you are the one teaching your child, and you know whether she gets it or not. If she doesn't understand the concept you can tell by the dazed look in her eyes. If she does understand, there's no reason to spend the next four hours re-teaching the same concept after dinner. You can always test the child over the material if you're not sure. Chapter 21 talks more about grades and testing.

Making homeschooling more than school at home

Homeschooling isn't really "school at home." Instead, think of it as independent tutoring sessions day after day. Most homeschooling can be done in two to four hours per day with no homework, and that includes high school. Because you teach one and not twenty or more, you can explain concepts in much less time than a conventional teacher. Sometimes independent reading or assigned projects fall outside that range, but the vast majority of homeschoolers find that they don't need to assign homework for their children to maintain their skills.

If a child misses a concept today, you can always re-teach it tomorrow. Teacher's manuals include re-teaching time nearly every day as they attempt to catch the learner who didn't quite understand the first time. If you wait until the following school day to tackle a particular skill again, you give the concept some time to settle. Within the next 24 hours you may discover a new and fresh way to present the skill, or your student may gain the extra processing time he needs.

For several years, one of my children refused to do math. Well, okay, he didn't actually refuse; he simply completed the pages as slowly as possible. After awhile, I got tired of waiting for him to finish daydreaming over his math page, and I assigned the unfinished problems as homework. That meant he put the math page with any incomplete problems next to him on the table, and it became after-school work.

It didn't take too many months before he realized that finishing a math page within ten to twenty minutes proved to be much more fun than staring at the math problems and thinking about all the other things he could be doing. Now he does his math quickly and well, within a decent time frame, and we move on to other things.

When you want to call the taxi

It's 8:15 a.m., and you'd rather do anything than open that textbook one more time. These are the mornings I look over the children's heads, catch my husband's eye, and ask if he thinks the taxi could be here by 8:25 — in time to take the children to the local school. Of course the answer is no: Who ever heard of a taxi arriving within ten minutes? But the question releases the tension, and I feel a little more ready to face the day.

Everyone has those can-I-call-the-taxi days. Sometimes the best antidote for low enthusiasm is to make yourself open the books and begin the day. The very motion of doing what you don't want to do acts as a kind of therapy, and you find that you become interested almost in spite of yourself. Sounds stoic? Perhaps, but it works.

If the taxi urge comes on you because your children wake up in a less than amiable mood, you may want to turn the day upside down and begin with an exercise in creativity. Pull out the construction paper and scissors, the clay, or the recorder flutes, and have at it. Dance and wiggle to some upbeat music. After everybody spends some time creating and the juices start to flow, math looks much less reprehensible.

Once in a while, nothing settles the nerves but a day off. This is the day to play in the snow, picnic in the park, or go to the zoo. (If you visit the zoo and talk about what you see, it counts as a field trip!) After a day of rest or field tripping, you feel more refreshed and ready to hit the books again.

If you really and truly took the day off without doing anything educational, remember that you may need to teach an additional day at the end of the year to meet your school days quota. However, when the doldrums hit in January or February, it's worth an extra day or two in late May. After all, who can put a price or time limit on sanity?

Using the extra time

If you opt for school without homework, what do you do with all the time you save? You suddenly have time to sit with your family and enjoy an after dinner movie — during the week. Maybe you find the time for those volunteer opportunities that you always wanted to do. Or perhaps you may fill the hours playing board games or card games with your children.

Children think of all kinds of things to do when they find themselves free from homework. They build contraptions and coliseums in LEGOs. They grab the clay and populate a pretend town. They draw paper dolls along with stunning wardrobes. They run, ride, and skate. Once in a while, they may even grab a book and read on their own, without you prompting them. When I want my son for some miscellaneous reason, I first look on the sofa to see if he camped there with a book. More often than not, my quick sofa search ends the quest.

Getting used to a lack of stimuli may take your children awhile, especially if you bring your kids home after they spend several years in the school setting. Everything is programmed in a school setting. You eat at a certain time, open your math books at a specific point during the day, and place all the day's homework into your to-take-home folder.

Homeschool isn't like that. After the day's work is done, children are free to pursue new interests or continue old ones. During the first few months at home, you may find your students wandering aimlessly around the house wondering what to do with themselves. When I see that behavior in my own kids, I present them with a list of available options, such as painting, crafts, dolls, model trains, and so on, to remind them that they do have activities that they can pursue if they like. I always end the list with "...and you can always clean your room." Funny — in all this time, they have never selected the room option.

Chapter 3

Addressing the Buzzword: Socialization

In This Chapter

▶ Introducing the issue
▶ Determining the question
▶ Socializing in the homeschool

*I*t's the first question you get from strangers who learn that you homeschool. Sometimes you even hear it from well-meaning relatives. Usually, however, anyone who actually knows your children on more than an, "Isn't that Rivkeh's kid?" basis, also knows better than to demand information about your child's social life. (At least, they should.)

Among veteran homeschoolers the topic is simply referred to as *The Question*. The dialog goes something like this: "Hey guys. I met somebody at the mall today who asked me if I homeschool and then asked me The Question." At this point everyone in the room responds in unison: *What about socialization?*

If the social aspects of homeschooling concern you, relax and enjoy this chapter. Here's where to start for the real scoop on The Question and what it means to you as a homeschooler. It means that you're doing fine, your children will be fine, and you don't need to worry (but feel free to continue reading if you want more details anyway).

Making the Question Clearer

How do you address The Question? Before you can answer, you need to determine the question at hand. Is the person asking about *social outlets*, the time we allot to spend with friends and do fun things together, or is he actually asking about *socialization?* These are two entirely different questions.

Social outlets

Social outlets are a no-brainer. In fact, so many opportunities exist for homeschool families to spread their social wings and meet with other homeschooling (as well as nonhomeschooling) families that a whole section later in this chapter covers the options in depth. If someone asks you how your child finds social outlets, list the myriad of activities that nearly every homeschool family involves themselves with. Religious organizations, sports, scouting, and so on fill our children's time and create excellent social opportunities.

Or do they? We think they do because we continue to sign them up for the classes and the organizations.

Do you find yourself seeking an endless roster of activities? What purpose does endless activity serve? Is it to meet an educational need or to pacify some unknown questioner who may peer over our shoulders at any minute? If not for educational purposes, or to fill empty hours, why do you feel that you need to satisfy anyone but your family with your activities? (I tried scheduling my days to pacify the family dog for a while, but that didn't work at all, so I gave it up.)

Socialization

The majority of questioners ask about something much more nebulous than scouts or Sunday school. The words are the same: *What about socialization?* However, they don't want to know what you do so much as where your children will stand when they mature.

Now when The Question is posed to you, and you truly understand the query, you are free to answer the question instead of providing a few fluffy comments or blindly running through your after-school itinerary. The question is really *How will your child fit into society if he doesn't go to school?* The answer, of course, is that your child fits into society just fine.

Your child learns from you and the other adults and almost-adults in his life. He gets a much better view of how life really works because he isn't incarcerated with a selection of age-mates all day long. Your child sees wisdom at work as she watches you plan and complete tasks, interact with people in your community, and schedule your life to get (almost) everything done. She learns your values and morals as she listens to what you say and watches what you do. In the meantime, your child learns to

✔ Interact with the people around him, regardless of age, sex, or social class.

✔ Observe and join adults in conversation that includes more meaningful topics than what the latest cute junior high boy wore to school.

✔ Work with others as a team for longer than an hour on the playing field. Working together becomes a way of life with homeschool students and parents.

✔ Spend concentrated time and effort becoming good at a skill, such as dance, engineering, or computers.

This is the kind of interaction that leads to healthy, independent citizens.

If this subject intrigues you and you want to read more, take a look at *The Underground History of American Education,* by John Taylor Gatto (a former New York State and New York City Teacher of the Year) or *NEA: Trojan Horse in American Education,* by Samuel L. Blumenfeld (who authored the *Alpha-Phonics* reading curriculum, among other things). You also may want to take a look at the books by John Holt, who wrote *How Children Learn* and *How Children Fail.*

Presenting the Issue of the Year

Socialization always appears as the homeschooling issue of the year, no matter which year it happens to be. Of course, it's only an issue among people who don't actually teach their children at home. The veteran homeschoolers know better.

By the time a homeschool family has a couple years' experience, its members understand that the best social place for its children is the home environment. Where else can you learn to relate to people from all different age groups, strengths, and weaknesses without resorting to insanity or institutionalization?

Families pass along values, morals, and standards as they interact together. Parents teach their young ones how to interact with society, how to tell right from wrong, and why they should avoid sticking their fingers in light sockets. (Ouch! That one hurt.) In fact, parents do a fine job through about age five, and then someone else comes along and tells them that they need to send their children to school to learn all that matters.

Take time for a quick trip back to introductory logic. If you did a great job when they were two, and you were magnificent when they were four, then why is it that all of a sudden you need help at six, eight, and ten? That doesn't make sense. How is someone who you don't even know more qualified to teach your children about society than you are?

You learn about society by living life. Sitting in a classroom for six hours each day while someone tells you to be quiet and listen isn't living life. Unless you happen to be a professional bank depositor for a large corporation, neither does real life consist of standing silently in a line several times per day.

So if these scenarios aren't real life in the adult world, why do we insist that our children fit a mold that we ourselves wouldn't be caught dead in? I don't know about you, but if I worked in a job where I needed to raise my hand to go to the bathroom and then marched there and back carrying a brightly colored tag that reads *Girl Bathroom Pass* in large block letters, I think I'd find another position. At home, my children don't raise their hands for permission to go to the bathroom. Do yours?

Letting Your Proverbial Hair Down

Homeschoolers who've been at this long enough to develop a network of homeschooling friends can readily tell you that finding something other than homeschooling to do is easier than staying at home and teaching. Not that working with the kids is boring, but the thought of spending the afternoon with other people always raises interest. We could be ice-skating with friends or lunching at the park. Maybe it's not too late to attend that field trip. But no, here we sit, finishing the daily math assignment. It's enough to give one the doldrums.

Math assignments have their place, but so do relaxation, volunteering, and group activities. All of anything makes your student lopsided. As Aristotle once said while gazing out the window at the other homeschool boys whose work was already finished for the day, "Moderation in all things is good."

Although your social adventures are only limited to your imagination and the number of hours that you're willing to leave the house each week, here are some general ideas to get the thoughts churning:

✔ **Join the scouts or 4-H.** Many communities offer homeschool 4-H groups, and a few areas contain scouting groups whose members primarily homeschool. (If you join a homeschool group, it generally meets when you're available during the day, instead of using evening or weekend hours.) Ask around.

✔ **Race miniature cars.** A retailer in our area sells small battery-operated cars called Tamiya 4WD Racers that fit on a special track and go a mile a minute. The retailer sells these inexpensive car kits and then offers free race nights once or twice a week. Kids change out motors, tweak with tires, and generally have a great time with the cars while learning about the basics of mechanics and gears at the same time. (Shh! Don't tell. They thought it was all for fun.) Maybe something like this happens in your community.

✔ **Volunteer for a local nonprofit organization.** Many organizations may appreciate helping hands. The animal shelter, library, and local food bank are only a few of them. Look in the nonprofit section of your local phone book and locate a worthy cause.

✔ **Play ball, tennis, or golf.** Regardless of your favorite sport, the local parks and recreation department probably offers some kind of spring or summer classes. It's a great way to meet other people and maybe even find someone to play with. After signing up for tennis lessons last summer, the parents in my time slot sat around the picnic table to get acquainted. It only took us a few minutes to realize that all but one of us taught our kids at home.

✔ **Meet a playgroup at the park.** Homeschool park groups incorporate all ages from preschoolers on up. Some families pack a lunch and stay most of the day, while others drop by for a bit to spend some time and then wander off to other activities.

✔ **Play in the homeschool orchestra.** And brush up on your note theory at the same time. If your community doesn't offer a homeschool orchestra, maybe it organizes a theater group, choir, or some other artsy conclave.

✔ **Join or create a field trip group.** Some homeschool groups meet once a month or so only to participate in field trips together. This is a way to meet other families, see new sights, and not feel like you're committed every week for the rest of the semester.

If you find yourself driving around your community from event to event several days a week, you may want to pick up a set of foreign language tapes. Pop one into the car as you head down the driveway and work on your foreign language skills as you ride together. It not only makes the travel time useful, but it also marks off one more subject from your daily list. Even if you can't look at the book (I certainly don't recommend it if you are the driving parent) you can learn quite a bit through listening.

They won't find only 34-year-olds on the job

Imagine working for a company that only hires 25-year-old workers. Everywhere you turn you see other 25-year-olds: in the mailroom, at the computers, in the warehouse. Each person is exactly your age.

Sounds vaguely *Brave New World*-esque, doesn't it? Thankfully, it's not reality.

Homeschoolers get a jump on this whole reality thing. Because they incorporate multiple ages into learning and life from the beginning of homeschool (whenever that may be), these students cope without shock if their first manager is old enough to be a grandfather (or, conversely, young enough to pass as an older sister). Homeschoolers grow up with the idea that people come in all ages, all sizes, and all shapes. After all, that's what they see at home, in the educational co-op, and in the community.

They learn to be kind to younger people and listen to older ones. They find out that a best friend can be several years older, several years younger, or the exact same age. And they understand that they can pursue interests and hobbies different from a close friend yet still share some things in common. They learn to be individuals.

This carries over into the workplace. These students think through problems and suggest solutions because that's what they do at home. They tend to follow instructions even though they may ask *why* the first time or two. If I ran a retail establishment, this is the kind of student employee I'd want working at my store. How about you?

Chapter 4

Complying with Uncle Sam

Homeschooling is legal in every state in the United States (also in Canada, if you happen to live in the northern half of North America). Really. It is.

What makes the home education process a bit sticky is that each state governs its own homeschoolers. That means that what I do in Indiana to comply with state law isn't what you may do if you live in California or North Carolina. If you live in one state and plan to stay there for a while, you learn the homeschooling ins and outs in your area and you know what you need to do. The interesting part comes if your family moves every few years or so; then you may find yourself homeschooling in a state whose requirements are radically different from the state you left.

In this chapter, you can find the ins and outs of dancing the state-law samba. Whether you need to know the number of days that your state requires you to homeschool each year or you're dying to read the educational code that pertains to you while you sip the day's last cup of coffee, this is where you begin. If you find that you still have questions after reading this chapter, those are the queries to take to your state homeschool association. (Much as I'd like to help you out, I can't take the time to memorize the laws for all 50 states plus the provinces of Canada. Like you, I have kids to educate.)

Conducting Yourself (Yes, Ma'am) in Accordance with State Law

The laws that you follow depend entirely on your state of residence. Wherever you live, that's the state legislature you listen to when you plan your school year. Because education legislation belongs to the state and not to the federal government, each state regulates homeschooling as part of its education laws.

Some homeschooling laws are relatively easy to follow and understand. They usually say something such as this: Teach your kids yourself, do it in a decent, orderly way, and we'll leave you alone if you leave us alone. (Not exactly in those words, mind you, but the gist of the content is there.)

Other states want more involvement in your homeschool. If you really corner your state officials and ask, you'll find that what truly concerns them is the almost-mythical homeschooler who removes the child from school and then sits the child in front of the television for the next five years only to return the child to school a year or so before graduation and demand that the schools, "Do something with this child." With a scenario like that rolling around in my mind, I'd be a little testy, too.

Unfortunately, there's a bad apple in every large barrel, and the *almost-mythical* homeschooler is just that. Once in a while, you get a weirdo in the bunch, and that's the family that usually makes the headlines. After all, who wants to report on the well-read children who struggle once in a while with math concepts, or the homeschool family down the street whose children nearly make it to the National Little League Championships every other year or so? That's not news. It's normal. And everybody knows that what's normal isn't news.

So, in an effort to document that you truly know what you're doing (even though you already knew that to begin with), many states require some kind of proof in the form of paperwork. It may be standardized test scores, attendance records, or a small collection of worksheets and writing samples from the previous year. Like filing your income tax with the government, filing this information may seem intrusive at the beginning. Everybody grumbles about having to file it, but everybody does it.

If you belong to a military family, then you follow the state homeschooling law where you *currently reside,* not the state that you declare as a residence when you file your taxes. When you're stationed overseas, talk to your local military community commander and tell this person that you plan to homeschool. For more information, visit the National Home Education Network Military Homeschoolers Web site at www.nhen.org/nhen/pov/military.

Many states have legislative watchdog groups who specialize in homeschooling laws. These organizations badger (also known as *lobby*) the state legislature for various laws that they think will benefit homeschoolers. If this type of activity interests you — whether you want to join the effort yourself or you'd like the group to inform you of their work — your state homeschool organization can point you toward these friendly folks. (If you find yourself wandering around your state or local homeschool convention, look for a table that says something like Homeschooling Freedoms or Legislative Alerts. These folks usually appear at such events because they rightly reason that they may meet a few convention goers who want to join the cause.)

Locating Your State's Law

Although you probably don't need to camp outside the front door of the state legislature building, having a working knowledge of the law as it applies to homeschooling is always a good idea. First of all, a thorough knowledge of the law and how it applies to you reduces your panic quotient. If you know without hesitation, for example, that your state requires 172 school days per year, the occasional flake that insists that homeschoolers need to teach 200 days won't faze you at all.

Now that you know you need a copy of your state requirements, where do you find it? Short of calling your local department of education (which may or may not be a good idea depending where you live), you have a couple solid resources available to you. You can contact your state homeschool association or, if you have Internet access, you can locate a copy online.

Some educational systems are still leery of homeschooling mostly because they see it as a threat. Local officials sometimes have little idea what the state law actually says and cause trouble without meaning to by requesting information or forms that they have no right to request. At the state level, most of the educators have a better idea of how homeschooling works and how it benefits the educational system as a whole. (For example, home-schooling tends to remove the "problem kids," such as the gifted, ADD, and unique learners, and leaves the students that the schools were actually designed to teach.)

You can obtain a copy of your state law through your state homeschool association. (For a list of homeschool organizations by state, see Appendix B.) This is one of the services that all statewide organizations offer, and in some cases, it's one of the main reasons the organization was formed in the first place. If the organization sends you a copy of the law, and you find it incomprehensible (because, like all laws, it will probably be written in law-speak), call them again. Most organizations take the time to explain the law to new homeschoolers, publish a what-this-law-means brochure, or keep a list of veteran homeschoolers from your state who volunteer to answer questions, such as, "What in the world is this trying to tell me?" Finding a copy of your state law online is quick and painless — that is, unless your cable system decides to reset the routers in the middle of your search. In that case, your cable modem goes down, the Web browser poofs into nothingness, and there's nothing left to do but start the kids on an art project while you wait for the cable connection to resume.

After you get back online, you can locate your state law in one of three ways:

✔ **Hop over to your state homeschool organization Web site.** If the organization has a Web site, and most of them do, you'll find it in Appendix B of this book.

Look for a link on the main page that leads to legal information, state homeschooling law, or the like. The link usually leads to a copy of the law on the Web site itself. Then you can either read it or print it out. Maybe the link leads to an Adobe Acrobat file (named something.pdf), which you can then save to your hard drive for later reading.

✔ **See the state homeschooling legislation information at the National Home Education Network Web site:** (www.nhen.org/leginfo/ state_list.html). Find your state in the list of links and click it to open the information that pertains to you.

One of the great things about this site is that it links you right into your state law as it is actually written. If you don't see a link to your state homeschool law in the Important Documents or other commentary section, note the number of the law in the Brief Overview section at the top of the Web page (it's always there), and then scroll down to the bottom of the page. There you see a Web link that takes you to your state legislature online. Here you can plug the law number into a search engine, and it pops up for your perusal. Isn't technology wonderful?

Most of the time, the site provides links that go directly to applicable laws, so you don't have to mess with the copy and paste process. If (in the opinion of the National Home Education Network) your state contains any statewide homeschool organizations that provide stellar legislative guidance to new or questioning homeschool families, you see a link to those groups as well.

✔ **Visit the Homeschool Legal Defense Association Web site:** (www.hslda. org/laws). After you're there, locate your state in the list and click the link.

The site serves up your state law in table form. In a glance, you see what's required for attendance, subjects taught, parent-teacher qualifications, information provided to the state or local school district, record keeping, and testing. Some states require quite a bit. Others don't.

This site provides you with summaries of your state law, but it doesn't reproduce your state law so you can read the words for yourself. On the one hand, the general information here is easy to read because it's written in plain English. On the other, if you've never even seen your state homeschool law, you may want to hunt up a copy through your state homeschool association or the National Home Education Network so you can at least say you've laid your eyes on it if anybody asks.

You can get more detailed information through the Homeschool Legal Defense Association site by clicking the Legal Analysis link near the top of the screen that shows the tabled requirements for your state. The Legal Analysis tells you your homeschool law by name (such as Iowa Code Ann. § 299A.1-299A.10) so you can track it down yourself if you want to. It also tells you what's in the law without resorting to law-speak.

If you live in Canada or are considering moving there, you may want to check out the Association of Canadian Home Based Education provincial laws listing on the Internet at `www.flora.org/homeschool-ca/achbe/legislation.html`. Much like the United States, Canadian homeschoolers fall under the homeschool laws governing each individual province.

Counting Out the School Days

Just how long is a school year, anyway? Good question. And the answer (surprise!) varies based on your state of residence. Your state may call a school year 148 days, such as in Iowa, 186 days, such as in Kansas, or somewhere in between. Most of the states hover right around 180 days.

Or you may live in a state such as Missouri, which counts hours of instruction instead of days. That makes life interesting. Where would you be without your handy calculator?

If you look at your state's attendance requirement and your head starts to spin, do not pass Go and do not collect $200. Turn directly to Appendix B and locate a homeschool organization for your state. Talk to someone from your state homeschool association and find out how home educators in your state manage the requirements in real life.

Table 4-1 in this chapter has a rundown of all the states and the required teaching days (or hours) required per year. Where you see *None,* no particular days are specified, but the state may have other regulations that you need to meet. Combining N with a number, as in N/180, means that your state offers a couple different homeschooling legal options. One option has no particular attendance requirement, but under the other alternative, you need to teach so many days.

Table 4-1	Homeschool Attendance Requirements by State		
State	**Requirement per year**	**State**	**Requirement per year**
Alabama	None	Montana	180 days
Alaska	N/180 days	Nebraska	1,032 hrs elementary 1,080 hrs high school
Arizona	None	Nevada	180 days
Arkansas	None	New Hampshire	None
California	N/175 days	New Jersey	None
Colorado	N/172 days	New Mexico	Same as schools
Connecticut	180 days	New York	180 days
Delaware	180 days	North Carolina	Nine months
District of Columbia	same as schools	North Dakota	175 days
Florida	None	Ohio	900 hrs
Georgia	180 days	Oklahoma	None
Hawaii	None	Oregon	None
Idaho	None	Pennsylvania	180 days
Illinois	176 days	Rhode Island	Same as schools
Indiana	180 days	South Carolina	180 days
Iowa	148 days	South Dakota	175 days
Kansas	186 days	Tennessee	180 days
Kentucky	185 days	Texas	None
Louisiana	180 days	Utah	N/Same as schools
Maine	175 days	Vermont	175 days
Maryland	None	Virginia	N/180 days
Massachusetts	900 hrs elementary 990 hrs secondary	Washington	2,700 hrs total* grades 1–3 2,970 hrs total* grades 4–6 1,980 hrs total* grades 7–8 4,320 hrs total* grades 9–12

State	Requirement per year	State	Requirement per year
Michigan	None	West Virginia	N/180 days
Minnesota	None	Wisconsin	875 hrs
Mississippi	None	Wyoming	175 days
Missouri	1,000 hrs		

Combined Total. In other states, this number indicates per year.

These attendance requirements are current as of this book's printing. Your best bet is to locate a copy of your state law and ensure that the attendance rules remain the same — if you find it changes, feel free to alter the requirement in the book. I won't know, but you will, and that's what counts.

Calling a Truce: Interacting with Your Local School

Most of the homeschool hassles occur at the local school level. Someone sends out a letter from the superintendent's office requesting all kinds of information that homeschoolers legally have no obligation to provide, and people get all stirred up. One person calls the state board of education, another calls the legislature, and a third calls a journalist — not to mention the several calls that go directly to the Homeschool Legal Defense Association. Before you know it, the school system has a huge mess on its hands, all because somebody got a little nosy.

Situations like this happen every single year in school systems around the country. The same school system usually doesn't do it more than once or twice (bad press is not good when you rely on the public for funds and you're seen as oppressing the poor homeschoolers), but it does occur. And it may happen in your community.

Or you may receive a phone call from your local school system demanding information or an interview. Usually the education folks leave the homeschoolers alone because they have plenty to do searching out the true truants. Once in a while, though, you may meet someone on a power trip, or an official who truly doesn't know what's going on, and that's where the misunderstandings begin. If this happens at your house, your best safeguards are well-informed and courteous answers.

This section is in no way intended to guide you legally. Organizations such as the Homeschool Legal Defense Association or the National Home Education Network do a much better job than I ever could. The National Home Education Association encourages homeschoolers to become informed about their educational legalities and supports their efforts in grassroots legislative reforms as necessary. The Homeschool Legal Defense Association, on the other hand, is a Christian group that provides legal defense to home-schoolers who are taken to court by state and local school districts. They also do some intense lobbying at the national level. Look for contact information for both of these organizations in Appendix A.

First: Know your law

If you know what you're supposed to do and what you aren't, you're already a long way toward resolving any potential conflict. Many times school officials demand to see curriculum, attendance, report cards, testing results — that they may *or may not* be entitled to by law. In my state, for instance, no one can ask me to show the curriculum I use with my children. (I'm not sure why they'd care anyway, but that's beside the point.) If someone in an official capacity did ask, and I didn't know that person well enough to know why they were asking, I would simply parrot my state regulations: "My state law requires this, and this, and this."

Do I have any personal reasons for not wanting to show my Greek curriculum? Not really, except that nobody outside other homeschoolers or genuinely interested persons need to paw through my books. It's not necessary, and it tends to leave fingerprints.

If you're like most homeschoolers around the country, you know your law a heap better than your local education officials do. Some of them simply assume that because they want to see this or that, you'll willingly hand it over — they think you don't know any better. Or they don't know enough not to ask.

Many areas have so many homeschoolers, and they've worked with the homeschoolers for so many years, that the local officials already know the ropes. They're so used to seeing portfolios and paperwork year after year that they glance through it looking for obvious errors, check it off, and move on to the next one. As homeschooling continues to grow, this will hopefully become the case almost everywhere.

Your goal is to become familiar enough with your state law that you know what is permissible and what isn't. Reading through the law (or even a reputable interpretation) may give you enough information to talk about it coherently. Knowing what the law says also helps when you get questions from fellow citizens. Most homeschoolers find themselves answering all kinds of questions when they meet strangers who realize they teach their children at home.

Second: Make sure your ducks are in a row

Make sure that anything the state requires is current. If your state requires an intent-to-homeschool letter or form, then you need to file it by the deadline. That way, if anybody asks, it's in. (And keep a photocopy for your own records so you know what's on it and the date that you filed it.)

A "Gee, we'd really like to see this from you" is *not* a requirement, and you are only required to do what the law says that you're required to do. If your state law says that homeschoolers need to register on request from the state education office, and nobody calls your house to ask you to register, then you don't need to do it. If your state law says that only children removed from a public school need to file form such-and-so, and you began teaching your children from the very start and they've never *seen* the inside of a public school, much less attended one, then that part of the law doesn't apply to you.

Only do what you have to do. This isn't a talent contest or a friendship contest. It's more like a small business filing the required no-I-do-not-sell-tobacco-products-in-my-store form that arrives each year. The government doesn't really care whether the small business sells tobacco products; it simply wants to know whether your shop carries cigarettes.

In much the same way, filing the required intent-to-homeschool letter or form each year enters your family into a database, and this is all your state may want from you. Sending test scores, worksheets, and art projects with the intent-to-homeschool letter tends to upset people. First of all, if your state doesn't ask for this information, *it doesn't want it.* Providing extra pieces of paper that the state officials have no means of tracking does not help. It only confuses people: They want to know why you sent the stuff, they have no place to put it, and it languishes on somebody's desk for weeks because nobody wanted it to begin with and now they can't remember who to return it to.

Don't bother creating the portfolio to end all portfolios each year. Your goal is to meet your state requirements that prove you actually teach the kids. Adding more than you need to may raise a red flag — either you're trying to hide something or you need more to do during the day. And basically, when you give the state complete access to everything you do, you allow an invasion of privacy. Why hand over more information than anyone asks you to?

Third: Know your law

I know that I said it before, but it bears repeating here. Knowing your state law gives you both freedom and security. It gives you freedom because you know what you can and cannot do. If the law says teach 180 days, it's not a suggestion. You're free to teach more than 180 days if you want to, but not less.

In much the same way, knowing your law gives you security. When you know you're doing what you're supposed to, it releases much of the stress that comes from uncertainty. If you live in a state that requires a portfolio, for instance, and you know the portfolio days are coming, then you prepare for it by taking snapshots of field trips and projects throughout the year.

Some state laws provide several options for homeschools. If your state provides two or three legal options, choose the one that makes the most sense for your family. In some cases, for example, enrolling with a private umbrella school releases you from some of the paperwork non-enrolled families file each year.

If you live in a state that prides itself on being a pain to work with (based on comments from homeschoolers around the country, a couple of states are actually a pain for homeschoolers), then you may want to enroll in a satellite school program and avoid much of the hassle. In California, you'd want an Independent Study Program, or ISP. With a satellite school, you're actually enrolled in a full school program, but you're doing all the teaching at home, thus ending many arguments with the local school officials. An ISP, on the other hand, gives you more freedom to teach whatever you want; yet you still have someone on the paperwork end of the spectrum that you can turn to. See Chapter 11 for more information about satellite schools and ISPs.

Chapter 5

Getting Everybody Involved

In This Chapter

▶ Incorporating the non-teaching parent

▶ Drawing on strengths

▶ Teaching skills that you lack

Homeschooling is a whole family adventure. You realize that homeschooling doesn't fit neatly into a Monday-through-Friday-from-8 a.m.-to-3:30 p.m. routine; instead, it becomes more of a lifestyle. Life itself becomes your classroom, and your children learn as they walk through it with you.

Much of what you teach them fits nowhere into your planning book: values, priorities, likes and dislikes — yet it's learning, all the same. If they weren't learning it from you, they'd certainly learn it from someone else. Aren't you glad they learn it from you?

In much the same way, homeschooling involves more than the primary teaching parent. It incorporates everyone in the household, and sometimes the extended family as well — parents, siblings, and maybe even grandparents or cousins, depending on your family structure. Pulling everybody together and getting it all done takes a bit of ingenuity, but the result is a family that travels together in one direction.

Dad's or Mom's Role in Your School

Generally, one parent takes the position as primary homeschool instructor or learning guide. Usually mom fills that role, but more and more dads are stepping up to the homeschool plate and teaching their children at home. If you foresee it working best for you if dad teaches the classes, then give it a try.

Working with your children each day gives you a relationship that few men enjoy, and the homeschool dads I've talked to absolutely love what they do and wouldn't want it any other way.

Sometimes the parent who doesn't keep up with the lesson book or explain the math problems feels left out of the educational experience. Often these parents think they're unqualified to make schooling decisions because they don't do it every year and letting their partners do it is easier. However, they miss much of the excitement and learning that goes on when they divorce themselves from the day-to-day homeschooling flow.

Incorporating the non-teaching parent as often as possible can help. Although holding math class until dad gets home from work may not be the most inclusive (or stress free) move you could make, you may schedule a school field trip to the nearest museum on a Saturday or the working parent's day off so that you can all go together. That way, you take advantage of both parents' knowledge as you tour the exhibits. If you know science inside and out, but your partner's specialty is history, you cover both subjects in depth during a trip, which increases the trip's usefulness for all.

Here are some other ideas to involve the parent who doesn't carry the primary teaching load:

- ✓ **Schedule vacation trips that involve some educational content.** This allows both parents to help with the learning, explain what the children see, and generally enjoy the experience.

- ✓ **Encourage the non-teaching parent to share what he knows about a subject dear to his heart.** If kites truly jazz him, then spend some time looking at kites, why they fly, and how they fly. You may even make a kite or two together from plans you can find at the library and spend an off-work day flying. One or two evenings a week for an extended period of time covers much ground — especially when the parent teaches what he loves.

- ✓ **Set aside an evening a week to pursue a topic you've always wanted to cover as a family, and make it part of your school time.** If you want to dive into a subject, such as gourmet cooking or amateur radio, you'll find it's much more fun when it's a whole-family adventure. And with a pastime, such as cooking, you automatically have more hands to help with cleanup when you schedule a family affair. Because parents like to learn too, this gives mom something to look forward to after a day at the office.

- ✓ **Change your weekly school schedule once in a while to incorporate both parents.** Although it may sound kind of strange, you can schedule a Saturday School and then take a day off the next week. Holding Saturday School once a month or so keeps the nonprimary teacher in the loop with everything you teach and gives the children the benefit of working with both parents every now and then.

✔ **Incorporate a sharing time into your routine.** Remember "Show and Tell," when kindergartners and first graders drag their favorite items to school — hopefully to bring them home again without losing them in the meantime — to share with their classmates? You can do the same thing at home by setting aside some time to share each child's progress with the parent who doesn't usually teach each day. What was the neatest picture your youngest made this week? Which new fact astounded your oldest? These topics make great dinner conversation as well as after-dinner presentation time. Children love to show their progress to the people they care for the most.

Regardless of which parent primarily homeschools, unless you're willing to make some additional personal time sacrifices and perhaps follow rather unique schooling hours, one parent needs to be available during the day hours for homeschooling to be effective. If you have the freedom to take your children to work with you, that's great — but if not, and they're too young to stay home and work on their own, then you need to be at home each day with them. Chapter 2 discusses special situations that require creative homeschooling solutions.

Drawing on Your Strengths

You have strengths. Maybe you play soccer well, exhibit a flair for flower arranging, or balance the family's financial books effortlessly. These abilities trace back to specific skills: in this case, an athletic ability, design skill, and prowess with numbers.

These are the things that you can pass on to your children. Although they may not be born with extreme athletic ability, you know enough about soccer (and probably some other team sports) to get them started in the right direction. You know that regularly moving your body for a period of time makes you feel better and enhances your general health. These are tidbits of knowledge that you share, and you don't need a textbook to do it. To you, this probably qualifies as part of life, but in the school setting they call this "education."

And if something is important enough to you that you spend the time to excel at it, you probably want your children to at least have a nodding acquaintance with the skills involved. Your child can learn to balance a checkbook and follow the stock market without needing to declare finance as a college major; there's a big difference between developing a life skill and a vocation. (Some skills and talents may develop into that vocational specialty, but they don't have to.)

Sometimes it's those things you learned the hard way that you want to pass on the most — I learned to cook from my college roommates, so I make a concentrated effort to teach my children nutrition, meal planning, and basic cooking skills. On the other hand, my mother taught me to make pies, so that's important for me to pass along as well.

Filling in the Gaps

What? You don't specialize in calculus functions and genetics? Let me tell you a secret: neither do I. Yet these are subjects I may want to cover, especially when my children reach high school. Thankfully, resources are available outside of running to the library and cramming for the calculus course that I *might* need to teach four or more years down the road.

A couple of my available resources live and breathe — maybe yours do, too. Many non-teaching homeschool parents who opt out of daily tutorial time with the children feel like they can't relate to elementary subjects, such as beginning addition and grammar. The closer you get to high school level courses, however, adult members of your family and adult friends may feel much more comfortable with sharing what they know with your soon-to-be-in-high-school children. They then function as some of your most valuable resources, as they help by teaching what they know. (Which, in turn, keeps you out of the library till the wee hours of the morning researching a subject about which you have no clue.)

Use the people and organizations around you to fill in the gaps that you perceive in your own knowledge. The help may be as simple as a self-teaching textbook that guides your learner into the knowledge he needs, or it may mean locating a personal tutor. Here are a few ideas to get you started. Hopefully they'll jumpstart your thinker and point you in the right direction:

- **Turn to local athletic groups such as the YMCA, Turner's, or parks department for courses.** These organizations teach tennis, swimming, fencing, basketball, aerobics, and a host of other sports and athletic skills.

- **Engage a volunteer homeschool parent who specializes in what you don't.** Maybe that mom across the city majored in biology, exactly the subject that you need for your ninth grader. Give her a call.

- **Trade skills and accomplishments.** Although your homeschool friend feels confident teaching advanced grammar, you love to teach various needlework techniques. If you need an English tutor and your friend wants someone to teach a home economics class, a trade is in order. Meet at one person's house and trade children for an hour or so until all the children learn the skills they lack.

- **Hire a tutor.** Many former teachers willingly tutor in their special areas, no matter where you live. Ask through the grapevine or check the community paper listings to find a local tutor.

- **Delve into a stack of library books.** If you want to learn a new skill, such as photography, take a trip to the library and pore over the books. A good local library usually contains enough resources to give you a good start.

✔ **Take a class.** Community colleges, studios, and private teachers offer courses in art and music if you want to pursue subjects such as these in your homeschool but feel a definite lack of talent coursing through your veins. Sign up for one and re-teach your student at home, or (especially in the case of music lessons) enroll your child and see how it goes.

✔ **Call a family member.** Maybe your brother or sister-in-law makes a living in the very subject you need and would be willing to tutor their niece or nephew in exchange for dinner once a week. You work out the arrangements however you like, but I know my brother and sister-in-law would *definitely* show up for hamburgers or chili, even if I asked them to help with our studies. (They may think twice about Tofu Helper, however.)

Coping with help that you don't think you need

We all come up against it sometime: that well meaning yet annoying help from those around us. Generally, it comes from family members indoctrinated into the educational scene, such as your sister the public school teacher or your father the assistant superintendent. Once in a while, you hear the horror stories that come from Aunt Mathilde who just loves to pass along anything gory, and bizarre homeschool stories top her favorites list.

Helpful family members and neighbors are enough to drive you crazy, especially when they're helpful in that nonhelpful sort of way. Demeaning your choice to homeschool and privately telling your children that their parents are wrong does *not* classify as helpful. This only places a wedge between parents and the antagonistic adult.

Your best bet is to quietly stand your ground and let time speak for itself. Anytime you walk outside of someone's frame of reference, you're bound to hear interesting comments from people. The bottom line is that this is your child and your child's education, which makes it your prerogative if you want to teach them at home. As your child makes progress, others will see it. It may take several years, but eventually they have to face the truth in front of them: Your child is learning, and she does it outside a traditional classroom setting.

Be patient with family members who truly try to be helpful but consistently miss the mark. They want to support you but don't know exactly how. In this case, sometimes inviting them over to watch a day or two of your school routine helps to show them what you really do — as well as what you *don't* do — it may even show them how they can truly be of assistance. Sitting with your child and listening to him read aloud, acting as an extra pair of hands during that trip to the zoo, or showing your child how to work with wood, paint a picture, or shoot a bow all qualify as helpful assistance.

Your goal is to redirect the interested adult to projects or tasks that actually add to your learning experience. Many times you mention a specific skill, such as gardening, only to hear "Why in the world would he want to learn that?" At this point, you want to show how gardening fits into your overall school plan. (Gardening can be a science topic, and its pursuit can show a child the skills that are needed to begin and complete a project.) At the same time, you assure this person that they're the perfect person for it. Because they are! If you find someone who wants to help you and offers skills that you don't have, it saves you time and effort to incorporate them. It also builds relationships and memories between your children and the adults in your lives.

Part II
Tackling Kids of Any Age

The 5th Wave   By Rich Tennant

"...and remember, no more German tongue twisters until you know the language better."

In this part . . .

How about some PE? Although you may feel like a rousing game of backyard flag football once in a while, this part is actually more about teaching children than actually tackling them. And it's a good thing. (We actually prefer squirt guns at my house.)

Whether you teach the first grade or eleventh, this section introduces the various subjects and record keeping required for various age levels. Beginning at the beginning (which is where all children seem to start), the chapters progress through preschool, elementary years, middle school/junior high, and high school. You even find a few gems here on guiding your homeschool student after graduation.

Start where your children are now or reminisce through the younger ages and work your way up. Or read in advance and find out how to tackle high school and beyond and stay sane. No matter how old your children may be when you begin homeschooling, you're bound to find some useful information here.

Chapter 6

Teaching Your Toddler While You Change Your Baby

. . . .

In This Chapter

▶ Getting through these precious but tiring years

▶ Using quiet time to everyone's benefit

▶ Taking turns with your toddler

▶ Navigating through preschool

. . . .

Congratulations! Your home contains a new bundle of joy, and now you're trying to figure out how to educate the rest of your happy brood while taking care of the almost endless needs of the new baby. You'll enter the preschool stage soon.

Look to this chapter for hints, tips, and suggestions for making it through this tiring time of your life. This section gives you ideas for merging baby duties with the need for teaching the older children that grace your life. After you wean your little one from the bottle and diapers, also check here for preschool pointers that help you have a good time with your child and learn too.

Hang in there! Although the view into your living room picture window may look bleak now (actually, it probably looks more exhausting than anything) this stage does end. You will regain your energy. They do grow up to fix their own peanut-butter-and-jelly sandwiches, and they even learn to use table knives safely.

Juggling Primers, Preschoolers, and Diapers

You're home from the hospital, the bambino never sleeps more than one hour at a time, and you already wish the little critter could walk. Which parent normally takes charge of the children during school time is pretty irrelevant at this point: Everybody's tired when a new baby comes to stay, and life goes on hold for awhile.

When diapers and feedings fill your life, it seems like one more thing will send you over the edge. Yet your older children need to put in a "good" school day; they need time and energy, too. You can make homeschooling work with an infant without earning your Super-Driven Parent of the Year Award or purchasing a one-way ticket to the funny farm.

Unfortunately, a new child generally doesn't choose the most convenient time to announce its arrival. If you plan to produce a child during the off-school summer months, you're dreaming or you have better planning skills than I ever did. So far, I've managed the oh-no-we're-halfway-into-fall child and the oops-it's-not-time-for-spring-vacation-what-do-we-do-now baby.

Although I can't do anything about the physical toll a new baby takes, these suggestions for homeschooling survival may make your way a bit easier:

- **Turn baby care time into home economics class for an older child.** Diapering, feeding, cooing, and cuddling are all considered a part of Child Development class in the public high schools. Take advantage of your homegrown opportunity to teach the basics to your other children. Giving an older child — one who is ready for such responsibility — the baby to care for one morning a week after a period of solid training frees you for teaching, paperwork, or a long hot bath. And it gives the older sibling the training most of us wish we had before we found ourselves caring for our own little drooling bundles of love.

- **Take advantage of natural down times.** You have to feed the baby on and off throughout the day anyway. Babies don't do well with cereal for breakfast and nothing to eat until that cheeseburger for lunch. Because feeding becomes part of your daily routine, take advantage of it! While you're feeding, listen to emerging readers strut their stuff, pile onto the bed together for an oral history lesson, ask an older child to read the next chapter of that book that you're working through together, or practice the foreign language you've been learning as a family. "I kiss my pig on the mouth" ("J'embrasse mon couchon sur la bouche!") may sound kind of strange in French, but if your youngsters have the vocabulary for sentences like that, such pronouncements are guaranteed to keep their interest while you feed the baby.

- **Put everybody under three feet tall down for a nap.** Then take that time to work with the older children on the subjects that require one-on-one attention or pull out the science equipment marked *Use Caution* or *Not For Use By Children Under X Years of Age* and conduct the experiments that you wanted to do for the past two months.

- **Institute quiet time for the entire household.** You don't *have* to jump up from the kitchen table and rush back to the schoolroom or computer. Sometimes, marking that hour or two after lunch as quiet time puts a little sanity back into your day. Put the tiniest family member down for a nap and distribute books to everybody who is both too old and too young to take a nap. You're allowed to lie down with a book, too! After everyone catches some well-deserved rest, *then* continue with your day. You may even find that your littlest ones (or you) face the rest of the afternoon with a better attitude.

A baby's arrival is a great time to take a vacation from school. One of the wonderful things about home education is that you can take a vacation when you need it rather than when the calendar says to take a break.

Although your neighbors may not be doing it, life still continues if you take a month or two off in February — or whenever your bundle arrives at your house. Then teach through the summer days to make up for "lost" time. Even if your house lacks air conditioning, learning outside under the trees creates memories that your students keep alive forever. They treasure the memories or laugh over them — depending whether they recall the warm breeze flowing over them as they read *Lorna Doone* aloud or the ant hill they mistakenly sat on.

You can also plan ahead and take two days off through the winter holidays instead of two weeks. That gives you eight days to play with when you need to take time off later. Drop those days into your planning schedule when you suddenly need time off or incorporate them into the infant arrival period. Those eight days give you almost two "free" weeks that you don't have to make up for later because the children already did the work.

Surviving Life with a Toddler

After a couple of years, your "new arrival" is no longer quite so new. He looks a little tarnished, in fact, from the bruises and dings sustained from running through the house at full speed and occasionally into a wall or piece of furniture. (Ouch! That one hurt.) But few things are more lovable than a toddler's face. So you grab him and kiss all those boo-boos away as you wonder how in the world you're supposed to teach with this bundle of energy in tow. Not quite old enough for preschool stuff, they spend most of their time getting into things and trying to elicit yet another "No" from the overseeing parental unit. Toddler hood ranges from just walking through the terrible twos.

Grab some hot chocolate, take a deep breath, and hold on for the ride. Although the toddler years aren't the time to begin that far-reaching toothpick project you promised to your 8-year-old child, you can still keep enough hold on your schedule and your sanity to make it through the year and know that everyone came close to meeting their educational goals. Who knows? You may even surpass your wildest expectations.

Teaching with a toddler

Teaching a group of other children (or even one or two) with a toddler in the mix guarantees some interesting days for the whole group, but it can be done. Many homeschooling families survive toddler hood each time and even go on to teach that youngest person at home when she becomes ready.

Forget the super-parent mentality. This may come as a shock — or a huge stress reliever, depending on your current state of mind — but with young children in the house, you can't do it all. Even if you *could* do it all before the youngster made his appearance on the scene, little guys require too much time, effort, and love to allow you to homeschool, lead Girl Scouts, become the head volunteer at the Humane Society, *and* provide a four-course home cooked meal every night. Enjoy the toddler years while you have them. The Humane Society will still be there next year, and I bet they'd love a new volunteer.

Whew! That much said, here are some ideas to streamline your life while you live with a toddler:

- **Use videos for those times when you must have 24½ uninterrupted minutes with an older child.** If your toddler loves *Blue's Clues* or *Winnie the Pooh,* those are the videos to keep back from general family usage for the sacred teaching hour. Pop one of the most-loved videos into the player and work with the other children to the sound of the *Winnie the Pooh* theme song.

- **Keep a stash of special toys in your school area.** Maintaining a small crate of "school time only" toddler toys gives your little person something to play with that he doesn't generally have in his hands. When my kids were toddlers, I rotated toys every couple of months; with a box on the floor and a box in the closet, the kids thought they got "new" toys quite often.

- **Use naptime to its fullest.** Most toddlers still need to nap. If you resist the urge to crash along with her, the toddler naptime can function as your main teaching time with the other children. You can get a good one-on-one instruction period into each day if you concentrate on teaching new skills while the toddler happily snoozes. Then, when your recharged ball of energy re-enters the scene, you can work on memorization skills, reading time, or other tasks that require less interactive attention.

- **Play "pass the toddler."** This may make your school days longer, but if everybody takes a turn playing with the toddler until naptime, you can work with the students who are left. Taking turns gives your other children a break from school time, and it keeps the toddler occupied.

- **Hold and cuddle if you have a lovey dove.** Some babies and toddlers love to be cuddled. Nothing says you can't hold your toddler on your lap while you teach. A little bounce once in a while and a nice warm hug may be enough to keep them occupied as they watch the siblings do their thing from the comfort of a parent's arms.

✔ **Go to bed early once in a while.** No one will report you to the Stay Up Late Police if you turn in at 8:30 every now and then. Putting the toddler to bed and leaving the other children in the care of Parent Number Two makes total sense if you're exhausted or simply need an hour or two by yourself.

Teaching your toddler

If you have more than one child, you know how much younger siblings pick up from their older counterparts. Much of it, thankfully, is even positive! Wonder what you can teach your first toddling homeschooler? You're probably doing just fine already.

Toddlers learn best as they bounce around their world. Exploring life, getting into the mud after a rain, hiding CD-ROMs in your best plants, and crashing for a nap after a hard morning's play — these are the things toddlers do best. They play hard, learn a great deal, and generally sleep pretty well (as long as you're willing to scoot over in your bed in the wee morning hours once in a while).

Incorporating your toddler into your day provides some of the best pre-homeschooling training she could receive. Talking to a little person increases her vocabulary when she's ready to use it. Letting a toddler watch you spread peanut butter onto crackers or pour the daily apple juice shows him how the world works. You teach things like beginning cause and effect (what happens to the empty glass when we tip the apple juice jar over it?) simply by living through your day.

Here are some simple ways to incorporate learning into your toddler's day:

✔ **Announce the colors of clothing and objects as you come across them.** Not too many months will pass before your toddler knows the difference between the red jacket and the blue one.

✔ **Talk about clothing as you dress your toddler.** Snapping, tying, buttoning, and Velcro may be old hat to you, but to your toddler it's a whole new fastener-filled world out there.

✔ **Listen to different styles of music and talk about them with your toddler.** While discussing musical motifs is probably more than your toddler has in mind, saying something like "Let's listen to some Beethoven," "Want to hear some Russian folk music?" or "How about some Fleetwood Mac?" fits right into the flow of things.

✔ **Talk about the people who come to your house regularly.** "Here's the mail carrier!" not only identifies that person who brings such cool stuff on a daily basis, but it also gives your toddler language that helps her identify that part of her day. By the time my children were preschoolers, they could identify UPS, FedEx, RPS, U.S. Postal, and Airborne carriers on sight simply because they came to our house nearly every day.

✔ **If you know a second language, begin identifying objects in both languages.** The younger a child learns a second (or third) language, the easier it is for her to assimilate that tongue. Of course, teaching a toddler or preschooler a second language guarantees some interesting sentences because young children use whichever word they think of first regardless of the language it comes from.

Covering the Preschool Basics

Your darling finally made it to the preschool stage. You've chosen your curriculum (see Chapters 11 through 17 for an overview of the options), painted the corner that you plan to use as a schooling area, and selected an assortment of pencils and crayons for the school adventure. Before you launch the educational adventure, step back a minute and look at your 4-year-old child again. Preschoolers barely sit through an afternoon snack without wiggling. You can't expect to plant that little body that wants to move so much. Pack up the curriculum, periodically dust your corner, and enjoy your child right now.

Preschoolers explore their world, and they spend an amazing amount of energy doing so. They watch bugs, dig in the dirt, and play dress-up. They create imaginative scenarios with stuffed animals and then act out their adventures. Because every child is different, individual preschoolers won't hit all the major milestones at the same time. One 3-year-old child counts to three, for example, while another may count to ten. Counting to number three is actually the three-year developmental milestone according to speech therapists. If your child counts past three, all the better! But don't stress if your preschooler seems to take her time about mastering a few things. Preschoolers relish their newfound individuality, and they tend to do things in their own time.

Teaching with a preschooler

Teaching with a preschooler around isn't as hard a task as it sounds. Although your little person may insist on individualized attention once in a while, most 3- to 5-year-old children can amuse themselves for a while if they have to. A school time box with old clothes for dress up time, some paper and crayons, a picture book, and a few favorite toys may be all you need to keep your preschooler happy while you work with the rest of the crew.

At our house, the preschooler decided that she needed to be in school, too. So, we took a little desk and stocked it with primary puzzles, pencils, crayons, paper, simple dot-to-dot pages, and some felt paper dolls. While I worked with her older brother, she sat at her desk doing her "very important school work." When she decided she was finished for the day, she wandered off to play with her toys. Who knows? It may work that way for you, too.

Teaching your preschooler

With individuality and exploration in mind, here are some ideas for introducing learning into your post-toddler's world. Your child may not enjoy doing all these things. Your best bet is to introduce a wide variety of activities and see what they like. Incorporate as many of the toddler ideas from the previous section as you think your preschooler would enjoy. Music, for instance, is ageless, and a preschooler enjoys music as much, if not more, than a toddler does.

While you don't want or need to create a structured learning environment for a preschooler, the child's energy level usually demands that you do *something* or risk finding her outside one morning jumping on all the plants in your flowerbed "just to see what they would do." A preschooler's creativity and curiosity will win out, whether you offer anything in the way of education or not. A large part of education is exposure to a wide range of experiences; offering these at the preschool level gives your little one something to do at the same time that it enlarges her horizons.

Introducing advanced concepts at too early an age does nothing but stress you and your preschooler. Instead, spend your days playing, exploring your world, and enjoying preschoolerhood. There will be plenty of time later to memorize the numbers to 100 or the color theory chart. Right now, enjoy your 3- or 4-year-old.

Observing what your preschooler doesn't like to do sometimes gives you more information than noting what he does enjoy. Watching one of my children shy away from play dough, ice cream, papier-mâché, and anything slimy told me that I had a *tactically defensive* child on my hands — a youngster who couldn't physically or emotionally handle a particular range of textures or tastes.

Here are some ideas for preschool learning. For the most part, choose the messiness level that you can tolerate and go from there. If the thought of finger paint covering your kitchen floor and your preschooler makes you cringe, try another activity altogether. If the thought only makes you cringe a little, how about finger painting with vanilla pudding? It doesn't stain quite as much. Whipped cream works, too, and while it's stickier than vanilla pudding, it hoses off nicely.

To liven your day:

- ✔ **Read aloud.** Preschoolers generally love to hear stories, and this is the perfect time to introduce them to poetry, stories, folk and fairy tales from various cultures, and family history. For the most part, younger preschoolers require shorter stories, while a 4- to 5-year-old child may sit through a folk tale or two at one sitting.

- ✔ **Finger paint with your preschooler.** Look for finger paint at educational stores, discount warehouses, or the local toy store. Special finger paint paper works the best, but isn't absolutely necessary if you aren't raising a budding Rembrandt. One box of finger paint paper took me through two preschoolers and I still had some left long after finger painting season.

- ✔ **Take walks outside and explore the world.** Go outside. Look at bugs and identify them for your child. Talk about the flowers, trees, grass, cement, and sidewalks — basically anything and everything that you see is enough to spark a conversation. Big city skyscrapers are just as exciting to a 5-year-old child as the wide open spaces of farmland, and vice versa. You can use the environment to increase your child's vocabulary simply by talking about what you see.

- ✔ **Wander out into the weather if your preschooler enjoys it and if you dare.** To most 4-year-olds, spring showers occur simply for entertainment. Put on your weather wraps and take a short walk in the rain. Smell the rain-soaked air, and talk about what you feel, smell, and see; go outside, catch snowflakes on your mittens, and show your child how different each flake appears; snuggle up a safe distance from the window and watch a thunderstorm. Although going outside in a thunderstorm probably isn't safe, you and your preschooler can still enjoy the show from inside.

- ✔ **Practice drawing circles, pictures, letters, and numbers if your child shows interest.** Some preschoolers think that learning to write their names is very important. Others could care less. Go with the flow — you still have several years to make sure they've got their numbers and letters down.

- ✔ **Complete puzzles.** Puzzles teach children to look at the way parts fit into a whole and they exercise a child's thinking cap. Purchasing and teaching your child to complete a few board puzzles helps her learn about project completion and strategic thinking, as well.

If you have friends who recently went through the preschooler stage for the last time, they may have a few puzzles stored away in a closet and may be willing to donate them to the cause.

Relax! She's 3 years old!

You hear the horror stories of parents enrolling their children in "academically acceptable" preschools in the nation's most competitive educational districts — sometimes even before the baby's birth! Unfortunately, some of that competitive spirit sometimes rubs off on the homeschooling community as well.

Before you run out to purchase "Teach Your Baby Fifteen Languages Before He's Two" tapes, stop, take a deep breath, and mentally count the years until your preschooler reaches age 18. Write that number down and post it at the top of your lesson plan book if you need to. You have that many years to get the basics into them.

Very few children already know astrophysics before entering college. *Very* few. However, most of them know how to read and compute. Some even know the basics of calculus. Some, but not all.

During the preschool years, the most important thing that you can do is teach the child how to learn for herself. And that skill comes through — you guessed it — play. Preschoolers pretend and act out what they know in their world. They

experiment with science: What happens when you throw a ball at the ceiling?

How about letting go of a raw egg as the dog passes underneath? Would the result be different if you let go of the egg without the dog there to catch it? (I'm not advocating these things, mind you. Those who live with preschoolers know that this is how the little guys *think.*) And this too develops scientific thought, regardless of the mess.

Memorizing childhood songs helps preschoolers develop memory skills. And they're much more likely to memorize *Twinkle, Twinkle Little Star* than the periodic table of elements. You achieve the same skill: memorization. But there are two ways to go about it. You can choose the fun way or the pulling-teeth way. Laughing through *Twinkle, Twinkle* or *John Jacob Jingleheimer Schmidt* gets you much farther with your preschooler than "Okay. Let's try it again: antimony, aluminum, arsenic . . . "

And with a whole arsenal of fun things in their preschool repertoire, you'll be classified as the greatest dad/mom ever by your little one. What more could you want?

Chapter 7

Covering the Elementary Years

. . . .

. . . .

Crayons, paper, glue, pencils, and Cheerios fill your days. You spend more time than you thought imaginable looking at ladybugs and subtracting with chocolate chips. (Wait! Don't eat it yet. The math problem isn't finished!) You must homeschool an elementary student.

Elementary students span such a wide range of processing, skills, and interests that categorizing them is hard. Some get a concept and take off, while others require slow and steady tutoring to get them over the humps. Keeping a watchful eye on your learner steers you past many a pitfall. When you know what your child is learning and how she takes in information, an occasional lack of understanding doesn't stymie you because you see it coming.

Setting out with Elementary Students

Students fill their elementary years with all kinds of learning. This is when your child learns the basics of living and builds the foundation of his education. He learns to make toast, read a book, multiply, and open a can of ravioli (skills we all need, right?).

A solid elementary foundation means that as your little one grows, he should tackle the upper grades with ease. Beginning with basic math, history, science, and social studies, and adding on any subjects that you want your child to learn (as well as those that your state law might require), you guide your learner into an impressive body of knowledge by the time he finishes sixth grade. Even you may be surprised at how much he knows!

Between the ages of 5 and 12, children amass an amazing amount of knowledge about all sorts of things. (Of course, some of it we wish they *didn't* pick up so readily, but who's counting?) This is the time to introduce your child to all kinds of information, be it historical, scientific, mathematical, or whatever.

Because children often learn best by doing, especially if you have a kinesthetic learner, hands-on experiences provide the most understanding (see more about kinesthetic learners in Appendix C of this book). You want to teach your child about inclines for math or science? Grab a handful of small race-cars, a sheet of cardboard or large book, and practice racing the cars down the surface when it's held at an angle or propped against something else to create a slope. Later, your child may forget what inclines are *called,* but she won't forget what they *do.* (Chapter 27 talks more about learning with toys and games.)

These are the cut-and-paste years when children make a dizzying number of things from construction paper. They learn to tie their shoes, and they happily reset the combination lock on your briefcase. Oops! That one wasn't quite on the list. Congratulations anyway.

Exploration also fills the elementary years. From the backyard to the neighbor-hood corner, the world provides a wealth of objects to explore. Mayflies or June bugs on the window become a reason for excitement with younger children, while older ones delight in turtles and frogs. Encouraging these interests and the excitement of discovery is one of the most important things that you do as a homeschooler. Sometimes encouragement is as simple as pointing out half-hidden denizens of the wild on a walk or steeling yourself when your 11-year-old proudly drags home a garter snake for you to appreciate.

Facing the Facts: It's Tougher Than You Suspected

Nope. You're not finished with schooling after you teach them to read. However, after you teach your first child to read, you'll feel like you can teach her *anything.* It's not that teaching a child to read is difficult — after all, most of us learned it with or without educational assistance. It does, however, require patience and the ability to stick with a project until you see results.

Nothing beats reading to your child to interest him in books. Letting him see that you read follows as a close second, and may be even more important in the long run. As we all know too well, it's not what we say that the children catch, so often as what we do.

It's as easy as A, B, C

When do you teach a child to read? If he asks you to teach him, then do it. I made the mistake of putting my youngest off for six months because I thought she was too young to read. Actually, all I did was underestimate her ability to trudge through a project until its completion (now I know), and deny her six months' pleasure reading time. Bad mom. No biscuit.

Many books promise to teach your child to read. All you really *need* is access to a public library and a list of the various phonics rules that you can find in the back of the book *Why Johnny Can't Read* by Rudolf Flesch. I used an out-of-print reader recommended by Flesch in his book, and it worked fine for both children. Regardless of what the educational theory of the week may declare, reading happens when you apply the sounds of words to the symbols that we call letters. Some children figure it out on their own, while others need to be shown the code.

If you want a more organized program, you probably want a reading curriculum. Here are a few tried and true teach-your-child-to-read programs on the market.

- ✔ *Alpha-Phonics:* (Internet: `www.howtotutor.com`) *Alpha-Phonics* lays out what children need to know in daily lessons. When you and your child finish this book, your child can read. I used an *Alpha-Phonics* book with my daughter after teaching her to read to ensure that she had a grasp of the basics. Available from most bookstores and homeschool suppliers.

- ✔ *Sing, Spell, Read, and Write:* (Internet: `www.pearsonlearning.com/singspell`; Phone: 800-526-9907) A popular program among homeschoolers, *Sing, Spell, Read, and Write* uses a raceway game, readers, and phonics songs to teach reading. After you learn these songs along with your children, you'll never forget them. Years later, we still periodically break into rousing choruses of "a-a-apple, b-b-ball" for no apparent reason. Available from most homeschool suppliers.

- ✔ *Teach Your Child to Read in 100 Easy Lessons:* (Internet: `www.startreading.com`; Phone: 541-485-1163) Based on the DISTAR reading approach that was popular in the 1970s, this book starts by teaching a modified alphabet that includes a symbol for each phonetic sound you hear. The student then learns to read with this alphabet, and it transitions into the normal alphabet by the end of the book. Many homeschoolers love this approach, and it works for them. But some children stress out about halfway through the book.

- ✔ *Ultimate Phonics Reading Program:* (Published by Spencer Learning; Internet: `www.spencerlearning.com`; Phone: 858-455-9818) This program promises phonics, and it delivers phonics. With no frills or added gimmicks, this book-and-CD-ROM package teaches words in solid phonetic order. Version 2.0 works on both Mac and Windows machines and includes reading paragraph exercises to solidify the student's skills as he learns. Because all the words and sentences are part of the CD as well as printed in the book, children hear individual words and the inflection a good reader uses when reading the sentences. Pausing the mouse over a word or letter combination reads it aloud to the student. If you teach more than one student to read at a time, you can include student names so the program tracks individual progress.

I have a houseful of voracious readers. My children read two or more hours per day for pleasure if I don't find other things for them to do. What created this love of words isn't necessarily that the children's parents are authors — it's that the children's parents are *readers*. We each try to steal away for a while each day and immerse ourselves in a book, whether the book is nonfiction for interest, research, or fiction for enjoyment and escape.

When the children were little, we instituted a 7:30 p.m. bedtime rule. Bedtime occurred at 7:30 p.m. with no arguments. The only exception was if the children wanted to read in bed. Then they still had to go to bed, but their lights-out time was extended to 8:30. This gave them a fair amount of time to immerse themselves in books, relax a little before trying to drop off to sleep, and pursue our goal of building good readers. The books they read during this time are free reading, not anything required for class work.

If your children have books in their rooms, you may want to rotate them periodically (the books, not the children). A couple times per year, I go into the bedrooms and pull out the generic reading material below their current reading levels, replacing these books with others just above their reading level. That way the handiest books, those next to the bed, are at least comparable to their understanding if not a bit challenging. The pulled books then get returned to the family library shelves so that if they *must* read Clifford one more time, he's still available. (Indiscriminately throwing out books in a family of readers is akin to mutiny.)

Is it worth the wait?

Children who learn to read the "Teach Your Child to Read in 100 Easy Lessons" way cannot read anything else (such as library books) until they nearly complete it. DISTAR books are long out of print. (When this method was first designed, it included storybooks rewritten using the DISTAR alphabet at several reading levels so the children could actually practice their reading with additional materials.) The book is available through bookstores, but you can get the complete learning kit (which includes video and audio training tapes) only through the author.

Once your child can read, she can read. Reading does *not* require eight years' worth of classroom readers to accomplish this seemingly awesome feat. Graded classroom readers are boring and they only introduce 200 to 300 new words per *year* on the average. Use your library card and practice reading for free.

Going on to the heavy hitters

After your child learns to read, an entire vista of possibilities opens to her. She can pursue a topic that she loves, whether it's ballet, bonsai, or bullfighting. And even more delightfully, she now does it without you reading each article in *Bullfighting Times* aloud to her. Isn't life wonderful?

Unlike reading in the schools, many of which continue to teach a memorize-each-word-at-a-time approach (the schools call it *whole language*), a child who learns to read by phonics starts out reading at the third-grade level or so after completing a good reading program. This may cause you some problems: That second-grade science book you bought with such anticipation is pronounced, "baby reading" by your child. Oops. If this happens to you, you can always cover a chapter a day or every couple days and finish the book in a week or two.

You still need to keep an eye on your child as he peruses the public library because when his reading level increases through the sheer practice of reading, he finds himself drawn to adult reading material. Although all adult material isn't bad, much of it is a bit unsavory — especially for your 10- or 12-year-old. Simply because your child can read at an adult level doesn't mean that he's ready for adult language, topics, and situations.

On the other hand, he really can go beyond *Curious George* when he's ready. Here are some authors who write kid-friendly novels in advanced language:

- **Lloyd Alexander:** Known for his medieval-themed fantasies, Alexander's *The Black Cauldron* was made into a full-length animated feature by Disney. Students who enjoy the series may like Alexander's Prydain Chronicles, a tale that spans several volumes and begins with *The Book of Three*.

- **Daniel Defoe and Robert Louis Stevenson:** Who can forget *Robinson Crusoe* or *Treasure Island*? These books spark the imaginations of readers everywhere.

- **Sir Arthur Conan Doyle:** His *Sherlock Holmes* serial mysteries are now compiled into several volumes, and provide great deductive reading for the mystery buff. My 10-year-old reads *Sherlock Holmes* with a magnifying glass in his pocket (to add to the atmosphere, I do believe).

- **C.S. Lewis:** *The Chronicles of Narnia* tell the story of four children on an adventure. Beginning with *The Lion, the Witch, and the Wardrobe,* the story unfolds book after book. C.S. Lewis also wrote a three-volume science fiction series: *Out of the Silent Planet, Perelandra, That Hideous Strength.*

- **Gene Stratton Porter:** A botanist as well as novelist, Porter wrote about the nature and land that she loved as well as immortalizing characters such as *Freckles, The Harvester,* and *A Girl of the Limberlost* in her books.

- ✔ **J.R.R. Tolkien:** *The Lord of the Rings* trilogy remains one of the most popular series ever written, and outside the trilogy, Tolkien's *The Hobbit* introduces many of the characters your child will meet in the *Rings* books while telling the story at a slightly lower reading level.

- ✔ **Laura Ingalls Wilder:** Although *Little House in the Big Woods* reads at about third- to fourth-grade level, vocabulary and reading levels of the *Little House* books go up as the books continue through the series. Because of this, it's a good series for the child who you can't keep up with.

- ✔ **Henry Winterfeld:** Two of his books, *Detectives in Togas* and *Mystery of the Roman Ransom,* follow a group of Roman schoolboys through mystery and adventure. Household favorites, I was delighted to find these still in print.

If you find yourself really stumped for good reading material, you may want to peruse the online 1000 Good Books List on the Internet at `www.classicalhomeschooling.org/celoop/1000.html` by grade level. It includes enough title ideas to keep your reader going for a while.

Eating Your Way through Math

For many children, math is a pretty ethereal subject. After all, you're working with symbols that may (or may not) mean something to the child, and expecting him to take these symbols, read the code sign between them, and correctly come up with a new symbol. Is it any wonder so many children have problems with math?

You understand the symbols because you've done math for years, but if the code doesn't click with your child, he's going to have problems discerning the answers to the numbers on the page. Your goal is to make those symbols mean something. After the symbols have meaning, then true math learning takes place.

Just because your child can count to 100 by rote doesn't mean that she understands what 100 may stand for. How many times did you hear the age-old ABC song before your child had any clue what those letters actually stood for? She sang the song, you applauded, and so she sang it again with even more gusto. The same can be true for counting by rote (1, 2, 3 . . . 98, 99, 100!).

You usually figure out your child hasn't put concept and symbol together when you try to show him how to add or subtract a few of those numbers that he's been chanting for weeks. That's when everything falls apart if it's going to — he may look at those symbols like he never saw them before. For all he knows, you may as well be teaching him to add and subtract Roman Numerals.

There is a way out of this dilemma. The solution is *math manipulatives,* an educational term for math help that you can get your fingers around. Math manipulatives can truly be anything that you can count or measure with, although some items function better than others:

✔ **Base-ten blocks:** These are counting blocks. Beginning with the one-centimeter cube and the ten-centimeter rod, just like the Cuisenaire rods, a base-ten set adds a 100 block that looks like ten of the ten-centimeter rods fused together, and a large block that represents 1,000. You can add and subtract large numbers with this set; all the blocks come in the same color so they look the same and the learner concentrates on the size instead of the color.

✔ **Cuisenaire rods:** These ten little rods range from one-centimeter cubes to pieces of wood that are ten centimeters long. Each rod is one centimeter longer or shorter than the others, they come in predictable colors (for example, the five-centimeter rod is *always* yellow), and you can use them to add, subtract, multiply, divide, and do fractions, among other things. One set of rods contains several of each rod length.

✔ **M&Ms:** You know them, you eat them, and now you can count with them, too! With a few bowls and a pile of M&Ms, you can add, subtract, multiply, divide, and have snack time all at once! (Fractions are tough with M&Ms.) Do it quickly, though; if you hold them long enough, they *do* melt in your hand.

✔ **Pattern blocks:** Using these little plastic tiles, your child learns about patterns, fractions, geometric shapes, and tessellations (patterns that fit into one another and arguably go on forever). Shapes include square, triangle, hexagon, rhombus, and trapezoid. If you want to play with these online before you track them down at your local educational store, visit the Pattern Blocks: Exploring Fractions with Shapes Web site at www.arcytech.org/java/patterns.

✔ **Pennies:** Although half-dollar coins are easier to find on the table, pennies are much cheaper if you happen to be counting to 100. These function the same as M&Ms, but you don't get the added thrill of eating the chocolate when you finish math class. To drive home the point, you can always make your own ten-count penny sticks by gluing ten pennies to a strip of light cardboard. This way, your child *knows* there are ten pennies per strip because she patiently sat and glued each one of them.

You can use manipulatives with any math program, but some programs are specifically designed for use with hands-on helpers. Math-U-See (Internet: www.mathusee.com; Phone: 888-854-6284) is one of them. Math-U-See actually uses its own manipulatives, which are not listed here. Math-U-See manipulatives look like a cross between Cuisenaire rods and base-ten blocks.

Another one is Miquon Math (Internet: www.keypress.com; Phone: 800-995-MATH). Miquon primarily uses the Cuisenaire rods as manipulatives. Using Miquon, the child learns how to use the rods as he learns the math concepts.

Miquon is a little weak in time (clock reading) and story problems, but it's designed to lay a conceptual foundation in the first three years of elementary school. Children leave Miquon with the equivalent of a fifth- or sixth-grade math education, and they then move on to another program. Here are some other math programs that you may want to take a look at:

- ✔ **Excel Math:** (Internet: www.excelmath.com; Phone: 858-578-2100) This is a relatively inexpensive math program for kindergarten through sixth grade. It's been around since 1976, and you purchase teacher's manuals (which include answers as well as teaching suggestions) separately from student sets. It incorporates story problems into each lesson after story problems are taught. Each daily page consists of a two-sided sheet of paper, and the page is divided into new material and practice problems.

- ✔ **Key To series:** (Internet: www.keypress.com; Phone: 800-995-MATH) This is where you go after Miquon if you want to stay with the same publisher. Described as a supplementary program, the Key To books present a single topic per page, and each set of booklets covers a particular topic: decimals, fractions, percents, measurement, algebra, or geometry. These books say they're for grades 4 through 12; however, the geometry curriculum is "proofless geometry;" therefore, it doesn't qualify as regular high school level geometry.

- ✔ **Saxon Publishers:** (Internet: www.saxonpub.com; Phone: 800-284-7019) Saxon prides itself on review. If you find your child needs daily concept review to keep the information fresh in her mind, you may enjoy this curriculum. Looking at the examples for the Saxon home study packages, this curriculum seems to drill a concept into the student rather than allowing the student to discover the concept and run with it.

Going Beyond "Our Community Helpers"

Every first- and second-grade social studies book that I know begins with "Our Community Helpers." If your child schools at home, however, she probably knows the mailman on a first-name basis. Nobody needs to tell her the friendly school bus driver comes through her neighborhood — she sees the bus go by her house each day while she munches her Marshmallow Wheetos.

If you want to cover community helpers in the first and second grade, be my guest. It certainly won't hurt your children, although they may be bored out of their minds. You could spend the time talking about your town or city, state, and region of the country instead. Take the children to look at the nearest river. If they've never seen a river up close before, you're sure to get a wow reaction when they see how big it is. And a good river view gives them a basis for understanding those squiggly lines on the globe.

Social studies generally begin with the local and move out; so you start with the interesting facts about your hometown and then, as your students progress, teach about your state, your country, your world. When you throw the history aspect of social studies into the mix, you also move through time, teaching from now to the past or from the past forward. But don't worry — you have 12 or so years to cover all this stuff, and several publishers create curriculum to make the task easier.

I happened to have a second-grade social studies book on the shelf when my children were five and six, so I opened it and we covered the entire book as a read-aloud in about six days. That way, I felt emotionally secure in the knowledge that I covered the material, yet the children didn't look at me with that glassy-eyed when-is-lunch stare because I attempted to stretch the book far beyond its rational limits.

Early elementary homeschoolers often take advantage of community field trips to avoid the community helper text and still introduce their children to the world. Most local homeschool support groups schedule trips such as this every year for the younger elementary students. Either join an organized field trip through a support group or organize your own. Consider asking another family or two to join you on your expedition. It adds to the fun and maximizes the company official's time.

If you decide to do your own field trip, call the establishment well ahead of time to find out the organization's rules for field trips. Some of these options are extremely popular, and you may find yourself in for a several week wait. Identify yourself as a homeschooler, and if you're available at virtually any time, be sure to tell the company official so. They appreciate it when you bend your schedule to fit theirs — especially when you visit a building whose main occupation is something other than providing field trips to students! With that in mind, you may want to

- ✔ **Drop by the main post office.** If you send packages and letters even on a semi-regular basis, you can probably explain what happens inside a post office from your own experience. But some branches offer tours. Call your local post office for details.

- ✔ **Pick apples or pumpkins.** If you happen to live within driving distance of an apple orchard or pumpkin patch, these businesses usually welcome small batches of homeschoolers, especially when compared to the huge busloads they usually receive. Although such a field trip also counts as science — because the fruit grows — the facility often includes some information about what happens to the fruit after picking. This gives your child a frame of reference for that apple cider he sees on the store shelves.

- ✔ **Tour McDonald's.** Okay, so it's not on the normal community list — but what 5- or 6-year-old doesn't know the golden arches when she sees them? McDonald's offers behind-the-counter group tours. They also have picture and Braille menus around somewhere, if you happen to be studying diversity or alternative communications. My children found the Braille menu fascinating — especially after finishing a biography on Louis Braille.

✔ **Visit a local bakery.** Small bakeries often give tours — as well as fresh, yummy samples.

✔ **Visit the fire station.** Firefighters are used to giving tours to groups of small children, and they stress safety at the same time that they show the kids around their huge fire trucks.

Older elementary students need basic information about maps, continents, rivers, hemispheres, peoples, and latitudes. An easy way to incorporate everything at one time is to pick a spot on the map and study that spot. After you settle on a country, find out everything you can about it.

✔ **Determine the country's longitude and latitude.**

✔ **Determine what the populace considers important by finding out the country's primary religion.** Does a measurable percentage of the population practice anything other than the primary religion? If they do, note that faith as well.

✔ **Find out about its people.** Who are they? What do they do for a living?

✔ **List or describe the country's major produce or production — from corn to cars, almost every country produces something.**

✔ **Name and give examples of the language or languages spoken by the population.**

✔ **Name its nearest oceans and outstanding topography (mountains, valleys, and such).**

✔ **Locate its continent.**

This, in essence, is social studies — learning about the world and its people. A nice portfolio or report on each country tracks your progress and proves to anyone who may be interested that you are actually covering social studies in a logical manner.

Several publishers produce social study guides, both in unit-study form (which is basically what is outlined in the preceding section) and in grade-level-textbook form, should you decide to use them. For more information on unit studies, see Chapter 13.

One option is to use a ready-made state or nation portfolio book. Your student does the research and creates a scrapbook on colorful, pre-lined pages. Designed for fourth through eighth graders, these books are available from A Beka Book (Internet: www.abeka.com; Phone: 877-223-5226). (Using one of these books for each country and state that you cover, however, may prove to be a bit cost prohibitive.)

Instead of social studies, I teach biography, history, and culture from various time periods. I also cover geography as a separate class. More of a classical education approach (see Chapter 12 for more about classical education), it starts with history and brings it to life. Then I answer any miscellaneous social studies questions that arise along the way.

Firing Up the Bunson Burner

Science is everywhere. Especially when you're four feet tall. Gazing at the clouds counts as science, particularly if some helpful adult (that would be you) identifies them by type for your child. Watching a favorite plant grow and flower is science. It's also science when you forget to water it and the plant dies — a way of redeeming all those plants I kill.

Although you can purchase elementary science books for your child as she passes through each grade level, you may want to concentrate on the real world and its offerings for the first six years or so.

- ✔ **Go outside and explore nature.**

- ✔ **Conduct experiments with household items:** I don't know how many times we've done the old baking soda-and-vinegar-volcano project, but it's still a family favorite.

- ✔ **Create a kite from a sheet of printer paper and fly it.** You learn much about wind this way.

- ✔ **Find a plastic can or honest-to-goodness rain gauge and set it outside to measure the rainfall**. If you remember to measure and then empty it after each good rain, you get a good idea of the precipitation in your area.

- ✔ **Hang an all-weather thermometer outside and graph each day's temperature in Fahrenheit and Celsius.**

- ✔ **Try raising an ant farm, brine shrimp, or mice.** This, of course, depends much on your general pet tolerance — your children will survive if they only see ants outdoors.

 Your library provides a wealth of books in the sciences. If you need a few fresh ideas, wander up and down the juvenile science section of your local library and pull books at random. (Remember to put them back when you're finished or your librarians will dislike me intensely.) You should find science biographies and books chock full of experiments as well as books about animals, plants, rocks, and so on.

Reading real books — the books on the specific subjects that you find in the library or at the bookstore — gives you far more information than one elementary level science textbook ever could. Instead of basic introductions to concepts, you actually get some useful history, data, and applications for specific topics. Reading an entire book on astronomy, for example, is much more interesting to the young scientist than reading something like, "Look at the night sky. Many stars twinkle above us. Each star is a sun far, far away."

Do I exaggerate? Not much. Most elementary science books are designed to hit a broad number of topics lightly throughout the year. Then the next year, you cover the same set of eight or ten topics a little more in depth, and so on until you finish sixth or eighth grade. Stars. Solar system. Plants. Rocks. Magnetism. Body systems. Water. Animals. Each the same year after year.

If your child loves science but doesn't yet read at the level she comprehends, you can always read the science books to her. In this manner, she satisfies her thirst for knowledge and skips the frustration of stumbling over the words that she's not ready to read on her own.

We found a couple introductory reader series that we enjoyed reading and discussing, and used them as our basic science curriculum for the first few years. We read about plants, space, animals, automobiles, boats, and goodness-only-knows what else. In three years' time, the kids probably read forty or more of these books. Because each title covered one specific topic, the children were introduced to a broad body of knowledge at their reading levels.

If you want one book written for elementary teachers that covers much ground, you may want to take a look at the *Handbook of Nature Study* by Anna Botsford Comstock (Cornell University Press, 1986). Originally written in 1911 as a guide for elementary teachers, it covers animals, plants, earth, sky, and even a page or two on magnets. You could use this as a teaching guide throughout the elementary years if you wanted to.

Timing Is Everything

Timing is essential — especially with elementary students. When your child is ready to read, she will read. When he's ready to divide, he'll divide. No amount of coaxing, prodding, wheedling, or screaming can force your child to do something that he's not ready to do.

When timing is off

If you get the famous "huh?" reaction day after day when you attempt to present a particular skill, or you see your child's stress level rise as she tries to apply knowledge that she's supposed to have, you may need to back off a while. On the other hand, if you get boredom signals day after day, maybe you need to skip a few problems or speed up the process before your child falls asleep on you. If you realize later that you went too fast through a topic, you can always back up and reintroduce it later. (That's one of the bonuses you get from owning your own schoolbooks!)

We covered second-grade math for five school terms at my house — with one child. By the fifth year I didn't care anymore — I was willing to teach basic addition and multiplication through high school if that's where my student topped out. We used everything I could think of — Cuisenaire rods, M&Ms, counting chips, dots on the paper, crayons, pictures — I was out of ideas. Then one day, my child got it. The light bulb went on. She ran into my office giggling and showed her brand new skill. And we were off!

She needed to grow to the point that multiplication and division made sense. Now they do, and my daughter flew through the second-grade math book and halfway through a third-grade book before she slowed down. Will we make it out of third-grade math? Sooner or later, we will. Still flush from the last mathematics victory, I really don't care how long it takes until we see fourth-grade math.

While you wait

If you're waiting for a child to grow into a concept, first of all don't fret. Even with a subject such as science or math, you can do plenty to fill your school hours while you watch your child mature a bit. Put on your creativity cap and use the time constructively, and you find you're building those skills at the same time you pretend to avoid them. Here are a few ideas:

- **Break open the GeoSafari, GeoSafari Laptop, or KnowledgePad CD-ROMs.** A GeoSafari is a computer that holds individual cards that quiz players on various topics. It's been around for a long time, and is rather antiquated as far as computing technology goes, but it's expandable, self-checking, and you can buy the card sets that review or teach whatever skills and information you like. Card sets cover everything from elementary science to life in Bible times to advanced geography to ecosystems of the earth. If you can't locate these at your nearest teacher education store, you can order them from Rainbow Resource Center (Internet: www.rainbowresource.com; Phone: 888-841-3456).

  The GeoSafari Laptop updates and scales down the large GeoSafari into a portable carry-along that comes with 126 different cards. The cards cover most of the favorite GeoSafari topics, and a new expansion provides cards for ages 3 through 7. When you purchase the laptop, you can buy one version with the cards and add the second card set later.

  KnowledgePad CD-ROMs takes the GeoSafari concept to the computer with four math titles and one general knowledge title. The math CDs are correlated to national standards: When you purchase the Grade 1–2 CD, its games cover the skills normally taught in first- and second-grade math classes.

✔ **Explore the world.** Watch bugs crawl and leaves turn for science. Break out the math manipulatives and simply play with them. Take the dolls and create stories and play with them for language. Visit a local landmark for social studies and learn about it.

✔ **Incorporate those LEGOs, blocks, or other building toys.** Objects such as these sharpen thinking skills and creativity. After your child has completed his creation, ask him to tell you about it as a language arts activity. If you want to track his progress, write his story as he tells it to you.

✔ **Use a Match Frame and the FunThinkers books to match your child's lagging skill.** These ingenious little gadgets from Educational Insights consist of sixteen numbered tiles in a plastic frame. Students open one of ten available books and move the tiles from one side of the frame to the other as they answer the question. Books include three levels each of math, reading, and thinking skills (logic) for ages 4 through 12. If you can't find one at your local educational store, several online vendors carry them.

When they don't fit into the box

Many homeschoolers find that their child doesn't fit neatly into the second-grade box. Or even the fourth-grade box. This child may be a little ahead in this subject and/or a little behind in that one. This is actually pretty normal, especially in the homeschool realm. Because these kids have no mythical standard to rise (or fall) against, they have the freedom to develop in their own time.

That development may be quick. Or it may be slow. You may have a child who is able to do math problems in her head at the same time in her life that she finds writing a chore. Or maybe your little one reads all the time but doesn't truly understand how 1½ cups of sugar fit into a one-cup measure and a half-cup measure. That's okay.

Walk with your child wherever he happens to be, and you both build a bond much stronger than you get through sharing a textbook alone. Teaching your child where she is may mean going through five years of second-grade math.

Or you may find yourself flying through two years in one because your child just seems to "get it" this year.

More than likely, your child's interests will develop, and he'll show strengths in various subjects while he remains at about grade level in others. Who cares if your child talks about dissection at age 12? Will the world end if he reads adult nonfiction before he learns to plot x and y on a graph? Not really.

Actually, it takes you longer to adjust than it does your child. To her, this is normal. She simply follows her interests and builds on them, and they strengthen her general knowledge at the same time that they add to her favorite hobby. This may mean purchasing an extra textbook or two in a year's time, or visiting the library more than you may otherwise, but in the long run you get a fascinating young adult, and you learn a great deal about the inner workings of the *Titanic,* for example, in the meantime.

Chapter 8

Handling Junior High

· ·

· ·

During adolescence, your kids' hormones go wild, and your kids fight for independence — at the same time that they still secretly sleep with teddy bears. Adolescents begin to think on a semi-adult level, and they're a joy to engage in conversation. For perhaps the first time, they not only have opinions, but they can defend those opinions with somewhat rational thought. If this is the picture that you look at over the breakfast table each morning, you have a junior high student.

Junior high school or middle school in many communities is the between time. Too old for elementary school, yet not tall enough for high school classes, junior high students spend much of their time sitting through classes that attempt to catch students up and fill in any gaps before high school. If you can grin at their quirks, appreciate a developing sense of humor, and accept some friendly criticism without losing your cool, you'll love homeschooling your middle grades students.

Beginning in the Middle

It's not unusual to begin homeschooling in the middle years, especially if behavior or less-than-expected school achievement sends up a warning flag to concerned parents. Some students jump at the chance to be removed from what they see as a no-win situation. Others may fret when you remove them from the social arena that concerns you.

You may want to spend a few weeks getting used to the new schedule before you dive back into the books, especially if you remove a junior high student from the middle of a school year. Older students don't adapt quite as quickly as younger ones, and the change in programming may throw a student for a bit. Although you don't necessarily want your student spending all her free time in front of the PlayStation 2, you may need to allow some detoxification time so that she has the emotional energy to respond to you after you begin classes at home. If you begin at the start of a school year, your student already has several weeks away from the system, so it's not as big of a deal.

Junior high students who school at home explore many more opportunities than their friends at school, simply because they have more time available to pursue activities. (See Chapter 3 for more information about socializing.) Although a public or private schooled junior high student spends the days at school and perhaps evenings at sports practice, homeschooled students can arrange their school time to

- Participate in community plays.

- Volunteer at the local animal shelter.

- Volunteer to help at the library.

- Assist at a local history or children's museum.

- Start a home business, whether it's babysitting, the gift basket biz, or another creative endeavor.

- Participate in community or competitive sports (such as ice skating, which takes hours of practice for truly competitive skill).

And that's only a quick list. Look around your own community for opportunities for these students. They generally love to help and want to feel needed. Plugging them into some type of community effort fills both those desires with a special activity or two.

Locating curriculum options

After you bring your child home, what do you teach? You have loads of options, and only time and money limit your choices. Because nobody has an endless supply of either of these (I know I wish I did!) by balancing the two, you can devise a pretty good curriculum that meets the needs of your student.

All of Part III looks at different ways that you can teach your child. You can purchase a full curriculum from an existing school and let that school form a protective umbrella over your

homeschool. Maybe you want to write a curriculum on your own. Perhaps you'd rather pull various books from a whole bunch of publishers like the schools do.

No matter how you think homeschooling should be done, Part III starts you on your way. If your middle schooler has trouble with reading or math, you may want to look at Chapter 7, which discusses various elementary school curriculums available for those subjects.

Keeping Track of It All

So now your middle schooler is at home and you realize that you need to track everything she's doing. When you start to think about the volunteering and other activities that actually carry educational worth, putting it all on paper becomes a bit overwhelming. Even if your state doesn't require it (see Chapter 4), tracking your middle schooler's courses and activities gives you great practice for the high school years, when transcripts become all important.

Start with the basics:

- ✔ **What subjects does your state require?** Math, English, science, and social studies usually begin the list.

- ✔ **What subjects do you think your student needs to learn?** Combining these subjects with the ones from the previous bullet gives you a nice, round group of classes.

- ✔ **What are your student's outside pursuits?**

  Does he participate on a traveling soccer team? Write it down under physical education or fitness. Did he set up a home business last year? That counts as economics, math, and business — you have to keep track of the money, which is math, and keep the process rolling, which requires general business knowledge.

  Some activities, such as time spent at the local animal shelter, may simply fall under "volunteer activities" unless your teen gleans some animal science knowledge along the way. (Then, of course, it takes its place beside the weekly science text on your planning pages.)

If your middle schooler tackles a subject early, such as Algebra 1 in seventh or eighth grade instead of waiting for high school, it still counts as a high school course. Be sure to keep track of dates and grades for any early high school classes because they end up on the final high school transcript (unless, of course, your student wants to repeat the class during the high school years just for fun).

The hardest part about keeping tabs on classes and activities is simply finding a method you like, sticking to it, and keeping the records in a place where you can find them when you need them. Beginning a file drawer cabinet — or even a folder — specifically for records and scheduling may help. I keep two files each year — one for attendance and one for lesson plans — that track all classes, assignments, and outside activities. It would be just as easy for me to roll both pages into one and store them together in one file. During the year these pages reside in a loose-leaf notebook, and at term's end, I transfer them to a file folder.

For additional guidance in homeschool organization, turn to Chapters 20 and 21. These chapters discuss testing, portfolios, scheduling, and daily planning. You may want to consider a computer-based planning system if you want to cut down on overall paperwork and still keep a hand on planned activities.

Putting Grades to the Test

If your child moves into the middle years with some homeschool time under his belt, then he may have little experience with grades. On the other hand, if you bring your child home to school during middle school, grades may be a painful reminder of the past. Even if you never graded work before, these junior high years are a good time to start.

For one thing, grading now gets your student used to grades in high school. Going from a completely nongraded eighth year to an all-graded ninth year can be a bit of a shock. Also, if you want your child to continue past twelfth grade, he needs some kind of transcript to take with him. That's where the grades come in.

 If you plan to use a correspondence high school program of some kind, you need eighth-grade scores and final grades to prove your student actually did the eighth grade work. Without this "baby transcript" the school won't accept your child. Chapter 11 tells you more about teaching your child at home with complete school programs from grade school through high school.

Many homeschool parents shy away from grading because they don't really understand how the grading scales work. Chapter 21 lays out a simple and effective grading system that gives you letters the colleges can deal with while being fair to your student. Advanced schools, whether colleges, universities, trade schools, or apprenticeship programs, don't deal well with *S* for satisfactory and *E* for excellent. They need a common language.

 If you feel more comfortable assigning comments rather than grades, such as *E* for excellent, *S* for satisfactory, *I* for improvement shown, and *U* for unsatisfactory, you can always translate these letters to *A, B, C,* and *D* (or *F*) if you have to. On one hand, they don't transfer exactly and an *E* doesn't really mean the student completed ten questions correctly out of a possible ten. On the other hand, how do you assign a letter grade, such as *A* or *B* to a project that a student worked on for weeks?

Extracurricular activities add depth

Although it's much easier to schedule a young teen who does nothing but traipse to the library to replenish an armful of books and then bring them home to read, the maxim that "all work and no play makes dull students" is a true one. In addition to meeting the social needs of your child (beginning with the teen years, this is no small matter) outside activities make your student much more fun to talk to. Varied activities help your teen to develop interests that make him a well-rounded individual.

One of your main goals as a homeschooler is to mold your children into creative, productive members of society — at least, I hope that's a goal. We all know people who read erudite books that make our heads swim yet cannot seem to grasp the main fundamentals of life. When your student steps outside his own "self bubble" to volunteer, join a sports team, or learn from an expert in an area of his choosing, he takes a huge step into real life. With any luck, he also stumbles on an interest or two that remain lifelong hobbies.

Unless your student enjoys conducting experiments or building models from matchsticks that test the laws of physics, pure textbook learning only goes so far. Living life is much different than reading about it. Your child branches into the living portion when she begins to engage in extracurricular activities.

Calculating the amount of paint that she needs to help redecorate the local county fair buildings brings math skills into the daily living category. So does noting how much dog food the local animal shelter uses on a weekly basis. Think about monthly dog food consumption and the numbers get huge!

Not only does your child get to practice what she learns in the classroom, but she also learns to interact with people of all ages, abilities, and strengths. She figures out what it is to join together with others to complete a goal. And she realizes the worth in reaching out to help someone or something else — without you ever saying a word.

Chapter 9

Help! I Have a High Schooler

Congratulations on reaching the high school milestone! You finally made it — your child survived. Deciding who deserves more kudos is hard : the children, for surviving years of macaroni and cheese, or you, for remembering to feed them three times a day for umpteen years. Now comes the fun part.

Whether you've homeschooled awhile and your students are ready to leap into high school or you're thinking about beginning the journey with an older student, high school homeschooling offers plenty of benefits. You get to spend your days with thinking, sometimes-rational humans. They can finally make their macaroni and cheese all by themselves, they know where to place the spoons at the table, and they remember to feed the dog. Okay, they forget the dog. Nevertheless, they're fun to talk to and fascinating to watch as they bloom into adulthood.

Here's where you turn for the ins and outs of guiding that blooming bunch. From individual class suggestions to high school record keeping, this chapter takes a look at the final homeschool years. Buckle your seat belt and get ready for the ride (because, after all, driver's education is part of the experience, and you don't want to miss it).

Starting at the Eleventh Hour (Or Eleventh Grade)

You see the same struggles year after year, and you wonder when something's going to give (at the same time, you hope fervently that what gives won't be your precious student). Perhaps you see new behaviors, new friends, and unique attitudes that don't mesh well with your home values. You want a solution that strengthens your family, and wonder if homeschooling may be the answer.

Believe it or not, beginning the homeschool journey at the high school level is a pretty normal solution. Not everybody does it, of course, but I know of several parents who brought their children home to school in ninth, tenth, or even eleventh grade. The students thrived, and the parents survived the experience, too.

Advantages of teaching at home in high school far outweigh the organizational disadvantages that you may encounter:

✓ **The disadvantage of beginning in high school: You have to get used to a new schedule, the tutoring process, and record keeping all at the same time.** Far from being insurmountable, the task provides that unique level of challenge that some parents thrive on. However, it does require more organization than if you begin in kindergarten and work your way up.

✓ **The advantages of starting at the high school level:**

• You begin with an almost-adult that you guide, rather than a child that you lead. Kindergartners (to pick on the really little guys) have no idea what courses they want to take. Give them scissors, construction paper, and glue, and they'll happily cut and paste for hours while you assemble the rest of their academic programs.

High schoolers, on the other hand, can tell you whether they prefer to take home economics or journalism. Because of the elective structure, you have more leeway when it comes to designing high school courses than you do at the lower grades. By sitting down together to design a program, you can discern which classes would work best for your student.

• You don't need to know it all. (Actually, you never did, but at this level it becomes even more important). If you happen to schedule a class in the area that you received your doctorate in, that's great. However, you can still schedule classes that you know nothing about, and you and your student can learn together in the course of the semester.

The main thing to remember is that nobody knows your child like you do. Even if this child happens to be taller than you are, the truth still holds. You know your children's interests, strengths, and weaknesses better than anybody else does. When you homeschool for high school, you can create a completely customized course of study that meets your student's needs.

Dancing the High School Subject Tango

High school is a little different from the other homeschooling levels. For one thing, you cover plenty of material in very little time in ninth through twelfth grades. This is where you hit everything one more time, while introducing new concepts, to ensure that your student knows the basics plus a little more.

High school at home doesn't have to take six to eight hours a day. It may — I know a parent or two who did it that way — but usually it takes four hours per day or maybe six once in a while. You may find that you swing through the day in two to three hours, but you have plenty to cover with six to eight different classes at a time. Even homeschoolers who embrace the school-without-texts unschooling approach (see Chapter 14) find that their children engage in learning activities for more than two hours per day.

Because high school at home usually requires less time than the traditional setting, students find extra hours that they can devote to outside interests. Volunteering opportunities, hobbies, skill building, apprenticeships, and part-time work all play as much a part in your high schooler's education as the two of you want them to. Schoolwork at home provides flexibility that most high schoolers don't enjoy.

If your student lands a part-time volunteering position with the local vet in the mornings, for example, he's free to pursue book studies in the afternoon after spending the morning with cuddly, fuzzy friends. On the other hand, if your friendly mechanic is up for a helper after lunch, your student can get book-work out of the way in the mornings and be free all afternoon — unhampered by time schedules if a mechanical emergency arises around dinnertime.

After you have free time scheduled, what do you do for the rest of the day? Most high schools require a certain amount of math, English, science, and history, plus an extra subject or two, such as a couple years of a foreign language. The classes that you teach depend much on where you see your child ending up after high school. On the one hand, you don't want to limit your child's choices by providing nothing but fluff high school courses. However, there's no reason to force your child through pre-calculus if he has his heart set on becoming a blacksmith (a science course that specializes in the properties of metals, however, may be an excellent idea).

Coping without college

Okay. It's time for a trip to the soapbox. Not every child needs to go to college. Not every child should go to college. If your child truly wants to become a chef, then college is *not* the best way to get there. The best chefs attend one of a few select cooking schools around the country and then complete an internship under a well-known personality in the world of chef-dom. They generally don't spend four years getting a bachelor's degree in French and *then* move on to cooking school.

Scientists, engineers, state-licensed teachers, computer programmers, and the like need a college degree. So do history professors, medical doctors, and business managers. Mechanics, however, receive specialized training outside the college walls. So do blacksmiths, bakers, house builders, and electricians. Some occupations, such as the military, place you in a different track if you have a college degree.

If your child truly wants a career that requires a college degree, then a university or college is probably the answer for you. It may also be the answer if your child loves learning for its own sake and threatens to major in a field such as philosophy. If your student shows no interest in school beyond the required 12 years, or she wants to pursue a specialty that lies outside the scope of the university realms, then pursue the alternatives. The absolute best occupation for your child is the one that makes him happy (while still falling within the guidelines of legality, of course).

The following sections give you an idea of the range of curriculum and electives available to the home high schooler. While this in no way gives you all the options available — other authors spend over 600 pages trying to do just that — you can use these ideas as a starting point. For some of the subjects, such as math and science, publishers have already developed homeschool-friendly textbooks. Other subjects, such as speech and journalism, leave you somewhat on your own to gather materials as you see fit. When in doubt, browse through the shelves of your library or local bookstore to get an idea of the materials available.

Math

Most high schools require two to three years of math. College-bound students often take four years of math, especially if they want to major in a field such as engineering or medicine after they get to the university. Although most high schools offer first-year algebra and geometry as the required two math courses, they don't have to be.

If your student does not excel in math, or finds math truly difficult, then homeschoolers have options other than algebra and geometry. You can start with a different subject altogether, such as *Mathematics of Budgeting,* and work your way into algebra by the end of high school. The options are completely up to you. Here are a few of the better (and better-known) math programs available for high school level math.

- **Key to Mathematics:** (Internet: www.keypress.com; Phone: 800-995-MATH) Designed as a supplemental or alternative math program, the Key To series covers fractions, decimals, percents, measurement, metric measurement, geometry, and algebra. These books can be used for grades four through twelve, and each consumable workbook presents one concept per page. Both the algebra and geometry curriculums contain enough workbooks to be considered a full year of instruction. The geometry series, however, is proofless geometry — the problems contain no step-by-step proofs, so it doesn't qualify as a college-prep geometry course. Various homeschool catalogs carry Key To books at slightly reduced prices, but as math texts go, they're a bargain at full price.

- **Math for Everyday Living:** (Internet: http://home.meridiancg.com; Phone: 800-530-2355) This series is for the ninth through twelfth grader who needs to know how math functions in the world of paychecks, taxes, and insurance. Use this as a supplement to a regular high school math program, as a math elective, or as an alternative for the student who doesn't think in the algebra-and-geometry kind of way. The publisher suggests using six books if you choose this option as a yearlong course.

- **Math-U-See:** (Internet: www.mathusee.com; Phone: 888-854-MATH) The Math-U-See concept continues through twelfth grade. Math-U-See is a manipulative approach to math, where students use plastic rods to work out the problems instead of relying on mental abstractions or calculators to do the work. High school level titles include *Basic Algebra and Geometry, Algebra 2,* and *Trigonometry.*

- **Saxon:** (Internet: www.saxonpub.com; Phone: 800-284-7019) Many homeschoolers use Saxon Mathematics each year. It incorporates a large amount of review into daily assignments. In addition, the Saxon lineup includes no geometry textbook. The publishers include geometry as part of Algebra 1 and Algebra 2 rather than giving the subject its own title. Saxon books include much theory but little real-world application.

- **University of Chicago School Mathematics Project:** Call 800-848-9500. Definitely a breath of fresh air in the mathematics world. This series meshes mathematics theory with real-world application, which effectively silences the cries, "When will we ever use this?" Each chapter includes a set of projects that bring the chapter's principles into everyday life. The seven books in the series include *Transitional Mathematics* (a seventh or eighth grade text); *Algebra; Geometry; Advanced Algebra; Functions, Statistics, and Trigonometry;* and *Precalculus and Discrete Mathematics.* Call and identify yourself as a homeschool parent for instructions on purchasing these books.

The math class lineup you generally see during the high school years goes like this, in order: Algebra 1, Geometry, Algebra 2, Trigonometry, First Year Calculus (in some book series, called Pre-calculus). The reason for this is so that students who opt out of math after the first two years get exposure to both algebra and geometry before they quit the math cycle.

Science

Science at the high school level should be part hands-on and part theory. Although you aren't going to construct all the possibilities that you read about in physics class, it's a bit of a shame to spend an entire semester reading about chemical reactions and never completing one yourself. Think of the smell — er, experience — you miss if you read a book on biology and never cut open a fish cadaver.

Thoughts of formaldehyde and dissection instruments aside, science is an experimental subject by nature. Sometimes you have to get your hands dirty. And if your student plans to continue education past twelfth grade, colleges and other higher institutions of learning want to see evidence of doing along with reading.

How do you accomplish this as a homeschooler without spending thousands of dollars on equipment and a home science lab? You have a few options:

- ✔ **Hire a tutor.** If your brother-in-law majored in biology in college, see if he'd be interested in tutoring his fine, upstanding nephews and nieces for dinner once in a while (or, barring that, for a fee). You buy the textbooks, and he teaches the class.

- ✔ **Join a co-op.** Some homeschool organizations offer high school level sciences as part of the weekly class list. The co-op tells you what text to buy, assesses a materials fee, and then a volunteer parent with experience or a hired tutor proceeds to teach the class.

- ✔ **Purchase a text that your student can work through independently.** The only high school science curriculum that I know of that meets this criteria and still manages to be college-bound level material and include lab work at the same time is the Apologia Science series. The current lineup includes *Biology, Advanced Biology, Chemistry, Advanced Chemistry,* and *Physics* (plus two texts for the middle school level). These books are written so that the student progresses through the material without parental tutoring. They are written from a Christian perspective by a former college science professor (Internet: www.highschoolscience.com; Phone: 888-524-4724).

History

U.S. History. World history. Geography. Government and economics. If you insert one course per year, leaving government and econ for the senior year (because that's when the schools teach it), you have a four-year spread of social studies courses. If you feel like you have a good handle on these subjects, or at least a good familiarity with the local library, you can do all of them without reading textbooks cover to cover. (And you'll arguably give your student a better education along the way.)

Parents who teach using a classical education model (see Chapter 12) alter this a bit, and generally begin the world history survey again in ninth grade, hitting ancient civilizations, Egypt, Greece, Rome, Middle Ages, China, the explorers, and the New World (all 200+ years of it) one more time before college. They sometimes incorporate the government curriculum into the history of the United States as they cover it. This ties everything together, and you still cover government during the twelfth grade.

Languages

If you plan to continue your schooling after high school, then two years of a foreign language is a must. (It's also a good idea if you want to communicate with a broad range of people in your own community.) Although you can take two years of any foreign language, colleges expect to see the most common ones: French, German, Italian, Japanese, Russian, or Spanish. Chapter 25 goes into more detail about foreign languages in your homeschool.

Although spending two years learning one language and then two years learning another may be more fun, you get more out of your language studies if you stick with one language long enough to read simple passages and ask where to find the bathroom in that language. Although I can identify the word "sale" in several different languages, for example, I lack the proficiency to determine the best route to the store in question. Thus, the usefulness of my multilingual sale-finding ability is limited. Spending more than two years with one language gives you a good chance of locating the store before I do.

Driver education

Whether you consider driver training to be a must or an elective depends mostly on your student's desire to drive. For some parents, it's a when-we-get-around-to-it kind of class, while others consider it a must at age 15½. At my house, we'll probably end up with one of each. This isn't that abnormal either.

You have a couple options for driver education, and your choice may hinge on your state of residence. One alternative is to sign your child up with a private driving course in your community. Alternatively, your school system may allow local homeschoolers to attend driver education courses through the school.

Another option may be to use a planned curriculum designed for parents to teach their drivers at home. A company called National Driver Training Institute sends you a package that includes a training manual, traffic safety videos, a student workbook, guidelines for 50 hours of behind-the-wheel training, and more. Although this curriculum is not yet available nationwide due to state driver education laws, the state inclusion list is growing. Give them a call at 800-942-2050 to see if your state accepts the National Driver Training Institute as equivalent to driver education class.

Electives

Electives make high school worth attending. Unless your student lives for prepositions or completes calculus problems in his sleep, electives add that spice and variety to the day that make you glad you're a junior. Just as all work and no play make a dull homeschooler, all high school core classes and no electives make for a disgruntled student.

Plug in a class here and there to add life and lightheartedness to an otherwise heavy schedule. If you were taking world history, government, trigonometry, and The Rise and Fall of the English Term Paper all in one semester, you'd be glad for a break, too. Although all the electives in this section certainly don't qualify as fluffy (take logic, for example), they do give your student a break from the core four: math, English, history, and social studies.

Art

Although art isn't required at any high school I know, unless it may be a magnet school for the arts, it gives your student the chance to be creative. Spending weeks on a really good drawing or painting produces a sense of accomplishment as few other things do, and if your student enjoys this type of endeavor then art class may be a good option.

Unless you want to delve into art history with a high school level textbook, take a look at the Walter Foster drawing and painting books for both children and adults. Take your pick on pencil, acrylic, colored pencil, airbrush, pen and ink, and more. Visit your local art store or their Web site at www.walterfoster.com for the scoop on these books.

Computing

This class can be as simple or as in-depth as you want to make it. You can use the time to help your student learn the essentials of word processing and spreadsheets, or you can take a computer apart and put it back together. These are two entirely different computing skills.

If you want a readable introduction to computer information, may I suggest the *For Dummies* series. As a rule, they're written well, and they cover the basics without drowning you in data. (I recommended the *For Dummies* series to others long before I wrote one.)

Another option is to look at the history of computing and delve into programming. *Bebop Bytes Back* is an 800-page book that takes your student through the equivalent of first-year college computing courses — it comes with a CD-ROM for your Windows 95 computer that turns your computer screen into a clickable historical machine. As you read about the various evolutions of computing technology, you can play with it yourself and see how it works. For more information, go to the Maxfield & Montrose Interactive Inc. Web site: www.maxmon.com.

Home economics

Home economics class can be as easy as accumulating various books on home skills from your public library. Throw in a book or two on budgeting and buying and you're there (see the earlier section on "Math" books). Nutrition, cooking, sewing, needlework, light home repair, housekeeping, childcare, and household money management could all qualify as home economics. However, trying to cover all these topics in one or two semesters will stress both you and your student. Pick one or two and go from there.

Journalism

Journalism counts as an English elective. The ability to condense information into little nuggets of data is a useful skill, particularly in our age of over-information. Students who find journalism and writing intriguing may be able to volunteer to help write (or lay out) a local organization's newsletter, or perhaps they may want to begin a homeschool newspaper that covers the homeschooling events and personalities in their own area. With the use of computers and simple layout and design software, many projects become possible with a little journalism training. Look for books on introductory writing at your local library.

Logic

Formal logic training helps your student think. Although you can introduce it at the junior high level, most logic courses take place in high school. Take a look at Chapter 12 for more about logic in your homeschool.

Music

High school music usually means choir, orchestra, band, or theater. You can do all this as a homeschooler, but it means thinking outside the box a bit. A search for high school level choir, orchestra, and band may lead you to private instrument lessons and either a homeschool co-op or community singing or playing group. Theater, on the other hand, could mean a group of homeschoolers or the community theater troupe. Although you can offer these classes at home yourself, group synergy definitely makes these activities more than the sum of their individual parts.

Track the hours that your student spends in these environments, and then record them as elective course work. More participation than book learning goes on here, as your student learns to function seamlessly as part of an assembly. He may discover a new talent or interest at the same time, especially if he joins a theater troupe to work on sets but becomes enamored with the art of stage lighting. (And pyrotechnics for the stage is a whole different discussion altogether!)

Religion

Part of the reason for including religion at the high school level, should you want to do so, is to cover the fundamental and advanced aspects of your family's tradition with a child old enough to think through the issues. Incorporating religion at the lower grade levels is fine, but younger children basically accept what you say because you tell them it's true. Now your child is old enough to think through the issues and determine *why* you think they are true.

If the idea of offering a survey of religion course one semester appeals to you, visit your local library for books on the various world religions and use them as the backbone of a general religion course. If your student writes a paper on each of the religions covered and then compares them with each other, they'll accomplish the same work as if they followed a course from a textbook.

Religion class doesn't need to be structured or scary. You don't require a tenth-grade theology text to teach religion. For my high school religion course, I collected a shelf of regular reading books that discuss different theological topics from the viewpoint of my religious community. This forms the basis for my high school religion curriculum; all these books are written at the adult level, and some may require interpretation from me, but I consider all of them to be solid historical or theological books. All are paperback, none were terribly expensive, and I picked them up through the years as I saw them on bookstore shelves.

You can do the same thing. Even if your community doesn't publish homeschooling religious books per se, you can still use the adult books and modify them wherever you need to. If your goal is to give your child a theological framework to base decisions on, then you probably don't want children's books anyway. By the time your child reaches high school, she's ready for some solid thinking material. The adult level books in your tradition provide enough theology to chew on without being overly philosophical (that is, unless you purchase seminary level treatises).

Speech

Although the idea of speech class may scare the words right out of you, taking a speech course at the high school level is a good idea. For one thing, public speaking is part of everyday life. Whether you talk in front of co-workers or present a project to your college business class, you find yourself in front of people more than you think.

One option for high school speech is to join a local homeschool co-op. These families often offer speech and debate class as part of their lineup, and they get a parent with speech training to teach it. Another alternative is to purchase the speech guidebooks from a public speaking organization, such as Toastmasters International, online at www.toastmasters.org, and work through those.

Other electives

Although you may have some trouble locating a homeschool philosophy text that you like, if you think philosophy is important, then cover it in high school. The same goes for home maintenance, small engine repair, electronics, or anything else that catches your student's interest. (Or that you feel is necessary for a well-rounded education.)

The only caveat is that you need to fill a semester's worth of work or more with the course so that you can include it as an elective on the high school transcript (more about records and transcripts later). Otherwise, it goes under the "Interests" section of the transcript, and all that work counts as playtime instead of education. Well, if not playtime, at least as interest and volunteering accruement.

Recording Records

High school is the first time you really need to keep records of schoolwork for The Permanent Record. (Remember that threat from grade school? *This will go on your permanent record.* Yeah. Right.) The records you keep now become the information that goes on a transcript later.

Before you panic, you don't need to mark down every time your lovely student sneezes. High school records mainly require that you start a folder that you can keep track of for four to six years without misplacing it somewhere. At our house, that's a trick in itself, but maybe you're more organized than I am.

Every semester, write down your student's

- ✔ Courses
- ✔ Final course grade
- ✔ Textbooks or materials for that course

Title your courses reasonably. At home you may call the class, "FruFru Elizabethan Poetry and Prose," but the transcript needs to say something like, "English Literature 1 and 2." College admissions officers have no frame of reference for FruFru Poetry and Prose from any time period, and you don't want to confuse them.

When you finish all four years, you have a list of course names and final grades, along with a grade-point average. (Chapter 21 goes into detail on how to figure grades.) To determine a grade-point average

1. **Assign a point value to the final grade.**

   Generally, $A = 4$, $B = 3$, $C = 2$, $D = 1$, and $F = 0$.

2. **Multiply the grade value by the amount of credit for that particular course. This gives you the number of grade points for the course in question.**

   Course credits, also known as Carnegie Units, are covered in the next section. To make it easy for everyone, most courses equal one unit. This gives a one-semester course that was worth one credit a final point value of 4 (assuming your stellar student got an A).

3. **Add up all the grade points for the semester, year, or four years, depending on the span of time that you want the grade average to reflect.**

   This gives you a total number of grade points. If our mythical stellar student takes two courses and gets an *A* and a *B,* the total grade points would be 7.

4. **Divide the grade point total by the total number of classes.**

   This gives you a grade-point average, otherwise known as GPA. Stellar student receives a GPA of 3.5 because 7 (the total grade points) divided by 2 (the number of classes taken) equals 3.5.

Keep the materials list in a file just in case anyone wants to see it. Some schools may want to see your list, but most of them probably won't. Also, keep a list of the extra activities your student immersed himself in for the past four years: volunteer work, part time jobs, the save-the-plants committee, and so on. This list generally goes on your college application forms. Colleges want to see leadership potential as well as activity. For some reason, bookworms who do nothing but sit at home and read physics texts interest them little.

Prepping for College

A college-prep curriculum really isn't high school on steroids. Think of it more like a well-planned recipe. If you follow the ingredient list using the right quantities and order, you end up with a tastier product than if you throw everything into a bowl, stir it together, and plunk it on the table. (Ewww . . .)

Colleges generally require that homeschool students show the same work as the other incoming freshmen they see. They want to see a common group of classes from all students that total 20 Carnegie Units (or in some areas of the country, you double each .5 Carnegie Unit to get a total of 40 for graduation).

A *Carnegie Unit* is a method of measuring a semester's worth of work. At the high school level, each Carnegie unit is worth half a point. Forty of these half-pointers total the 20 Carnegie Units that most schools require for graduation. Therefore, these are the classes most colleges scour the transcripts to see.

A normal lineup of high school courses looks like this:

- **Computer Technology:** One year for 1 Carnegie Unit. Some colleges require an Intro to Computers course these days. If your student doesn't know the basics of keyboarding and word processing, now is a great time to start.

- **English:** Four years or 4 Carnegie Units. One of these courses, usually a semester of senior-level English, should be a research-based course.

- **Foreign Language:** Two years. Most colleges want to see two or more consecutive years with the same language for 2+ Carnegie Units.

- **Math:** Three years or 3 Carnegie Units. Usually college prep math includes Algebra 1, Geometry, and Algebra 2. If you can squeeze in a fourth year of math, colleges look upon the transcript kindly.

- **Physical Education:** Many schools require one year of physical education for 1 Carnegie Unit.

- **Sciences:** Three years for 3 Carnegie Units. At least one year must be a lab science, such as biology, chemistry, or physics. Generally, college prep science includes at least biology and one year of chemistry with a year of physics if you can manage it.

- **Social Studies:** Three years or 3 Carnegie Units. Include one year of American history for 1 Carnegie Unit and a semester of government and a semester of economics to total 1 Carnegie Unit. Throw in a third year of world history or a semester of geography and an elective, and you're there.All these courses add up to 17 Carnegie Units. Generally, the basic requirement is 20 Carnegie Units; if your student carries a full load of seven courses for four years (which would be about six hours of instruction each day if every course lasted for 50 minutes), your student achieves 28 Carnegie Units.

Add extra courses to fill out the basic 20 Carnegie Unit requirement: journalism, health, additional foreign language, home economics, or a speech class. In addition to filling the transcript roster, electives like these broaden your student's horizons. They make your student a more well-rounded individual. (Who knows? She may discover a new love when she takes that speech class.)

Generally, a Carnegie Unit equals 120 hours of instruction, in case you care. This number helps you to convert other activities into educational terms for your transcript, such as the time your student apprentices with a friendly accountant.

ACTing on Your InSATiable Desire for Standardized Tests

The ACT and SAT are the tests that you take to get into college. They are offered at schools all over the country several times each year. To take the test, you register in advance, selecting a testing location when you register. On the date of the test, you show up with your registration confirmation in hand, take the exam, and hope for the best.

Take the exam in the fall of your senior year (or earlier) so that the results are processed and available when you begin the college admissions process. Waiting for your test scores to finish an application is, at the very least, a bummer. (If your score qualifies as a bummer after you receive it, you can retake both the SAT and ACT. Giving the exam an extra try before college is yet another reason to take the test early.)

SAT

The SAT I, otherwise known as the Scholastic Achievement Test, gauges how well you take tests (visit online at `www.collegeboard.com`). It also ranks you on your answers to multiple-choice questions about math and language, but mostly it tells how well you take tests. Because colleges need some kind of scale to compare incoming freshmen, the SAT I and ACT exams give them a benchmark of comparison.

Some colleges require that students take the SAT, while others prefer ACT (American College Testing) scores. Check with the institutions that your student has in mind to determine which test the school wants to see.

The book *How to Prepare for the SAT I* offers test-taking strategies as well as several full-length tests that you can use to prepare for the exam. Part of the Barron's Educational Series, this 800+ page book includes vocabulary lists, math problem strategies, and more. Hungry Minds, Inc. also publishes *SAT I For Dummies,* 4th Ed. by Suzee Vlk.

If your student wants to qualify as a National Merit Scholarship winner or finalist, which means college scholarship money, then she must take the PSAT/NMSQT (Pre-SAT/ National Merit Scholarship Qualifying Test) in the spring of her junior year. Although it's billed as an introduction to the SAT, your student's main reason for taking the exam is to see if she qualifies as a National Merit Scholar or Finalist.

ACT

The ACT Assessment covers math, English, reading, and science — it's a completely different test than the SAT I, and your favorite college may not accept both. Visit the ACT online at `www.act.org/aap` for information on registering for the test and locating a center near you.

Barron's Educational Series offers a *How to Prepare for the ACT* book that contains the same type of information as Barron's SAT book, only geared to the ACT exam.

Do I need to take the GED?

Deciding whether or not to take the GED is an "it depends" kind of thing. Contrary to popular belief, GED does *not* stand for General Equivalency Diploma. It stands for General Education Development and tests whether you possess what the test considers to be high school level competencies in language arts, math, science, and social studies.

If you plan to go to college, most colleges don't care whether you have a GED. As long as you produce SAT or ACT scores and an official-looking transcript, the college will be happy. Check with the college for any special admissions requirements. If you need a GED, the school can tell you.

Some employers may require a GED before they will hire a prospective employee. Most employers do consider a GED to be equivalent to a high school diploma. Stating that you are a graduate and that you were homeschooled may do the trick. In all the jobs that I've ever held, no one asked me to drag my high school diploma into the office to prove that I graduated. Plus, times are changing; not too long ago, homeschoolers were members of a rare breed, but now, so many balanced homeschool graduates precede your children that they may find no difficulty at all.

Chapter 10

Completing Twelfth Grade Doesn't Mean It's Over

In This Chapter

▶ Identifying your options

▶ Learning a skill

▶ Going to college

Celebrations are always the same no matter where you hold them. A home-school graduation brings mist to your eyes when your child stands among the few dozen graduating students just as it would if she stood with hundreds. Actually, there's a good chance your eyes will be even mistier because you know every hurdle your child jumped, every barrier she crossed, and every project she completed along the way. You were there.

As a homeschool parent, graduation brings a bittersweet day to your life. On the one hand, you're glad it's over! All the assignments, teaching, and educational oversight can now come to an end. But you also stand at the end of something precious, that amazing opportunity and privilege that you enjoyed when you took your child's hand and you learned through the school years together.

Now that the first twelve years are complete, where does your student go? These are the pages to turn to when those nagging questions nip at your heels, and you wonder what your student will do after the school years. Whether you're at that brink now or you have many years to go, look here for ideas and post-homeschool options.

Spreading Their Wings and Earning Their Keep

Homeschooled students have just as many avenues open to them as other students after they finish their high school years — maybe even more! Because homeschool students tend to be independent thinkers by the time they finish their educational track, they often opt for some unusual alternatives. Although many homeschool students move on to college after twelve years of schooling, certainly not all do. Homeschool is no more a guarantee that your child will attend (or even want to attend) a college than any other type of education.

I have a child who fluctuates between wanting to work as an engineer and as an historical blacksmith. Both are full-time positions. One requires a college degree, while the other requires a relatively intensive apprenticeship. What will he decide? Only time will tell. I hope that by homeschooling him I prepare him for both.

Continuing to college

Homeschoolers generally do well at their colleges. Some colleges and universities welcome homeschooled students more than others; one college professor noticed such a difference between his homeschooled students and the students from normal streams that he stopped teaching college classes and began writing textbooks for homeschoolers!

Even the colleges who welcome homeschoolers often require that they take additional entrance examinations to get into the school. A college that requires the SAT I (the test that most people know as the SAT) may also insist that a student take one or more of the SAT II Subject Tests, which are specific exams in writing, history, sciences, or foreign languages.

You can only take a maximum of three SAT II tests at a time, so most colleges who require the tests only ask you to take up to three. The reason that they require them at all is so your student can prove that she knows what she says she knows. Although singling out homeschoolers may not seem fair, admissions offices want to ensure that they accept truly qualified candidates — especially if scholarship money is involved.

Marching in the military

If your student wants to join the military after homeschooling, he needs an official high school diploma from a school. Enroll in a high school *umbrella* (or distance) program for high school and use the diploma your student earns from that school. Then there is no question. (See Chapter 9 for more on high schoolers and see Chapter 11 for a discussion on umbrella schools.)

To apply for acceptance into a military academy, the rules are a bit different. The U.S. Air Force created a whole list of suggestions for students who want to apply to the Air Force Academy. These recommendations cover extracurricular activities and athletics as well as academics. Take a look on the Internet: www.usafa.af.mil/rr/hs.htm; these suggestions can start you on your way towards the military school application process. If nothing else, they let you know what you need to be considered.

Studying at a trade/vocational school

Going into a trade or vocational school after high school is complete gives your student the best of both worlds. She gets the extra training that she needs to step into a skilled position after she leaves the classroom, and yet she's not tied up for four years (or more) at the local university. If your student has her heart set on working as a mechanic, computer troubleshooter, or electronics specialist, then a program specifically designed to teach those skills saves her plenty of time.

My local technical college offers programs in interior design, machine tool technology, medical assistantship, and accounting — plus a whole range of programs that fall in between those broad categories. Maybe your area school does, too. Look them up in your phone book and give them a call. They'll be more than happy to send your student a brochure or direct you to the official school Web site.

Entering the work force

Part of productive citizenship is moving into the working public to provide for self and family. Although you don't particularly want your 10-year-old hawking hot dogs on the corner, when your child reaches age eighteen or older, wage earning should probably be a topic of conversation.

Many homeschoolers move directly into the work force. If this is the case, they basically have two options: They work for someone else, or they begin their own enterprise.

Working for someone else

Homeschoolers prove to be popular hires in the workplace because they know how to work independently. This is a huge boon for supervisors and managers who would much rather get the job done than baby-sit a new hire. Some national companies and restaurant chains actively recruit homeschoolers because of their work ethics and independence.

Taking a job right after high school ensures that your student has some money in her possession right away. If your student opts for this route, don't overlook community colleges as a place to get extra training when needed. Relatively inexpensive in the huge scheme of things, these local institutions (sometimes called state vocational or technical schools) teach everything from algebra to computer programming.

Starting a business

A second option in the work realm is to begin your own business. What kind of business? The best options for small business are those jobs that no one else wants to do or that no one gets around to completing even though they should. Computer backups, fish tank cleaning, and outdoor window washing are examples of jobs that often get pushed to the back burner. Another good option is to capitalize on strengths. If you love dogs more than anyone else you know, a dog-sitting service sounds like a small endeavor but in some areas of the country you can make a killing. Devising and starting a small business while still in school allows your student to test the waters with her idea before making it a full-time occupation.

Small businesses don't have to require huge bankrolls to get started. My husband began four or five different small businesses in the past several years, and not one of them needed a business loan to get it going. With a little research and an abundance of ingenuity, your student can start a profitable business with very little cash in hand. When you do it this way, the money you earn goes to your Uncle Sam and into your pocket instead of back to the banker who really owns it to begin with.

Strapping on the Tool Belt

One movement gaining momentum in the homeschooling arena is the internship or apprenticeship as a training tool. Usually, an *internship* takes a semi-trained student for a specific period of time, such as the university internships that engineering students pursue, while an *apprenticeship* trains a learner from the ground up. These options don't get much press, and you probably won't hear much about it. The truth is, though, that a few people are looking up and realizing that the teenagers aren't getting the training they need.

Business people and others are taking notice of the problem, and they quietly offer a solution. You aren't going to enter the medical field as a doctor through an apprenticeship program. That is neither realistic nor wise. If you want to learn how to run a retail shop without losing your mind, however, that's another matter.

A friend of ours currently works with one 14-year-old homeschooled boy and a 15-year-old homeschooled boy as interns. He works with one of them in Web design and graphics while he trains the other in programming skills. He looked at their interests and skill sets, and is quietly helping to refine those skills so they can go on to excel in their fields. This arrangement gives the teens some spending money and much experience.

This is only one example of how an internship can work. Poke around the Internet or ask friends of friends. They may know of someone doing this in your community. Does your child love animals but unsure about going to college? See about an internship with your favorite vet to test the waters.

The point of an apprenticeship is to hone skills and interests already present. If your child shows a fanatical interest in something that doesn't require a college degree, ask around and see if someone would be interested in taking your child as a learner. Experts love to spend time with people who love their field of work, so an apprenticeship is often a good match for someone with a mature skill set and a younger student.

If you do a Web search, the term *homeschool internship* gives you more positive results than *homeschool apprenticeship*, but you may check both to get it all.

Here are a few endeavors that benefit from apprenticeship programs:

- **Baking or the restaurant biz:** If your student is interested in foods for sale — whether as a baker or confectionery expert (also known as candy maker), a cake decorator, or a restaurant staff member — an internship introduces him to the basics of the business along with some of the necessary details (such as contracting with the nightly cleaning crew).

- **Blacksmithing and related occupations:** Some skills, such as blacksmithing and pottery, are best taught one-on-one. These jobs are tailor-made for an apprenticeship program, and many working experts use internships to train the next generation of skilled workers.

- **Journalism:** Although you generally need a college degree in writing or journalism to work for the large city papers, smaller communities and some newsletters only require a love for and facility with words.

- **Retail:** There's much more to retail than standing behind the counter. A retail apprenticeship teaches your student about keeping the books, ordering, supplies, stock, overhead, and the myriad of other details that keep a shop running.

- **Service and hospitality:** If your child wants to work with guests or loves hospitality, perhaps you could find a bed-and-breakfast interested in taking an intern. This would give her hands-on experience before she goes into the world to seek her fortune in the hotel industry.

A while ago, I met a student who worked at our local grocery store. She was taking a class in hotel management at the local college, and as part of her class she arranged an internal internship with the grocery store where she already worked. For two-week rotations, she worked *every* department in the store, just as the management trainees did before taking their final positions. I thought this was a great idea. Not only did it introduce this student to all the areas required to keep a grocery up and running, but it also gave the management a chance to see if she truly excelled in a department she normally didn't inhabit.

Continuing Homeschool through College

With a tear in your eye, you wave goodbye while your recent graduate pulls out of the driveway. Car packed to the brim, she's on her way to college for that exciting freshman year. Or maybe not.

Although many homeschool students take the opportunity to attend college away from home, a few decide to stay near the nest even when the option to leave presents itself. College at home presents quite a few advantages:

- ✔ A familiar living environment
- ✔ Friends you find comfortable
- ✔ People you know who care

Staying at home

You or your teen may opt for college at home for several different reasons. These include, but certainly aren't limited to:

- ✔ **The age or emotional development of the student dictates that they really should stay at home for college.** Most colleges don't know what to do with 12-year-olds, for example. Although a school may be delighted to teach to an exceptionally bright pre-teen, the institution knows that it has no place where it can guide that child's emotional or physical development.

  Even if a student should be old enough chronologically to attend college, if that child still shows emotional development well below his years, then keeping him home for a year or two while the emotions catch up may be a good idea. If you wouldn't send a 14-year-old to college, and your student still functions at a 14-year-old level emotionally (regardless of book knowledge and aptitude), you may want to re-evaluate the decision to send her halfway across the country to college.

✔ **The student decides to stay close to home.** He has no desire to live on campus. He enjoys the town he lives in and wants to stay there. He has access to a full university program close to home, and it offers what he wants.

✔ **You can save plenty of money if your student lives at home instead of residing on campus.** Housing and meal costs are high; add to that the weekly (sometimes daily) dinners out, and you may have a hefty bill on your hands. College is a good time for a student to spread her wings and start to fly on her own, but if she's not ready, you can certainly find a college program to pursue from home.

Finding a suitable program

If you live in a community that offers one or more local colleges or universities, you're already well on your way to solving the problem. Your student may want to take classes at a local college while living at home. This gets her out of the house and onto campus during the school hours (whatever those may be this semester), but at home for nights and weekends.

Looking down the road

What will your children need in the future to survive in the work world — or even in the real world? Some individual skills, such as touch keyboarding, become more and more important every year. Although a company may provide a computer to a new hire, it certainly won't take the time to teach that person to type. In fact, a lack of keyboarding skill may keep your child out of various segments of the job market.

One of the benefits of homeschooling is that parents with foresight can guide their children into that place where they can become the most productive adults. When you think of where your child wants to go and what he desires to do after he graduates, keep in mind that being is much more important than doing. You *do* many different tasks throughout your working years — how many people do you know who work in the fields they were trained for? I know very few, including the adults in my own household.

When you expose your students to many different experiences and learning opportunities within the homeschool framework, you enable them to become a person worth knowing. You also allow them to pursue any avenue they wish — both interior decorating and a career with the Navy is possible for the student who explores his world to the fullest. Guiding your student into pastimes and occupations that develop skills and interests while you still teach him gives him the freedom to spread his wings and become the person he's meant to be after he leaves the fold.

Many colleges offer distance programs these days. Some of them offer complete distance programs where you never need to set foot on the university campus, while others expect to see your student's sunny face for a week or two each year. Requirements depend entirely on each school and its setup. When you read about a school's distance education requirements, they tell you the amount of time (if any) that the school requires bodily student attendance.

To determine the best distance program fit for your student, you may want to do a Web-based search or visit the Peterson's Distance Learning Web site at www.petersons.com/dlearn and browse through the list of degree programs offered at various accredited institutions around the country that have no on-campus requirements. If you want a print version of the information in the Web site, you'll find it in the latest edition of *Peterson's Guide to Distance Learning Programs.* One of the nice things about the Web site is that you can browse through specific intended majors, while the book provides the information school by school, and you have to use a special index to track down your interest.

Part III

Choosing Your Cornerstone: Basic Curriculum Options

The 5th Wave   By Rich Tennant

"I SUPPOSE THIS ALL HAS SOMETHING TO DO WITH THE NEW MATH."

In this part . . .

Every time you embark on an adventure, how you travel determines the accessories that you pack along. For a motorcycle ride, you grab your helmet (and maybe a leather jacket as well). A canoe ride requires a lifejacket. The beginning of an airplane flight finds you locating the air mask, detachable seats, and exit doors. (Depending on what airline you travel, you also may spend some time stowing the bottled sodas, water, and snacks you brought along.)

Just as your mode of transportation dictates the goodies and safety gear that you bring with you, your ideas about education and children determine the curriculum and resources that you buy and how you use them. If you believe that children learn on their own because they're born with the desire to learn, your school days look much different from the parent who thinks that children need to be led, step-by-step, through the learning process. In the same way, various homeschool resources and books are designed to meet the different educational goals.

This part takes you into the realms of classical education, unit studies, unschooling, and operating as a satellite school. Along the way, you also find out what it takes to design your own curriculum from scratch if you decide that's a project that you want to undertake. Also, look in this part for tips on homeschooling special learners and finding the stuff that you need to make it all happen.

Hang on to your library card because you'll need it along the way.

Chapter 11

Orbiting as a Satellite School or ISP

During one of your springtime romps outside in the neighborhood, your neighbor announces that he's decided to enroll as a satellite homeschool next year. You smile blankly and nod, all the while wondering what in the world space travel has to do with education.

Relax — you probably won't see your neighbor's kids building actual-size rockets in the back yard. As a satellite school, your friend will purchase an entire curriculum package from a private school that also promises to help with testing, lesson plans, and general teaching information should he need it. Instead of launching out with nothing but a teacher's manual and workbook to guide him, your neighbor decided to pay a little extra and get the whole package, which includes a human on the other end of the phone or e-mail system if he needs one. Think of it as technical support for homeschooling.

Riding the Satellite

A *satellite* homeschool (also called an *umbrella program*) functions as a tiny one-room schoolhouse under an established, usually private, school's oversight. You choose which school you want to use, pay your tuition for the year, and the school sends you the books, tests, lesson plans, and workbooks — virtually everything you need to do that school's version of education from your own home.

ISPing it

An independent study program, or ISP, can be much like a satellite school. Generally, ISPs are accredited schools that function as paperwork clearinghouses for homeschools. ISPs file required state forms, collect grades, and generally keep your homeschool paperwork organized in case the state or local education department wants to know what you're teaching. Often an ISP goes to bat for you if the state or county educational gurus try to challenge your right to homeschool.

An independent study program may, or may not, provide curriculum for the homeschool, so if you register with an ISP, you may still be responsible for gathering your own curriculum. Most ISPs, though, give you ideas of where to look even if they tell you that you're on your own. Many homeschoolers in California use an independent study program because it meets the California state requirements and frees the family to teach the children rather than spend time filing forms for the state. Most other states, however, enjoy less restrictive laws than California, so while a family may opt to enroll as a satellite program for a year, they don't actually need the help of an ISP.

Several nice things abound about choosing to be a satellite school:

✔ You receive everything you need. It's like school in a box.

✔ You choose the school that stresses what you think is important.

✔ Because you do the teaching, you pay much less than you would to send your child to a local private school.

✔ Because you can enroll as a satellite school from anywhere in the country, you could purchase a year's learning from a school in Baltimore while you live in Mississippi.

Opting for a Complete Curriculum

When you enroll as a satellite school, you receive the established school's complete curriculum for the grade you need. Math, science, language arts, social studies, history, spelling, art, and sometimes music and foreign language — the complete curriculum comes to your house ready to use. The school offers everything, including pencils, paper, drawing paper, crayons, and whatever else the student should need for the school year. The school keeps the records, too.

Prepare thyself. Wondering whether you get all this stuff at once? How long it takes to get it all? How far in advance you should plan to participate in such a school? If you have to return anything? In what format do you usually have to send your records (disk, paper)? The unfortunate answer is that each school does it differently.

The textbooks and lesson plans that you receive should carry you from September through the end of May or the number of teaching days required by your state. At least, that's how it works in the best of worlds. Because each family is different, some families take a little longer than two semesters to go through one year's materials while other families may finish the year's work early and fill the week or two left in the school year with various educational field trips.

A little-known fact, even among veteran homeschoolers, is that you don't *have* to finish all the textbooks every year. Some texts, such as spelling books, are designed for one-unit-per-week use, and these texts include 34 to 36 lessons so that you finish the book by the end of the year.

Other texts, such as math, give you more material than you could probably use in two school semesters. Finish the book if you want to, but if you run out of days before the last page of the text, don't stress. The review pages at the front of next year's math book are designed to take up the slack. Think about it for a minute: What would happen in a class of 25 third graders if they finished all the books with a week of school still to go? Textbook authors envision the anarchy, too — so they include a little more material than the amount needed to fit into a regular year.

Pinpointing a Satellite Program

Now that you know these schools exist, and you think you may be interested in finding out more, where do you turn? If you have an Internet connection, you can always search on the terms *homeschool satellite program, umbrella program,* or *homeschool independent study program.*

Or take a look at the schools listed in this chapter. If a school that's listed in this chapter specifically offers courses through high school, then it also provides your child with an actual diploma when she graduates.

To qualify for the diploma, however, you generally need to work with the school at least three of the four high school years.

Elementary through junior high

Some schools cover the entire range from kindergarten through high school, while others offer programs for only a portion of that time. Each school's requirements, fees, and offerings vary from the others. These schools all base their curriculum on different educational theories, yet I've heard various homeschool parents give almost every one of them rave reviews.

Take the time to look at several of the schools. If a complete curriculum and some teaching oversight interests you, give them a call if you have any questions. All these schools currently offer Web sites, so you can peek at them that way too, if you have Internet access.

The following list provides only a few of the full curriculum providers out there, but they give a good picture of the available range of services, curriculum, and prices.

- ✔ **Calvert School:** 10713 Gilroy Road Suite B, Hunt Valley, MD 21031; Phone: 410-785-3400; Internet: `www.calvertschool.org`. Calvert School has been involved in distance learning since 1905. Calvert offers homeschool programs for kindergarten through eighth grade, and they have a reputation for excellence. Calvert actually operates a day school that began in 1897. With Calvert, you can opt for a complete curriculum or choose your own math program if you like. They also offer optional elective courses.

- ✔ **Christian Liberty Academy School System (CLASS):** 502 W. Euclid Avenue, Arlington Heights, IL 60004-5495; Phone: 847-259-4444; Internet: `www.class-homeschools.org`. CLASS offers several options for students from kindergarten through grade twelve, including enrollment as a full satellite school. CLASS assembles an appropriate curriculum based on your child's current achievement levels. CLASS also offers parents assistance when and if they need it, and the program intervenes with local school officials if necessary.

- ✔ **Laurel Springs School:** P.O. Box 144, Ojai, CA 93024-1440; Phone: 800-377-5890; Internet: `www.laurelsprings.com`. Laurel Springs School offers textbook curriculum for pre-kindergarten students through twelfth grade. A project-based curriculum is available for kindergarten through eighth graders, and Laurel Springs also offers optional programs for special learners, honors students, and college prep.

- ✔ **Oak Meadow:** P.O. Box 740 Putney, VT 05346; Phone: 802-387-2021; Internet: `www.oakmeadow.com`. Oak meadow offers a curriculum that integrates various subjects as much as possible, so that students experience learning rather than simply work through a textbook. Lessons are divided into 36 weekly components, and students may work on one concept or many related concepts throughout a given week. Oak Meadow serves children from kindergarten through twelfth grade and bases its primary curriculum on the education theory that guides *Waldorf* schools (see Appendix C for more on "Waldorf" schools).

✔ **Seascape Center and Malibu Cove Private School:** P.O. Box 1074, Thousand Oaks, CA 91358-0074; Phone: 805-446-1917; Internet: www. seascapecenter.com. This is two schools in one. Seascape Center serves students from kindergarten through eighth grade, while Malibu Cove Private School offers high school courses. Both schools use curriculum from a variety of standard publishers, while most of the private schools that enroll satellite homeschools write at least a portion of their own curriculum for their students. Seascape Center also offers a specialized curriculum for hearing-impaired students, which is unusual, and both school divisions are willing to customize curriculum for individual students.

High schools

You say that you don't want to wing it when it comes to high school? In addition to the multigrade options listed earlier, you also may want to look at the full curriculum programs that these schools offer. Each one organizes its program a bit differently, but all of them offer diplomas to qualifying graduating seniors. These schools also qualify as accredited institutions.

Although you can find many more correspondence high schools on the Internet, and you can probably locate some really good ones, the following listing shows a few of the tried and true.

✔ **American School:** 2200 East 170th Street, Lansing, IL 60438; Phone: 800-531-9268; Internet: www.americanschoolofcorr.org. American School has been around since 1897 and has granted over 200,000 diplomas within the past fifty years — a pretty high number for any high school. American School provides correspondence courses for grades nine through twelve and offers both a general high school curriculum and college prep track.

✔ **Indiana University High School:** Office of Academic Programs, School of Continuing Studies, Owen Hall 002, 790 E. Kirkwood Avenue, Bloomington, IN 47405-7101; Phone: 800-334-1011; Internet: http://scs.indiana.edu. Indiana University High School allows students to take as many or as few individual courses as they need, so full-time registration is not a requirement with Indiana University High School. The high school allows students to take college and high school courses simultaneously.

✔ **Keystone National High School:** School House Station, 420 W. 5th Street, Bloomsburg, PA 17815-1564; Phone: 800-255-4937; Internet: www. keystonehighschool.com. Delivers almost all its courses either through correspondence or the Internet. Enrollment options include taking a single course, taking several courses at one time, or enrolling in the full diploma program. With Internet courses listed as the most expensive option, course costs vary.

✔ **University of Nebraska-Lincoln Independent Study High School:** Clifford Hardin Nebraska Center for Continuing Education, Room 269, Lincoln, NE 68583-9801; Phone: 402-472-4422; Internet: www.unl.edu/ishs. Dates back to 1929. A division of the University of Nebraska's Continuing Education program, the high school offers both a general high school level track and a college prep option. Independent Study High School also allows interested students to take high school and college courses simultaneously.

Independent Study Programs

These ISPs provide a paperwork umbrella for homeschooling families but require — and offer — no set curriculum. Thus, families who enroll with an ISP such as these not only get the state's required paperwork taken care of, but they're free to teach their children however they feel is best. This takes a load off the parent who wants to teach without specific curriculum yet still has an obligation to the state of residence for various homeschooling forms. Available independent study programs are shown in the following list:

✔ **Branford Grove School:** P.O. Box 341172, Arleta, CA 91334; Phone: 818-890-0350; Internet: www.branfordgrove.com. Branford Grove School offers a program for students in grades one through twelve. The school gives you a curriculum guide, attendance sheets, and other organizational forms. Branford Grove also deals with an enrolled family's local school officials if necessary. Homeschool families are free to use a complete packaged curriculum from a publisher of their choice or assimilate their curriculum from Branford Grove's resource list.

✔ **Clonlara School:** 1289 Jewett, Ann Arbor, MI 48104; Phone: 734-769-4511; Internet: www.clonlara.org. Clonlara School runs a home education program derived from the private school they've operated for thirty years or so. Using Clonlara's umbrella system can serve as an intermediary between families and school officials when necessary. The school advocates an unschooling approach and functions as an ISP for kindergarten through grade twelve.

✔ **Family Learning Center:** 3590 Peralta Boulevard, Fremont, CA 94536; Phone: 510-818-9864; Internet: www.familyplayce.org. The Family Learning Center takes care of all forms, helps families locate programs, such as driver's education and work permits, and provides a calendar of scheduled field trips.

Keep your own records and save money

Sometimes a school that offers a satellite program also allows parents to purchase the books and materials without buying into the entire program. If you feel comfortable keeping track of assignments and grades, this may be an option to pursue with your curriculum provider. Basically you follow the school's program, but you don't get the same level of support as a true satellite homeschool.

You assign the work, grade the papers, give the tests, grade the tests, and post the grades in your own grade book or computerized grading system. Then at the end of the quarter, semester, or year — however you decide to assign grades — you record final grades for those courses, which go onto a report card form that you can often purchase from the school as well.

Keeping your own records offers a few benefits:

You save quite a bit over the full satellite tuition price. Because you're only buying the textbooks and not all the teaching support that goes with them, you see monetary savings that are directly related.

You can tackle the books at your child's pace rather than setting your pace to match the school's calendar. For some families, this means taking a school year and a half

to get through the material. Other families may have a child who finishes two years' work in one school term.

On the other hand, purchasing only the materials and keeping the records yourself can pose some challenges. For one thing, some states require that you register as a satellite school or deal with increased state involvement or paperwork. In addition, when you purchase only the books and not the support, you're pretty much going out on your own. If you don't understand something in the teacher's manual, for example, no one sits patiently on the other end of the phone to talk you through it as they would if you registered as a full satellite school.

Also, if the school offers some type of formal school graduation from its high school program, and you only purchase the books and not the whole box of goods, then your child doesn't qualify as a satellite school graduate. This means no diploma from said institution.

If the freedom and savings mean more to you than full accountability and a certificate, and your state gives no limitations to homeschools, then purchasing the materials and completely teaching the courses yourself may be a viable option.

Matching Your Needs with Their Offerings

If you locate the greatest program in the world, and it doesn't match your child's needs, and then it may as well be written in a completely foreign language for all the good it will do you. Children thrive when they feel loved, cared for, and challenged at their level. Unfortunately, for some families this means selecting different curriculums — maybe even totally separate programs — to teach individual children in the ways they learn best. Lest you throw this chapter down in stark terror, I need to tell you that this doesn't happen very often. But it does happen.

Before you plunk down your money on a complete program, take a good look at the school's offerings.

- ✔ Do the subjects match what your child needs to learn?
- ✔ Does the school offer a placement test to ensure that your child is placed with the right grade-level materials?
- ✔ Is the school willing to give you textbooks from multiple grades if your child shows different ability levels for various subjects?
- ✔ Does the school have a history of being flexible with ending dates if something should come up during the year and you find yourself teaching past June?

If you have a child who whizzes through math but can't write a complete sentence by fourth grade because language just isn't his strong point, plopping him into fourth-grade curriculum across the board will hurt both his language skills *and* his math, unless you're willing to do some extra work in both subjects.

If you really, really like what the school offers and the school seems inflexible in its grade requirements, you always have the option to be flexible in yours. Whip through the math as quickly as your child wants to do the work, for example, and spend twice as much time on the language, grammar, and spelling to try to even out the skills.

Chapter 12

Does Classical Education Mean Teaching Vivaldi?

In This Chapter
▶ What is this classical thing?
▶ Assembling classical curriculum
▶ Gathering information

*V*irtually every homeschool book and magazine these days mentions the virtues of a classical education. If visions of togas dance through your head at the mention of the word classical, you certainly aren't alone. I use a variation of a classical curriculum with my own children, and the dancing toga sometimes crosses my mind, too. Then I focus on the day's tasks, and we work through our Greek vocabulary words one more time.

Tailor-made for the homeschool, classical studies focus on presenting education much as it was taught during the classical period of history — the way England and other European countries trained their scholars from the Middle Ages and Renaissance onward. Some (albeit few) private schools do provide a classical education, but it waxes strong in homeschool households. A classical education requires much work, much thinking, and exposure to a broad range of historical, scientific, and mathematical ideas.

If this information doesn't click with you the first time through, then we're in this together. Classical education is completely different than any other homeschool method, and it took me a good length of time — plus several different writers — before I figured it out.

Classifying It Classical

When people talk about classical education, they're talking about both a way of presenting information and the nuggets of knowledge offered. Classical education seeks to unearth the questions that stumped humanity since the beginning of the ages — beyond the ever-present, "What's for dinner tonight?" Classical education studies both the questions and the various answers to those queries.

Classical learning looks at the education of ancient Greece and Rome, the Middle Ages, and the Renaissance, and models a modern liberal arts education after these. It divides information and learning into three stages. All together called the *trivium,* these stages give information to students in a way they can handle it. The stages are

- ✔ Grammar
- ✔ Logic
- ✔ Rhetoric

Trying the trivium

The trivium's three stages of learning are called the *grammar*, the *logic*, and the *rhetoric* stages. Each stage focuses on learning in a different way as a child's mind matures and he can think more clearly and more abstractly. The complete trivium covers the entire range of elementary and high school.

Grammar stage

Generally the grammar stage covers the beginning of school through grade four or five. It concentrates on exposing children to a wide range of information, even if they don't yet understand how it all fits together. Later, with the data in their memory, they pull it out when they need it and assemble the puzzle pieces.

Little children usually memorize facts well — how many children at your house *don't* know the words to "Twinkle, Twinkle Little Star" or "The Alphabet Song?" Yet when your child memorized the letters of the alphabet in song, she didn't understand why those individual letters held meaning. It was simply a great song with a cool tune, and the older people in her life seemed to really enjoy listening to her sing it.

When your child needs to use the alphabet later for arranging books or words in an a-b-c order, that information is hardwired into her brain. She simply retrieves it and uses the alphabet to accomplish the task. This is the idea behind the grammar stage of learning. Students learn various pieces of information while they're young, and to do that you introduce them to history, literature, geography, science, mathematics, and foreign language. Then when they need it later, the information comes to the surface.

Logic stage

Children who function in the logic stage are usually in fifth or sixth grade through eighth grade. (Sometimes you see this stage listed as the *dialectic* stage, but *logic* is much easier to say.) Asking questions along the way, these children take the information that they know and begin to fit it together.

For example, they know that Julius Caesar met his end on the Ides of March 44 B.C. They also know that one of the reasons behind Caesar's assassination was the Roman people's fear of change. Taking all this in, the child in the logic state of reasoning can then ask or answer these questions: What kind of a ruler was Julius Caesar from the people's viewpoint? How did he rank on the ruler scale from history's viewpoint? How do we see him today?

Like all the stages, movement into, through, and from the logic stage depends much more on the child's thoughts and mental development than on ages. Some children may be ready to move into the logic stage a bit early, and they ask questions as they assimilate the information they've stored away. Others may not move into the logic stage until sixth grade or so, when they're ready to put the pieces together.

Asking logical questions when your children are still in the grammar stage gets you nothing but really blank stares. It took me awhile to figure out the difference. I needed to step back a little and ask them to retell the story I just finished relating rather than draw any deep and meaningful conclusions for me. When I asked for deep and meaningful, the question that usually arose was, "Mom, is it time for lunch yet? I'm getting hungry."

Rhetoric stage

From ninth grade and beyond, your student should function at the rhetoric stage. Your student learns to communicate in an expressive and persuasive manner when your student tells you and anyone else who may be listening what's on his mind, thus putting all those years of memorization and thinking to good use. The rhetoric stage also gives your student the time and freedom to pursue the subjects he loves.

After spending the first eight years exploring a broad variety of subjects, such as math, science, language arts, foreign language, art, music, and the like, the rhetoric level student can finally focus on what he enjoys. If he shows little skill for foreign languages, for example, then there's really no reason to continue advanced study in Latin, French, and Greek. The student who excels at languages, however, finds joy and purpose in continuing forward with these subjects. He may even decide to concentrate on them in college.

Students fill their rhetoric years with debate, writing, speaking, and conversation as they continue down the road toward a liberal arts education. Taking a look back at Caesar and his times, this student may articulate a well-designed argument for Caesar's unintentional role in the demise of the Roman Empire. After all these years of study, classically trained students generally function well at the college level after they arrive. Many find the first couple years of college a breeze compared to their high school studies!

Forming the foundation with literature

Classical education looks at the philosophers of the ages and the classic books that stand the test of time. These create the curriculum's written foundation. Students read from the collection of literature known as great books to spark their minds and show them how other people thought.

What are the great books? That's a really good question, and almost anyone you ask will give you a different answer. Mortimer J. Adler, a professor at Columbia who coined the term "great books" in the first place, put his own list together. You may agree with his list, or you may not, and that's okay. If you want to take a look at what Adler called the great books, you can find it in *Encyclopaedia Britannica's Great Books of the Western World* collection (Internet: www.Britannica.com). The Web site lists all the authors included in the collection.

By reading the works of the past, the student wrestles with the same problems the original writer contended with. The material world, the questions of philosophy, the beauty of mathematics, and the order of science all find their place in a classical curriculum. Students often explore these subjects through the literature created by the mathematicians, scientists, and philosophers as they grappled with their problems and reported their discoveries. One popular way to approach these writers with older students is to read an author's works as you study the time period in which they lived; thus, students studying ancient Rome read Plato, Aristotle, Cicero, and so on.

Assembling Your Classical Curriculum Components

A classical curriculum covers all subjects for the child's entire twelve years of school: language arts, math, science, history, geography, art, music, and . . . um . . . Latin. Okay. So you don't actually start Latin in first grade. You usually wait until third grade or beyond to begin Latin. But Latin composes part of a classical curriculum, and some families also add Greek and one or two modern foreign languages, such as French, Spanish, or German, to add variety to the mix.

Keep in mind as you read through these recommendations that they are only suggestions. This is your child and your curriculum. If the all-out classical curriculum doesn't work with your child, but parts of the system jazz you, go with what works. (Excuse me while I dodge flaming arrows from the diehard classicists over there.)

Language arts

Read. Write. Spell. Conjugate . . . er . . . explore grammar. The classical curriculum puts a huge emphasis on the written word — primarily because Socrates and Plato didn't have access to video recorders, I think. Teaching your child to read becomes your primary language arts goal. After she masters reading at a second- or third-grade level, you can begin to explore good books with abandon. (For ideas on what to use to teach her to read, please turn to Chapter 7.)

Reading

Everything your child reads doesn't have to display *Classical* in gold letters on its cover. Because your goal is to teach your child to think, however, it helps if the books are decent literature to begin with. Introducing your child to Robert Louis Stevenson's *Kidnapped,* Sherlock Holmes mysteries, Louisa May Alcott's *Little Women,* or the Greek myths opens new worlds to them.

If your child isn't quite ready for the unabridged version of whatever book you want her to read, most classics are available in children's versions from various publishers. A trip to the library or local bookstore should unearth plenty of options. Although many parents disagree with me, I made these children's versions readily available to my kids. By age eight they both declared Jack London's *The Call of the Wild* one of the best books they ever read, and their exposure to the classics rivals that of many college graduates.

A trip through the 800 section of your local library (if your library follows the Dewey Decimal System . . . if it doesn't you can search for the 800s for days and never find them) unearths tons of classic literature. Find an author you love or recognize, or try someone new to you.

We often use electronic versions of the classics because housing bound copies of every classic we own would soon book us out of house and home! When I need a new classic that doesn't reside on our home library shelves, I pop an electronic text CD into the computer and print out the text. On the Internet, visit one of these two sites for thousands of classic electronic texts:

- ✔ Pink Monkey: www.pinkmonkey.com
- ✔ Project Gutenberg: www.promo.net/pg

You can also get the latest copy of Project Gutenberg burned onto CDs from Walnut Creek CD-ROM, Phone: 800-786-9907.

Writing

Although your final goal is to teach your child to write the well-organized persuasive essay or research document, getting there takes some time and perseverance. Beginning with sentences, your child then progresses to one paragraph, and then puts paragraphs together with meaning. Before you know it (several years later), he's writing for a specific purpose, and you realize he learned to write after all.

Writing Strands, a writing curriculum mentioned in Chapter 15, covers all grade levels and teaches writing in a progressive manner. In fact, any of the writing programs in that list would work for writing.

Unless you find yourself (or your child) permanently chained to a computer keyboard with red licorice, an actual handwriting program is in order. As with everything else in homeschooling, you have a choice of curriculums.

Spelling

Although some children hate spelling and others love it, most parents agonize over *the* spelling curriculum to introduce to their homeschool. Before the angst hits you too, take a deep breath, step back a moment, and ask yourself these questions:

- ✔ What are you actually trying to teach with spelling?
- ✔ Do you want your children to actually learn to *spell*?
- ✔ If that is the case, what words do you want them to spell?
- ✔ Should they spell words from their world and their reading?

Then assemble your own spelling lists each week from life as you live it and use those words.

If you want your children to learn to spell almost any word (and you have dreams of your Myrtle becoming the next International Spelling Champ), then look at a curriculum such as Excellence in Spelling (Internet: `www.writing-edu.com/spelling`). Excellence in spelling breaks down words phonetically and your student spells them after multiple practice repetitions.

On the other hand, you may look at spelling as one of the required "rules based" subjects of the grammar stage. If spelling makes you think of a subject that lays down the rules in a no-frills way yet gets the job done, then peek at *Webster's Blue Back Speller and New England Primer,* by (The Man himself) Noah Webster. This reprint from the late eighteenth/early nineteenth century starts easy, but progresses to a raft of words that most adults can't spell without their handy-dandy dictionary.

You can use the Webster book as a basic grammar guide, too, or branch out into a program such as The Shurley Method (discussed more fully in Chapter 15) or the Easy Grammar/Daily Grams combination (Internet: `www.easygrammar.com/EZGrammar.htm`; Phone: 800-641-6015) that teaches and then reviews grammar skills each school day.

Math

Your classical math program teaches the flow and structure of mathematics. Beginning with the easy stuff, such as addition, your student climbs the mathematical ladder as far as he can go before the end of twelfth grade. Classical students usually go beyond second-year algebra, although your student's math progress is up to him.

To begin your progression, you can use any math program that teaches solid concepts. Chapter 15 suggests several math curricula that may work for your child. Early focus in math, as a classical homeschooler, needs to be on fact memorization (such as multiplication, division, addition, and subtraction facts) as well as a good knowledge of how math *works* in addition/subtraction, multiplication/division, fractions, geometry, and algebra concepts. With a good base, your student can then tackle higher math courses more easily.

Although they may begin in the low grades with another math curriculum, most classical homeschoolers switch to Saxon Math and follow Saxon's recommendations at age 10 or 12 through the end of high school (see more about Saxon Math in Chapters 7 and 9). Saxon contains plenty of review in every single lesson. (For some children, I'd go so far as to call it math busy-work). But it does seem to get the job done. And you don't have to assign all the problems each day if your child doesn't need to do them all.

Science

Classical science places an emphasis on the traditional sciences: biology, chemistry, and physics. But you can't start there with a first grader. Your goal is to build a scientific basis so that when your child gets to formal biology age, she'll be ready for the challenge.

Explore nature. Watch the stars. If you want a manual to guide you, many in-print science books explain the basics of astronomy, the earth, and nature. For a one-volume guide, you may want to look at Anna Botsford Comstock's *Handbook of Nature Study,* covered in detail in Chapter 15.

After you get to high school science, in the best of all possible classical schools, your student reads the original treatises by scientists such as Galileo, Copernicus, and Aristotle. (I know that Aristotle is usually considered a philosopher. But because he's the author of *Physics* and *On the Parts of Animals,* he's a scientist, too.) At the same time, your child works through high school textbooks on biology, chemistry, and physics, continuing on that foundation she built through elementary and middle school science.

The Great Books Academy, a classical school listed at the end of this section, uses Glencoe Science books as the basis for their advanced science courses. You can purchase these texts directly from the Great Books Academy. Call 800-521-4004 or visit their Web site: www.greatbooksacademy.org.

History

The best way to explore history in the classical tradition is to read the stories of the men and women who made it. Beginning with ancient civilizations, the student progresses through ancient Egypt, Greece, Rome, Vikings, Middle Ages, Renaissance, Explorers, and finally the New World. (Of course, if you want to cover ancient China, Japan, Africa, Aztecs, Maya, or any other civilization, go ahead and slip them in wherever you want to emphasize them, but a classical history curriculum generally follows the history of Western Civilization.)

Reading biographies and writings of explorers, statesmen, philosophers, artists, leaders, and inventors gives your student a well-rounded feel for the time. Of course, no one could possibly cover it all! Even college professors limit their expertise to one portion of history rather than trying to be an expert in everything.

Here are a few resources you may want to consider when you chart your history curriculum. Like every other subject listed, this gives you a small sampling of the resources out there:

- **Bluestocking Press:** This company (Internet: www.bluestockingpress.com; Phone: 800-959-8586) sells various United States and world history resources in addition to other material. This company's catalog provides good browsing or bathroom reading.

- *Calliope, Cobblestone,* and *Footsteps* **magazines:** All brainchildren of Cobblestone publishing (Internet: www.cobblestonepub.com; Phone: 800-821-0115), *Calliope* focuses on world history, *Cobblestone* presents American history, and relatively new *Footsteps* centers on African-American history. All designed for readers age 9 through 14, these magazines are topical and *Cobblestone* keeps most, if not all, back issues in print. When you want to teach a subject, see if *Cobblestone* offers a back (or current) issue on that topic.

✔ **Greenleaf Famous Men series:** If you feel more comfortable with biographies in hand, you may enjoy this series. Individual books cover Greece, Rome, Middle Ages, and Renaissance/Reformation, and the Greenleaf Press catalog lists enough extra history resources to keep you busy with history for quite a long time. Although the optional study guides that go along with each volume are written from a Christian perspective, the Famous Men books themselves (titled *Famous Men of Greece,* Rome, and so forth) are edited revisions from a 1904 series on famous people from history. Thus, the Famous Men books (along with many of the other history books in the Greenleaf catalog) aren't specifically Christian in content.

✔ **History coloring books:** Although these are primarily for the younger scholars, history coloring books provide something for little hands to do while you read aloud and they give your child a visual impression of the time. For history coloring books in all time periods, look at Dover Publications (Internet: `www.doverpublications.com`; 31 East 2nd Street, Mineola, NY 11501-3852), which you should find samples of at any bookstore, and The Color & Learn series from EduPress (Internet: `www.edupressinc.com`; Phone: 800-835-7978). The EduPress books feature times and places, such as Ancient Egypt, Japan, Africa, and Ancient Greece.

Geography

Geography can be as simple as sitting down with a globe or good atlas or as complicated as purchasing a full geography curriculum. You decide. If you want to go the globe-and-atlas route, you can spend some intensive time studying each region as you cover it in history. On the other hand, if a curriculum interests you, check out some of the ideas in Chapter 15.

A classical curriculum usually incorporates geography into history rather than teaching it as an alternative subject. Introducing your grammar-stage student to maps, globes, and the measurement mystique that surrounds them both (as in latitude and scale) is a good way to get the rudiments of geography into your child during the memorization stage. After they have the basics down, you can introduce the geography of a place as you introduce the time you plan to study.

Any quality local education store should carry introductory workbooks on maps, longitude, and the like. I spent a year covering American Education Publishing's *Maps and Geography* workbook with my elementary-age children, which laid the foundation well enough that we can now move on to more interesting topics than isolated physical maps and room layouts.

Art

Classical art instruction takes two forms: art creation and art appreciation. As part of a liberal arts course, students learn the *doing* part of art as well as the *looking* part. After all, looking at an impressionistic painting is much more fun when you understand the method because you experimented with impressionism yourself at one point.

In some countries, such as the United Kingdom, learning to draw and paint still marks you as an educated individual. Talent has nothing to do with it. Every child learns basic drawing skills in a classical school in the same way that each child learns to read and write. And just as every student who ever took piano lessons doesn't turn out a concert pianist, so each child in art lessons doesn't become another Picasso. (And the world is grateful. After all, how many Picassos do you need in one world?)

When you teach a child to draw, you are teaching them to *see* — to look at the world around them with new eyes. That's the goal of art instruction. Art appreciation, on the other hand, teaches them to see the effects of culture on art, and art on culture, as they study art history through the years.

To enhance your art curriculum, you may want to look into

- **HomeschoolArts.com:** This Web site (www.homeschoolarts.com) offers more art books than I knew were available. Sections include information and recommendations for art with pencil, pen and ink, colored pencils, watercolor, pastel, and acrylics, to name a few. This site also offers free art lessons to get you started.

- **Your local library:** Libraries generally carry a nice selection of juvenile and adult art books. Select one or two and work through them as a basis for your art curriculum.

- **Local art lessons:** Does your community offer continuing education courses through the local high school or community college? A class or two in drawing, painting, or perspective may entice your older learner into a love of art. They generally aren't expensive and give your student a different perspective on art than working through lessons at home.

Keep in mind that your finished product is only as good as your materials. Although you don't need to run out and spend hundreds of dollars on art materials, starting with a few decent drawing pencils and perhaps a small box of Berol PrismaColors (if you plan to do colored pencil drawings as well) can make the difference between joy and drudgery.

Music

Most classical homeschoolers use private piano or violin lessons as part of their curriculum. If they find that their children absolutely hate lessons after a year or two, they — get ready . . . radical thought here — *stop* the lessons. That's right. They stop. End. Finis.

Some children really love music and music lessons. Those kids generally continue in lessons for years. But everybody isn't born with a perfect ear and rhythm. (Unfortunately, I know this because I was one of those children. Even as an adult, I am rhythm-challenged.)

Music doesn't *have* to consist of private lessons. You can teach a love of music without teaching all the theory and practice behind it. Composer biographies and classical and folk music selections can function as an add-on to your history curriculum (call it *culture* if you want) in addition to stand-alone music lessons. Turn to Chapter 25 for even more discussion of music and its appreciation.

Latin

Ah, Latin. The language of love . . . or is that Italian? The language of wonderful food . . . nope, that's French. The language of — hey, why *do* we study Latin, anyway?

Scholars (that includes your child if she follows a classical curriculum) study Latin because it forms the basis of so many languages, including a hefty portion of English. They also study Latin because many of the philosophers wrote their original thoughts in that language, especially if they happened to be Romans. Rumor also has it that many classical educators of the past — the way past — taught in Latin, but I'm not sure that's enough reason to run out and learn a new language.

In a pure classical curriculum, Latin takes one of the prime subject spots. When you begin Latin is up to you. You can find curriculum for students as young as third grade if you want to start Latin that early, or you can wait until your students grow a bit taller before you begin reciting the beloved Latin conjugations of yore.

You may want to consider these Latin resources in your planning:

✔ **Artes Latinae:** Written for 10-year-old students on up, this curriculum includes cassettes or CD-ROM, graded readers, a reference notebook, and tests. The curriculum meets the requirement for two years' of high school foreign language, and it's been around long enough to be recommended by a homeschool generation. Available online from Bolchazy-Carducci Publishers at www.arteslatinae.com.

- ✔ **Latin Primer series:** A beginning Latin course for third grade on, these books sport titles such as *Latin Primer I, Latin Primer II,* and *Latin Primer III.* Look for it from Canon Press (Internet: www.cannonpress.org).

- ✔ **Latin's Not So Tough:** You can begin this Latin curriculum at grade three, or maybe even a little younger. Available in five levels, students progress from the Latin alphabet to five noun declensions and various verb conjugations. The Greek 'n Stuff Web site, www.greeknstuff, tells you more.

- ✔ **The Latin Library:** This online library (http://patriot. net/~lillard/cp/latlib) groups a collection of Latin texts for your reading pleasure. This site contains everything from commentaries by Caesar to a Latin translation of Lewis Carroll's *Jabberwocky.*

- ✔ *Wheelock's Latin:* Originally written in 1956, this hefty little volume contains grammar, Latin reading selections, and (in the newest sixth edition) maps to help you orient your learning. Written for college-level instruction, homeschoolers use it at high school level on up.

- ✔ **Workbook for** *Wheelock's Latin:* This companion volume gives you drills and vocabulary exercises to help cement your Latin learning. Also available at high school level on up.

Foreign language

Contrary to popular opinion, children who learn more than one foreign language will not die. In fact, they live even if you go so far as to introduce a new language while they're yet young. Preschool language learners actually provide quite a bit of merriment because they select whichever word means what they want to say, regardless of the language.

French and Spanish make good companion languages for a classical curriculum because your child is already learning Latin, and Latin forms the root for these languages. Foreign language is foreign language, however, and if you have your heart set on another one, the Classical Cops won't show up at your door next Saturday demanding to know

1. Why you aren't doing school on a perfectly fine day; and

2. Why you think you must teach Russian to your youngster instead of French.

Chapter 25 goes into more detail about foreign language programs available to homeschoolers.

Certified classically crazed

If you like the idea of classical education but reading the information presented in this chapter makes your head swim, take a chocolate break and try it again later. The words still look blurry? Then you may want to enroll in a school that puts the parts together for you.

Take a look at what Calvert School offers for kindergarten through eighth grade. Calvert comes pretty close to classical education in a box. This school, which has been around since 1897, operates satellite programs for home-school families, so look for more information about Calvert in Chapter 11.

Great Books Academy (Internet: www.great booksacademy.org) is another school that offers a classical liberal arts education. Serving students from preschool through grade twelve, Great Books Academy offers lesson plans, end-of-the-year grading, and access to a human if you have questions with the course of study. The school also provides eighth grade and high school diplomas to graduating students. Contact them at The Great Books Academy, 1213 Piedmont Road North, Suite 107, P.O. Box 360, Piedmont, OK 73078; Phone: 800-521-4004.

Even if you don't enroll your child in the Great Books Academy as a student, the school's online bookstore sells a wonderful assortment of solid classical curriculum for various subjects. Anyone can purchase books online from the academy.

Gathering More Information

Although classical education generates much interest, not many people write books about it these days. The best all-around book in print today is probably *The Well-Trained Mind, A Guide to Classical Education at Home,* by Jessie Wise and Susan Wise Bauer. A mother and daughter team, they tell how Jessie created and implemented a classical curriculum in her homeschool. The book gives you a framework for creating a classical curriculum yourself. At the same time, the authors tell you what works in a classical setting and what doesn't.

If you have Internet access, you may want to do some online reading. Search **classical education** on the Internet at www.google.com. Some of the Web sites and links that will turn up as a result are useful while a great number of them aren't.

But Mom, I don't *want* to learn Latin!

Sometimes opposition comes from the most interesting corners. First your mother isn't too sure about this foreign language thing. Then your child announces that Latin is a dead language and she is *not* going to learn Latin this year!

You don't absolutely have to study Latin, but it sure helps. For one thing, spending some time with Latin and Greek now means that you don't have to exert as much effort mastering Greek and Latin derivatives later. Besides, what better secret language could the teen homeschool club find than Latin or Greek? They're practically undecipherable — the prime goal of teen and pre-teen gatherings everywhere.

Of all the ancient languages, Latin is one of the easiest to learn. Unlike Sumerian, Egyptian Hieroglyphics, Hebrew, or Greek, you don't need to learn an entirely new alphabet to master it. This alone saves you weeks of time! Plus, much of the English language traces its roots to Latin words. So Latin looks at least vaguely familiar. How many Sumerian-based nouns do you know off the top of your head?

Plus, after you get into the swing of things, you can pick up some Latin leisure reading. Honestly, I do not jest. *Cattus Petasatus, Winnie Ille Pu,* and *Quomodo Invidiosulus Nomine Grinchus* are all available for your reading pleasure. Who'd a thought? (For your pre-first-year Latin readers out there, these books are Latin translations of *The Cat in the Hat, Winnie the Pooh,* and *How the Grinch Stole Christmas.*)

Chapter 13

Teaching Them What They Want to Learn

According to your 9-year-old son, weather is the most important subject in the world. He tracks the phases of the moon. You have a handmade monthly rainfall chart tacked to the refrigerator door — always complete by the end of the month because he studiously empties the rain gauge into the flowerbed after marking the current water level. He reads books about tornadoes, monsoons, and other natural disasters with relish and waxes poetic about his favorite topic at the slightest invitation.

What do you *do* with a child like him? Well, you could present him with a brand new stack of textbooks each year and insist that he work through them. That is one option. Another, perhaps more palatable idea, is to take what he loves and what he's good at and build from there. This type of learning is called *unit study* or *theme-based* education.

Unit studies take a topic — virtually any topic will do, as long as your students show some interest in it — and build a whole curriculum around the topic, rather than treat each subject as an individual, stand-alone entity. If you build on interests the students already have and teach one large topic at a time rather than isolated subjects, then teaching becomes easier for you as the parent and your children generally become more involved in the learning.

Unveiling the Integrated Unit Study

A well-designed unit study takes information from all subjects and fits them together like the pieces of a puzzle. Going back to the weather example, the child writes a story about a spectacular thunderstorm for language arts, draws cloud formations for art, and calculates the differences in wind velocities for math. For social studies, he looks at the way in which different cultures experience storms, and the science portion of the unit study allows him to read about antique and modern weather instruments and their inventors. Spelling and vocabulary both focus on weather words, and if you sing or play songs about weather, you include music as well. (Think *It's Raining, It's Pouring* and *Stormy Weather.*)

When you take a step back and look at the whole package, you have a complete curriculum for a week or two — or even longer — that highlights one particular subject. While you learn about one subject in depth, you also hit the other required subjects along the way. The main subject could be almost anything: Art, music, reading, math, science, and social studies all make great jumping off points for unit studies. To do a whole unit study on a topic such as grammar, however, requires a diehard little grammar lover. And to date, I've never met one. My kids roll their eyes when I begin to extol the virtues of the prepositional phrase; they'd think that I had lost my mind if I suggested studying grammar for two whole weeks!

Unit studies are spectacular for teaching children whose ages vary widely. The 4-year-old and the high school student can both study a topic such as weather as long as you include information, tasks, and projects appropriate to both learning levels.

All unit studies, all the time

Many homeschool families opt to build their entire curriculum around the unit study concept. Most unit studies are designed to be completed in a week or two, so they select 18 or 36 different topics to fill a year and go from there. Or a family may choose the first six units or so and see how the year goes. If the kids really get into one particular subject, such as horses, you can track down additional information at the library or visit a horse breeder. Or watch a movie or two that feature horses as main characters and talk about the movie's plot and special effects. With additions like these, you could easily take a unit study designed for two weeks and stretch it for a month or so.

We did something like this with just one subject, history. Two years ago we began studying ancient Rome. We took a curriculum that was supposed to last one year or less — possibly as little as a third of a school year — and stretched it to two years by adding historical novels, architecture, CD-ROMs, art projects, such as mosaics and Roman-style lamps, and authentic recipes.

We not only had a great time, but the kids have a much better understanding of Roman life, culture, and history than they would otherwise. (We are, however, a bit behind on our Viking studies because we had such a good time in Rome.)

Locating unit studies

You decide to try the unit study route, and you have no idea where to track these elusive books down. Unit studies aren't too hard to find if you know what you're looking for. This section gives you a starting point by listing some of the better-known and more prolific unit study publishers available, along with an idea of the subjects they cover.

Look for words such as *unit*, *theme*, or *integrated* in the title or subtitle of a unit study when you browse through the local education store or search the Internet.

Almost all unit studies these days contain *reproducible black line masters,* which is education-speak for, "Buy one book and make as many copies as you need." Where homeschooling is concerned, you can make the number of copies that you need to teach the children in your homeschool. And if you find yourself visiting that unit study again, perhaps to cover the topic more deeply than you did the first time or to teach younger children, you have permission to copy the pages all over again.

Making copies of your new unit study for all your homeschooling friends is *not* what the curriculum designers had in mind. In fact, to do that is an infringement of the copyright laws. Tell your best friends where you got the book so they can purchase copies, too.

On the other hand, if you volunteer to teach the unit study to a group of homeschool children — homeschoolers all volunteer for this kind of thing sooner or later — you're perfectly within the copyright laws to photocopy the unit-study pages for each child in your class. Because you purchased the book, you're teaching the unit study, and you plan to teach this whole cadre of children, that makes photocopying the unit-study pages okay.

Instructional Fair

Instructional Fair/TS Denison (Internet: www.instructionalfair.com) publishes what they call *theme units* for grades one through six. Some of the nearly 100 unit studies are appropriate for two or three grade levels, although others say they're appropriate for a larger age range. These unit studies cover topics such as the human body, ecology, and the weather. More than half the unit studies introduce various countries of the world, such as Israel, China, England, and Kenya. Look for the country units in a collection called *The Time Traveler Series.* You should be able to find many of these books in your local education store or order them directly from the Internet site.

The Learning Works

Part of the Creative Teaching Press family, The Learning Works (Internet: www.creativeteaching.com) produces unit studies on a variety of topics for all kinds of learners. Some of their units are designed for early childhood, and other units are made for special needs learners or the gifted and talented. Topics include advertising, communications, economics (one title with three units included), celebrate, and create a city.

School Express

This little company (Internet: www.schoolexpress.com) provides downloadable unit studies. Sign up for the free service that sends a Web address to your electronic mailbox each Friday and download the unit studies one week at a time, or — if you really enjoy these like I did — you can order and download science, social studies, and geography collections for six to seven dollars per subject. Each collection contains between 10 and 25 individual unit studies. You can also download any of the individual weekly units. School Express writes these units for ages 7 to 10.

Teacher Created Materials

Teacher Created Materials (Internet: www.teachercreated.com) has designed more than 240 unit studies for early childhood up through high school — the company calls them *thematic units* — on topics ranging from ants or chocolate to the Industrial Revolution or oceanography. Teacher Created Materials also sells more than 80 downloadable thematic units on their Web site if you need a unit study right away. Most education stores carry Teacher Created Materials books, but if you can't find them in your area, you can also order them individually on the Web. With 241 unit studies, no store is able to stock everything this company makes, and unit studies are only one portion of their curriculum offering.

Making them last

Sometimes you find a unit study designed to carry you through an entire year or more, but you can finish most units within a two-week time period — unless the subject matter has so enamored you that you extend the time that you spend on it. Extending a unit study is easy as long as you keep integrating math and language arts along with the fun. Some topics lend themselves easily to math problems (such as figuring arcs, distance, and speed in baseball) or language (writing stories, poems, or sentences) and others require a bit more creativity. Nothing says you can't extend a unit study that's supposed to only last two weeks. The Unit Study Police won't track you down and demand that you begin a new topic as long as your child is learning, and you're both enjoying yourselves.

Getting sidetracked

If you find that you particularly enjoy a subject, take a trip to the library to find books related to your topic. Perhaps the library even loans educational computer programs. If so, browse through their computer listing to see if anything fits your topic. An afternoon exploring a computer program about the oceans may present a welcome change of pace after you just spent several days talking about the sea and perhaps creating clay models of ocean animals or food chain models.

You say that you know an oceanographer but haven't had the time to give her a call? Most people love to talk about their passions, especially if they're fortunate enough to pursue those passions full time. Schedule a lunch date with your friend, or invite her over to see what your brood's been up to the past few weeks. With a few chocolate chip cookies and a glass of milk, I bet you can convince her to talk about the ocean and why she loves it. That, in turn, can fuel the fire in your children so that they want to learn more. You may feel a little left out before the end of the afternoon, but watch your kids' eyes sparkle as they talk about a topic they feel strongly about with a professional in the field.

The same holds true no matter what your child's passion may be. If your child displays a hearty interest in cooking, whom do you know who really loves to cook and does it well? That person could really fuel your child's interest — as if it needed any help! And a visit or conversation with an expert can help fuel your own imagination, showing you where to take your unit study next. With a little persistence, if your child really enjoys the topic, your unit study doesn't have to end after 48 pages. Much like our study of Rome, it could go on for a year or two.

Changing Pace with Unit Studies

Even if you use textbook curriculum for most of your studies, breaking out of the print mold and jumping headlong into a unit study is nice every now and then. For one thing, it makes your students think a little more about how the different parts of life actually fit together. For another, it gives you a break from the middle-of-the-year doldrums.

Waxing and waning

We hit the low point of our year in late February. It never fails: Valentine's Day passes, and our interest in schoolwork does, too. And the kids aren't the alone in this — I don't want to walk downstairs and pull out the books, either. To combat the February grubbies, we spend a little more time making chocolate chip cookies for home economics class, creating hands-on art projects to supplement science or social studies (or simply for the joy of making something new in art class), and drag out the old GeoSafari electronic game cards for math and geography. Or I dip into my filing cabinet and pull out a unit study that takes two weeks to complete.

If you find that your children are deeply interested in one or two subjects but for the most part enjoy textbooks, then those subjects are the ones to pursue with unit studies when you decide to take a breather. Sometimes while you work through a year's studies, *you* see a hole in subject matter that you think should be filled. Find a unit study on that topic, and take a week or two to teach it. Do your kids find black holes fascinating, and does the science text cover them in a paragraph or two? Looks like a unit on astronomy may be in order.

Or to present another scenario: You think that economics is fascinating, and you know the library contains several juvenile books on the ins and outs of money management, basic economic theory, and business practices. However, you'll be hard pressed to locate economics in any textbook outside of consumer math in most elementary or middle school curriculums. Again, unit studies come to the rescue. With a little investigation, you're sure to unearth a prepared unit study or two that you can use. (Teacher Created Materials publishes a Money curriculum, and The Federal Reserve Bank of New York offers a free downloadable unit study, *Econ Explorers Journal,* at www.ny. frb.org/pihome/educator on the Internet.)

Local history, events, and landmarks make a wonderful topic for a unit study, but you probably need to design it yourself (see the next section for some hints). It's a topic that no textbook covers — a topic that adds a native polish to your children's education and heighten your own appreciation at the same time.

Taking my children to see the Johnny Appleseed gravesite turned out to be one of the highlights of moving to a new town recently. Crazy about American history, the kids thought that moving into the town that became John Chapman's (Appleseed) last stop was incredibly cool. Without the pressures of settling in a new place, that trip would be a wonderful beginning to a unit study on local history. Your area has places like that, too.

Designing Unit Studies

Of course, with a little time and creativity, you can create your own unit studies. Assembling your own curriculum around one topic sounds like a big deal — if it didn't sound so hard, an educational company such as Teacher Created Materials, probably wouldn't publish and sell as many great unit studies as they do. Designing your own unit studies presents two drawbacks:

✔ **It takes time.** For a busy parent who needs to get dinner on the table, teach several children, and still make the other wheels of life turn on a daily basis, this could be enough of a reason to take an extended trip to the nearest education store with your credit card in your pocket.

✔ **It may require access to a couple of grade-level subject books.** This includes science, language arts, or math, so you know which skills are typically covered at a particular grade level. If you have a good library — or better yet, a nearby college library with an educational books department — this could be a great excuse for the Unit Study Developer (that would be you) to spend a long Saturday and a pocketful of change at the college library with a stack of books. This leaves parental unit number two in charge of the kids for the day while you browse . . . ummm . . . *work* to your heart's content.

The good part? You can teach *anything* you want. If you want to teach bug genetics as a unit study, then grab some books from the library and go for it. Creating your own unit study on economics almost takes less time than tracking down a study that someone else already created.

Subject-ing yourself to this?

When you make your own unit study from scratch, your unit study needs to cover all the subjects you'd normally teach, unless you plan to skip the math, for example, and work through a math text along with the unit study (also a fine decision in the unit study universe). To be complete, each unit study needs to include the first two subjects from the following list and as many of the others as you can fit in logically:

✔ **Math:** Create math problems at your child's level. If you're working on second-grade addition, for example, and your unit study is baseball, then you can add bats and balls, write a story problem that talks about number of pitches thrown until the team reached the final out, and so on. For the same unit, math for an older child may talk about speed of the bat, distance the ball travels, or the number of hot dogs that individual team fans eat..

✔ **Language Arts:** Reading, comprehension, grammar, writing skills — the whole kit and caboodle — can be included in language arts. Although you don't need to include *all* this in every unit study that you write, most units do ask students to write a little bit about the topic. Perhaps your child wants to create a story about the topic at hand. Or read a book or two about the topic and talk about it.

✔ **Science:** Sometimes a unit study shines in science. Other times you may need to work a little. If you just designed that unit on bug genetics, you're off the hook for science. The entire unit study qualifies as science. On the other hand, a unit on ancient Egypt may take some time to look at the creations of the Egyptian engineers, mummification, ancient medicine, or the tools that the Egyptians used to get the job done.

✔ **Social Studies or Geography:** Much like science, social studies may be your main topic, or you may need to work some information into the topic at hand. Some questions you may keep in mind as you work: Where was your topic first seen or invented? What culture surrounded the time or event? Where did this take place? What are the residents associated with your topic used to?

✔ **Art:** Draw. Build. Act. Design. Create. These all fall into the art category. Design a Roman mosaic. Sketch an insect's genetic makeup. Build a temple from clay or LEGOs. Create a tapestry to illustrate the unit that you're studying (felt shapes work for quick tapestries when needlepoint takes way too long). Paint the flowers that you're learning about.

✔ **Music:** Sometimes music fits into a unit study nicely. Listening to folk music while you explore the civil unrest of the 1960s may be a natural fit. On the other hand, you may need to work a little harder to fit music into that bug genetics unit study. (I sure can't think of any genetics songs!)

✔ **History:** Adding history to a unit study may be as simple as researching when an event began or an item was invented. On the other hand, history could be as complicated as talking about the events and times that affected an item's inventor. It's your unit study and your call.

✔ **Physical Education:** You may need to be a bit creative with this one, but if P.E. fits into your unit, then use it! Run footraces like the ancient Greeks, or gather a group of homeschool students to finish that baseball unit with a rousing game.

Digging for topics

If you need ideas for unit studies, follow your children around for a couple days and watch what they do. If one spends all his time engrossed in books, think about a literature-based unit study, such as *How Books Are Made*. If another child hits the door to unearth rocks from the back yard, you may have an archeology or rocks and minerals lover. Both topics would make great unit studies.

Some topics are evergreen. You can present them more than once as your little group grows older. Perhaps your student is interested in

✔ Animals, horses, or mammals

✔ Baseball, basketball, fencing, or sports in general

✔ Cooking or catering (which may include business and economics information)

✔ Kites, flight, transportation, or weather

✔ Medieval history, ancient Egypt, or any historical culture

✔ Starting a business

Let their interests guide you

As your children mention an interest, write it down somewhere. If you keep a running list of interests as the younger set talks about them, soon you'll have more topics than you could use in a three-year time span! Even if your child only shows a deep interest in one or two topics, explore those. You may find that you create several unit studies based off the first one as new secondary and tertiary fascinations develop.

Do you have a chocolate lover at your house? Explore the history, recipes, and creations and the part chocolate plays or played. Chocolate development in the United States was completely different than in Europe, and the story is fascinating. Joel Glenn Brenner's *The Emperors of Chocolate* gives you an inside look at two of the United States' largest chocolate companies if you want a jumping-off point for that chocolate unit.

Does your child play only video games? Then take an in-depth look at graphics, animation, computer programming, and the hardware that makes the videos go. Including the histories of the companies that produce the games counts as business class, and you can get as involved in game programming as you want to. Look at the history of video games and learn about Nolan Bushnell and Atari, the little company he founded. Then go from there. Even with a seemingly tiny topic such as video games, you can create a unit study that will keep your students involved for hours.

Chapter 14

Unschooling: A Walk on the Relaxed Side

*W*hat would you do if you could throw out all the dry textbooks and teach your children by guiding them through their days? You watch them flower as they take the initiative to explore the ideas and subjects important to them, and you answer questions as they arise. Is this your idea of chaos, or does the idea make you sigh inside and think warm, fuzzy thoughts?

If the idea of turning your children loose to learn and explore life appeals to you, you're not alone. Thousands of homeschoolers join you in this adventure that educator John Holt coined *unschooling*. Unlike most of the other options currently available, unschooling gives you complete freedom to do whatever you want as long as you're confident that your children are learning.

More than anything else, unschooling needs to be *fun*. One of the basic tenets of unschooling, sometimes unspoken, is that more learning takes place when the students actually enjoy what they're doing. That doesn't mean that everything needs to be rosy all the time, but it does place a high priority on fun. As Ben and Jerry once plastered onto a bumper sticker, "If it's not fun, why do it?" (Ben and Jerry would've made great unschoolers.)

Raising Eyebrows and Suspicions

Outside of the term *socialization* (see Chapter 3), no word raises more excitement in the homeschooling community than *unschooling*. Some parents become downright hostile in favor of — or against — this type of education, and they defend or attack it hotly, depending on their views. After taking a long, hard look at what teaching children actually *does,* however, most homeschoolers would probably have to admit that they use unschooling methods at least some of the time. They just don't call it that.

Born out of educator John Holt's research and experiences, unschooling basically says that children learn on their own because they're wired that way. Give them a warm learning environment, and they'll take off, assimilating experiences and ferreting out information without any preset curriculum or schedule.

Along with this, Holt also believed that children are sensitive to adult intrusion, and one of the best things adults can do to help youngsters learn is to stay out of their way. You see this concept in action when you ask some leading question of your 7-year-old daughter, and she looks at you as though you have a cantaloupe on your head. The look on her face says, "When you ask me that question, it sounds like I'm too dumb to know the answer." If you ever experienced that look, then you instinctively know one of the basic tenets of unschooling.

Parents who successfully unschool their kids trust their children's learning instincts. They have an innate trust that these kids have valid opinions, true internal drives to learn new concepts, and the inquisitiveness to experience life until the learners find the answers to their questions.

Although we generally follow a curriculum during school time, unschooling takes over after the texts are shelved for the day. As I write this, my 10-year-old son sits cutting out and assembling paper soldiers and tanks so he can explore World War II while the 9-year-old sits in front of the computer, glued to *Sim Safari,* a geography, nature, and economics simulation for children. These activities are not listed as scheduled tasks, yet they're highly educational. The kids just don't know it. They call this type of amusement *fun.* I hear the question roaming around in your head. How well do these kids function? Do they learn anything, or do they simply play all the time? As unschoolers move into adult life, some attend the nation's leading universities, and others opt for military schools, trade schools, or entrepreneurship. Like all homeschool families, unschooling graduates fall within the full range of post-high-school life — at least, that's what I gather from talking to their parents.

Fitting the Bill

Unschooling may be the perfect educational match for your family. After all, homeschooling is all about deciding what fits *your* family the best. Before deciding to pitch all those textbooks, however, you may want to do a little personal and library research:

1. **Read these books written by John Holt:**

   How Children Learn (Perseus Press)

   Learning All The Time (Perseus Press)

   Growing Without Schooling (A compilation of the first dozen issues of *Growing Without Schooling* magazine, which Holt created in 1977 to reach the families who embraced the concept of learning without walls; published by Holt Associates.)

2. **Ask these questions about your kids:**

   Do they thrive on loose structure and individual exploration?

   Are they self-motivated when they explore something that interests them?

   Do they spend most of their free time exploring what you'd consider educational in one form or another?

Reading, drawing, crafts, design, games, and computer programming all fit into this category, but think of this list as a dynamic beginning rather than a static perimeter. If you're forever dragging your son out from under the kitchen table to start school because that's his favorite place to read before noon, then you could have a potential unschooler on your hands!

Unschooling requires both children who love learning and parents who are willing to let them do it. Our house contains the children but not the parents. As time goes on, I incorporate more and more unschooling into our program, but I still feel secure with a textbook in my hand.

Like every educational method, you don't have to jump into it with both feet — no matter what anyone tells you. If unschooling looks great but you, like me, feel better with a textbook in your hand, then take a year or two to explore the option. Purchase books to guide you in the subjects that you feel need books, and schedule one or two subjects as "unschooling subjects" for the year. Then turn your kids loose and see what happens. You may be surprised at what they do.

Learning through the Course of a Day

How much learning do you really fit into a typical day? You may be surprised, if you sat down at the end of a week to catalog everything you do. Informal learning takes up a large portion of a homeschool family's time as parents explain how the world works by living it.

Although every unschooling family looks different, here's a set of suggestions to start your imagination as you ponder education outside textbook walls:

- ✔ **Beginning with breakfast, let your older children fix bacon and eggs for the family while the younger ones set the table.** In educational terms, everyone just spent time in home economics class — especially if you stand by to answer any questions that may come up.

- ✔ **Spend the morning building with LEGOs. Engineering, science, and to some extent, math classes have begun.** Playing with LEGOs may not seem very educational, but when your 11-year-old shows up an hour later with a collection of small robots that move their arms as you rotate the heads, you begin to see it as time well spent. These robot creations require a gear system almost like a car steering wheel. How do you figure this out? By playing with LEGOs!

- ✔ **Use lunchtime to listen to foreign language learning tapes.** This takes advantage of natural down time. The kids are all stationary for a change, so you can work on something educational with everybody.

- ✔ **Use the library to research the children's latest interest, whether it happens to be ornithology or oceanography.** Then later, perhaps you can follow up the study with a relevant field trip to the local aquarium or bird preserve.

- ✔ **Incorporate strategy and thinking skills by sitting down to an early evening family game that teaches strategy and thinking skills.** Although Siesta looks like an easy board game — after all, you only need to place your sun-and-roof pieces so that you cast shadows and gain points — keeping track of everyone else's moves and taking advantage of the holes they leave takes a sharp eye.

- ✔ **During your next trip to the grocery, take the children along and work on cost-per-ounce as you select items to fill your cart.** This counts as math.

- ✔ **Keep a journal of the day's activities as they happen, or jot them down at the end of the day.** This ensures you that you did accomplish something until you get the hang of the unschooling lifestyle. A family who incorporates the suggestions in this section finds that although the kids opened a textbook not once, they still covered home economics, science and technology, some math, foreign language, more science, and strategy and logic (which you could also classify as math).

Every unschool day won't look like this because the days tend to be as varied as your life is. Enrichment classes, such as swimming, horseback riding, or art, may take a portion of your week. But overall, the unschooling family exchanges textbooks in favor of *real* books and class time for life experiences.

Filling Your Home with Unschooling Tools

You'll know an unschooling household on sight. The home usually overflows with books, games, videos, and maybe a computer or two. Hey! Wait a minute. Isn't that what *all* our houses look like after the first few years or so? When you attempt to get a handle on the educational plethora in your life, turn to Chapters 18 and 20 for organization tips.

The love of learning tends to take over in an unschooler's space, and you'll hear these parents talk about pulling the Russian tapes from the shelf because somebody showed interest. Already thinking that their children may be interested in languages at some point, they amass an assortment of introductory language materials. Or you may find them foraging through the local library's collection, making mental notes so they know where to find the language in question.

Unschooling families learn to look for educational content in almost everything. An unschooler may pounce on a game that more traditional home-schoolers have abandoned because they don't yet grasp the value of fun in learning. Teaching the geography of the United States and business basics through a railroad board game, such as *Empire Builder,* is much more fun than working through two textbooks simultaneously — especially if you're the one expected to write out all the answers.

Your collection of educational tools can be as varied as your imagination. As long as you keep real life in mind, and the things your children will eventually need to live life on their own, you'll be fine. The following sections offer some ideas for unschooling toys and gadgets . . . er . . . um . . . tools and manipulatives.

Books

With a book in your hand, you can go anywhere. Walk the streets of Turkey or Turkmenistan, view Arabia through the eyes of Scheherazade, or follow the latest in virus research. Children who see books as holding the key to the world will embrace them. They'll turn to books when they want to know something.

If you watch your own children when they have free access to books and time to read, you'll notice that they don't always run for the books written at their current reading level. Sometimes they choose a challenging book, and on other occasions they seem drawn to books well below their reading level. Their choices depend on their reasons for reading, what looks interesting to them, and their moods at the time. Adults react to books the same way. Sometimes, for example, you want to read James Michener, and other afternoons you'd rather browse through "The Far Side" cartoons.

If you follow unschooling, you should have an ample number of books at your house or free access to a good library. And if you refrain from culling the *baby* books every time you notice that your child is reading at a new level, your child's reading collection can encompass a wide range of levels. Reading is reading no matter what level book your child grabs from the shelf, and giving her a choice of books above and below her reading level allows her to stretch her mind when she wants to as well as relax and read simply for pleasure.

We have a *Titanic* lover at our house. I started it — I bought him a second-grade reader about discovering the Titanic. Now, he still has that beginner book along with several adult treatments of the Titanic, a few reprints from 1912 that give him a true feel for the time, and some juvenile titles sprinkled in between. If I tried to throw away the introductory book now, he'd mourn for it. He sees it as the book that launched him into a new, exciting hobby. And he still reads it, battered and bent as it is, from time to time.

Keep in mind that both fiction and nonfiction are important. Arthur Conan Doyle's *Sherlock Holmes* stories develop thinking and deductive skills while they enhance vocabulary (let's see . . . that would be science and math and language arts), but no fictional account truly explains the intricacies of laser science to a child who wants to learn them.

To build your library with less outlay, you may want to keep a list of books that your children want as birthday and holiday ideas. Scout the remainder tables at the bookstores. All the books at the bargain table aren't out of print; some of them simply got a ding or two on their way from the print shop to the warehouse. If this is a book that your child can drag with him for the next six months in and out of the car, under the bed, and waaaaay too close to the swimming pool, then a scratch on the back cover probably won't bother him at all.

Games

Gathering around the table for a game night, in some cultures, is still very much the way things are done. Children can learn cause and effect, strategic thinking, economics, business, sportsmanship, and creativity — all good things to have if you plan to survive in the world as an adult — from playing games.

Your game collection can range from small decks of cards to large intricate board games. The choice is up to you. Your available storage space, budget, and personal preferences decide whether you want to go big or small. Some ideas for your game closet include

- ✔ **Girl Genius, Set, Chronology, and Aquarius:** All card games, playing Girl Genius can teach strategy, playing Set enhances your mathematical ability to see likes and differences in attributes (what color, how many, and which shape), and playing Aquarius challenges you to complete a secret goal before your opponent figures it out and blocks you. In Chronology, you become a time traveler who looks at events from the past and sees what happens if events change — for example, how would history be different if the Titanic *didn't* sink on April 14, 1912? Most of all, these games are fun, which is a major requirement of any good game.

- ✔ **Ricochet Robot, Empire Builder, Formula De, Acquire:** Board games, such as these, require a larger beginning investment, but they pay you back in replay value. Playing our bedraggled version of Empire Builder taught my husband about the major railroad companies of the nineteenth century, geography, and business. Twenty years later, we still use that same copy. Playing Ricochet Robot teaches skills and thinking mindset needed for computer programming, Formula De is a realistic Formula One racing game, and Acquire deals with real-estate acquisitions.

- ✔ **Button Men, Vowel Play, The Farming Game:** A little off the beaten path, these games focus on math, vocabulary, and, well, farming. Button Men uses various polyhedral dice to play a game with numbers, and Vowel Play contains several different levels of vocabulary cards that you use to fill in missing vowels, identify the words, and play the baseball-like game. Playing The Farming Game realistically teaches the ins and outs of running a farm from purchasing grain and cows to paying the taxman and harvesting your crops. Plus, it includes Colorforms, those fun plastic stick-ons from the '50s. What could be better?

Finding these games may prove to be a challenge. Full-fledged specialty game stores are the only shops that carry most of them. You won't find these games at your local Wal-Mart or Toys "R" Us. If you can't find a store that sells them in your area, you could try one of the game sellers on the Internet: More Than Games (www.morethangames.com) or Fun Again Games (www.funagain.com) should start you off, and you can find many others through a Google search (www.google.com).

Software

Computer software helps to build a well-rounded home library. Although you don't need to run out and purchase every new title on the market, a few well-chosen titles can add much depth to your growing, inquisitive learners. Again, knowing what you're looking for guards against unfortunate purchases.

To round out your unschooling software library, you may want to consider:

- **A quality, current encyclopedia on CD-ROM:** When you think of the sheer space a print encyclopedia takes, an electronic encyclopedia is worth the money. Encarta Reference Suite and the current Grolier Encyclopedia are two of the packages on the market that give you much for your money.

- **Foreign language software:** For the 12 and under set, KidSpeak 10 in 1 Language Learning gives you an introduction to ten different languages in a three-CD-ROM set. Older learners may appreciate a total immersion program, such as The Rosetta Stone.

- **The word processor that came with your computer:** With it your children can design newsletters to send to friends, neighbors, or extended family members; write essays detailing their latest discovery; or create that novel they always wanted to write. They'll experience less hand cramping than if they tried to write it by hand, and they'll learn the intricacies of word processor usage at the same time.

- **A good typing program:** If your children don't already know how to keyboard, a typing program can save them incredible levels of frustration in the future. When you truly learn how to type, you can get the words on paper almost as quickly as you think. The frustration of having to hunt and peck out each individual letter is alleviated.

- **Computer games for strategy:** Whether you want to explore economics through a program, such as Sim City or Rollercoaster Tycoon, ancient civilizations through a title, such as Age of Empires or Sid Meyer's Civilization, or compete against the computer with a chess program, the number of game titles out there is almost endless.

Tie video, technology, and software together in one package with stop-action videos that you create yourself. The LEGO & Stephen Spielberg MovieMaker uses LEGO pieces (or anything small that you want to take pictures of), a camera, and software to create your own animated movies.

Technological and building toys

If it fits together with gears, you can make something out of it, or if it runs on batteries, you can probably call it a technological or building toy. LEGO and LEGO Dacta, mostly because they're available and you can do so much with them, stand among the leaders. What household doesn't have at least a few LEGO bricks lurking around? Dacta is the LEGO educational brand, and Dacta sets include way cool gears that you can't get anywhere else. These sets explore simple machines, manufacturing processes, robotics, and much more. You can locate Pitsco LEGO Dacta, the only company that sells LEGO Dacta in the United States, on the Internet: www.pitsco-legodacta.com or call 800-362-4308.

If you want to give the idea of LEGOs and simple machines a try without purchasing a full set, Klutz Press publishes *LEGO Crazy Action Contraptions: A LEGO Inventions Book.*

K'Nex, Fischertechnik, and Capsela all give children the chance to create, build, motorize, and design. Little hands busy for hours on end with these sets, and because they're made up of components that depend on your imagination, they develop creativity, engineering, and thinking skills as the child creates. (To locate a good selection of Fischertechnik products, try The Construction Site on the Internet at www.constructiontoys.com.)

If your child enjoys racing but isn't ready for an upscale remote control car, plane, or boat, she may enjoy the Tamiya Mini-Racers. These battery-operated cars race on tracks with raised sidewalls, and you can change everything about them: gear ratios, wheels, motors, weight, the works. For a ten- to twenty-dollar investment your child can assemble her own snap-together car and then race it with other area youngsters. (Can you say socialization?) And when she takes the car apart, changes components, and reassembles it, she learns quite a bit about simple mechanics and problem solving. Look for the Tamiya Racers at your local hobby store.

Videos

Why include videos in an unschooling curriculum? Videos provide a starting point for all kinds of discussions. Want to talk about history and propaganda? Check out a few 1940s musicals from the library and discuss how these movies helped paint a picture of America to the audiences who watched them. Interested in the science of special effects? In addition to documentaries that tell you how these stunts are arranged, locating a couple of the movies that have actually received recognition for their special effects enlarges your child's understanding.

We recently located a documentary on movie effects that traced the history of special effects from the nineteenth century to the present. The kids had already seen movies, such as *Star Wars,* so they were keenly interested in how the effects were done. To add to the evening, we pulled out a couple of the oldies-but-goodies that the documentary also mentioned, such as *A Trip to the Moon* from 1902.

Watch cartoons from the 1930s onward for an overview of animation history or trace one actor's career through three or four films. You can also use a movie as a jumpstart to cultural study, as a companion to the original book from which it was derived (this is an excellent time to talk about artistic license), or to give visual, moving images to science topics, such as bacteria or animal life. As in all other areas of unschooling, let your children's interests guide your selections.

Recording Their Progress

Making your adventures fit into a typical educational mold may require some creativity when record-keeping time comes. How do you record three afternoons spent building with LEGOs, volunteer time at the zoo, listening to foreign language tapes over lunch, and an in-depth study of the neighbor's newly hewn tree? Although at first glance, it may look like these activities have no educational content, you *can* create a logical-sounding list of activities from your children's life explorations.

If you live in a state that requires a performance portfolio or some other regular documentation, you need to use *education-speak* to explain what your children do and what they learn from it. Public and private school educators do this all the time to justify what they know are learning experiences — especially if those experiences don't fit into the required activity list for the year. So your field trip to the zoo that you took this week because the weather happened to be nice enough becomes an offsite exploration into worldwide animal behavior, socialization (you ate lunch with a group of friends), and retail practices (you hit the gift shop before you went home and took note of its contents).

This may sound like you're fluffing up the trip, but you're actually not. You're taking the experiences from life and putting them into a form that educators can understand when they reference them against a list of state requirements for a particular grade. If everybody uses the same vocabulary when you file a report or portfolio, understanding what you covered in a year is made easier.

Many unschoolers sign up with an *independent study program,* or *ISP,* if they live in states that require portfolios or other yearly documentation. The ISP keeps records and explains how to document daily doings so they fit into an educational report. Chapter 11 gives you more information on ISPs.

Chapter 15

Charting Your Own Academic Course

"*I*t's new, improved, and guaranteed to teach your student everything she needs to know for life — at least for this subject at her current grade level." Curriculum publishers try really hard to pull together a comprehensive collection of subjects that appeals to you as the parent/teacher *and* that teaches your student at the same time. Most of them do a great job — every now and then you find a losing proposition but not often.

The truth is that any publisher's curriculum must meet the needs of a certain group of children or that publisher doesn't stay in business long. So if a publisher presents a set of textbooks or unit studies, and they've been around for a few years or more, then that publisher's curriculum matches what the nation's teachers (including homeschoolers) want to buy for their students.

That much said, please keep in mind that no particular publisher had *your* child in mind when it created the latest way-cool homeschool curriculum. Why? Just like every other child, your child is completely special and unique. Although you may be able to find a set of books off the rack that meets your child's needs, you also may find yourself frustrated and attempting to create "the perfect curriculum" for your child.

Assembling your own curriculum for your child doesn't need to be frustrating. It can be plenty of fun — especially if you give yourself enough time to check out all the options before you make any big-ticket purchases or system-wide changes. This may mean choosing an inexpensive curriculum that almost meets your needs the first year while you research, assemble, and pull everything together during a summer break.

Sometimes assembling the "perfect" learning package is as simple as adding to (or subtracting from) a full curriculum system from one publisher or private school's satellite offering. For example, if you find a large unit study that you'd really like to use for the year, but it seems a little light on math and details, you can add a good math program and visit your local library to collect books that provide in-depth information about your topic.

On the other hand, if you find a great curriculum that adds a bit too much for your taste, you can always subtract what you don't like and replace it with something else. After all, it's your curriculum.

Knowing Whether Your Kid's Kinesthetic

Does your child learn best through her ears, eyes, or hands? Known respectively as *auditory*, *visual* and *kinesthetic learners* in education-speak, how your youngster picks up information is important. Channel the child's learning through her best receptor, and you find much less frustration in the long run. Short term, though, presenting information in the best way can be challenging. Here's a quick rundown on the different types of learning:

- ✔ **An auditory learner listens to song lyrics, old radio shows, and commercials once or twice and then repeats them verbatim to you.** Auditory learners respond well to videos, computer games, and CDs or cassette tapes — as long as they don't get bored. They also listen well when you tell a story from a subject such as history, especially if you give them a page to color while you relate. Proving that they really heard what you said, they can then tell the story back to you.

- ✔ **A visual learner learns through written words and pictures.** Although visual learners may pick up some information through their ears, you can give them a story on tape, ask them to tell you the story, and they'll probably miss some vital parts of the tale. If you give them a print version of the same story, on the other hand, they can tell you what happened and when. These children learn well with textbooks, workbooks, and the like.

- ✔ **Kinesthetic learners explore the world through touch.** *Telling* a kinesthetic learner about fractions may not get you anywhere, but if you take a piece of paper and show the child how to fold it into fourths, and then ask him to do it, the concept clicks much better. Kinesthetic learners can be a challenge to those of us who learned mostly from books. They require an abundance of creativity, but they're also plenty of fun. After all, where else can you play with (and eat) M&Ms as part of math class every day?

I have two learners, and between them, they run the whole learning style gamut. My son is an auditory learner, and my daughter is visual/kinesthetic. When I explain things to them, I use the talk-while-I-write approach because the information clicks best with my son when he hears the information and my daughter understands when she sees it. Sometimes it can be a bit confusing for me, but they do fine.

We found that math needs to be a pretty hands-on class for my daughter, so we took a break from books for a while and invaded the kitchen to learn fractions. She understands how fractions work much better now that she cuts butter by the tablespoon and measures dry ingredients into ¼-, ½-, ⅓-, and 1-cup measures. Conventional education? Nope, but it works, and the rest of the family loves her cookies!

If you want to see a quick checklist of various behaviors that point to particular learning styles, the Learning Styles and Multiple Intelligence Web site at `www.ldpride.net/learningstyles.MI.htm` offers an online test that shows you which learning style may be dominant in your child.

Pulling from Different Publishers

The easiest way to create your own curriculum is to find out which publishers excel at certain subjects and to purchase those. Although a full curriculum lineup from one publisher looks really nice (all the books are color coordinated and suggest an overarching order to your life), the truth is that one publisher usually doesn't excel at every subject. If they did, why would the world need a second curriculum publisher or a third?

I use a different publisher for almost every subject I teach. Through trial and error, I found some keepers, which I happily pass along. Others didn't work so well; when I get a book that doesn't work with my children, I offer it to another homeschooler who may be able to use it.

Starting with what you know

If you want to wade through the incredible wealth of curriculum choices out there and assemble your own, where do you start? Actually, that's a really good question. You'll feel much more confident if you start with what you know and move to the subjects that you don't know as well.

For example, if you're really good with numbers yourself, start by deciding which math curriculum that you want to use. On the other hand, if foreign languages are your forte and you want to include a language or two in your homeschool, begin by deciding how you want to impart that love to your children. Starting with your strengths lessens the "I don't know what I'm doing" blues because you *do* know what you're doing.

Here's another tip the educational pros don't tell you: No one is good at every subject, but — at least at the elementary level — one teacher is expected to cover it all. And in many situations, the teacher in the classroom doesn't have expertise in the course that they find themselves teaching. Perhaps the school's administrators hope to move a teacher into her area of expertise when the school finds a space, but meanwhile the school had an opening and that's where the teacher filled in.

After you have one or two subjects out of the way, and you feel surer of yourself, move on to the areas in which you don't feel as confident. This is where an idea or two from a veteran homeschooler or a friend who knows your children comes in handy. But keep your wits about you, even when you ask for suggestions. Veteran homeschoolers, no matter how long they've done this, don't walk through life in an impenetrable halo of light any more than you do. They make mistakes and purchase the wrong curriculum once in a while, too.

Pulling from the stacks

Searching through a narrow list of curriculum providers gives you the option of choice without the overwhelming knowledge that you need to siphon through 36 different math books before you find something that you like. If you try to tackle too much at one time, your brain goes numb and even chocolate won't revive it. Nothing works but a break from the task at hand while you recharge.

In an attempt to save you from chocolate overload and prolonged breaks, the following sections list various curriculums (and their publishers) that you may want to look at when you design your own textbook collection. By no means exhaustive, this cadre suggests the broad ranges available to today's homeschool family. Use them as a starting point, a guide for your first year, or as a definitive list of what you *don't* want for one reason or another.

Some of these curriculums I use with my own children, and I elected to skip others in favor of another program. Also take a look at Chapters 7 through 10, which cover elementary education through high school and beyond, for other curriculum ideas.

Math

Every homeschooler and textbook publisher has his own ideas about what constitutes a good math curriculum. Basically, you want to get from counting to algebra in twelve years or less. If your curriculum looks like it will do that and you can supplement the places it misses, then your child will be fine.

Every textbook can't possibly cover absolutely everything in one year. Do you think experiencing math is important? If you do, then you'll be happier with some of these publishers than others. If, on the other hand, you prefer to go about it the rote way and feel that strict memorization is the key to math skills, then different math texts will appeal to you.

Here are some of the basics, the tried and trues, and a new face or two thrown into the mix:

- ✔ **Excel Math:** (AnsMar Publishers, Internet: www.excelmath.com; Phone: 866-866-7026) Covers grades K through six. Excel's math comes to you on individual padded worksheets, one per grade. You can also get a teacher's edition that includes teaching suggestions and answers. Excel Math is also available in Spanish.

- ✔ **Math-U-See:** (Math-U-See Foundation, Internet: www.mathusee.com; Phone: 1-888-854-6284) Incorporates manipulatives, such as stackable blocks and transparent overlays, to teach math concepts for grades K through twelve. Doing the math and actually using pieces that you can pick up and manipulate helps those hands-on learners pick up the concepts.

- ✔ **Miquon Math:** (Key Curriculum Press, Internet: www.keypress.com; Phone: 800-995-MATH) Covers the first six years of math in three years by teaching concepts rather than stressing review. If your child seems to jump from concept to concept without forgetting the earlier information, Miquon Math may be a good math for them. You may need to supplement story problems and some time review with Miquon; the curriculum features little of either.

- ✔ **Key To Math workbooks:** (Key Curriculum Press, Internet: www.keypress.com; Phone: 800-995-MATH) Miquon's "big brother" continues where Miquon Math leaves off. Concentrating on one skill at a time and teaching one concept on each page, these little workbooks cover decimals, percents, fractions, measurement, geometry, and algebra. The Key To Geometry series does not contain geometric proofs, so it isn't equivalent to a college-bound high school geometry course.

- ✔ **Saxon Math:** Saxon Publishers, Internet: www.saxonpub.com; Phone: 800-284-7019) The current darling of the homeschooling movement, Saxon Math harkens back to the traditional days of mathematics for grades one through twelve. Each page presents three or four new problems, and the rest of the work consists of review problems from past sections. Thousands of homeschooling families swear by it, but if your child hates never-ending review, she will swear . . . well . . . near it.

Language arts

Reading, writing, grammar, and spelling — language arts include so much, and yet educators lump it all together under one heading. In a world where people communicate primarily through the spoken and written word — from newspapers to e-mail — language skills form a basis of a solid homeschool curriculum. For those of you with teenagers, there is more to language than "Huh?" "Yep," and "Nope."

A trip to your local educational supply store provides you with loads of ideas for language arts books, from spelling to writing practice. Many publishers provide language arts helps for busy teachers (and that includes you!) who need to supplement grammar or writing.

Although I can't begin to include all the available options for language arts, here are a few to make you think. None of these resources qualify as light and fluffy, but they are excellent:

- **The Shurley Method:** (Shurley Instructional Materials, Inc., Internet: www.shurley.com; Phone: 800-566-2966) Using this method, a student learns intensive grammar. With the help of the Shurley Method's singsong jingles and a set way to tackle each sentence, the student is exposed to parts of speech (subject, verb, adjective, and so forth) to every word in every sentence. Children who enjoy talking and singing typically do very well with this first-through-seventh-grade program.

- **Structure and Style in Writing:** (Institute for Excellence in Writing, Internet: www.writing-edu.com; Phone: 800-856-5815) Covers all grades with one video course and a reference notebook. This program teaches students how to write well by first imitating well-crafted prose. They then take those skills and create their own paragraphs. Paragraphs turn into research papers as your child matures, and a writer is born. Whew! Wasn't that easy?

- **Writing Strands:** (National Writing Institute, Internet: www.writing strands.com; Phone: 800-688-5375) With Writing Strands, your student can learn levels one through seven writing skills for four genres: persuasive, expressive, research, and creative writing. Designed in a set of books that guide ages three to eighteen, this made-for-homeschooling series covers the entire homeschool age range. The program covers both vocabulary and spelling in the course of writing but not as individual subjects.

- **Excellence in Spelling:** (Institute for Excellence in Writing, Internet: www.writing-edu.com; Phone: 800-856-5815) Reviewing phonics rules and respelling target words until the child can apply them to the words, a child can learn spelling. Children at the third-grade level though high school use Excellence in Spelling; it incorporates both vocabulary from their personal lives as well as preselected spelling words.

Library books form a great basis for reading material. You can purchase reading textbooks, but if you use library (also known as *trade* or *real*) books, you expose your child to complete stories, real authors, and good writing. A child who reads real books also learns a wider vocabulary because grade-level reading textbooks only use a certain number of words per grade but library books have no such limitation. They also cost less!

The books and authors that your child loves from her reading time, if you use library books exclusively, make great gift lists for family members.

Science

No one could possibly learn everything about science in twelve years of school! We have a name for those people who tried — research scientists. Even lab scientists devote their lives to one small science area.

Now that the pressure's off, what do you need to know in twelve years? Learners need to observe the world around them and draw conclusions. They need to see how basic aspects of the world work — physics, chemistry, botany, and astronomy, for example. Understanding in botany can be as simple as watching colored water creep up the veins of a celery stalk or as complicated as explaining Mendelian genetics. You begin with simple stuff while your children are young and work into the more difficult concepts as they grow. Here are some examples of the wealth of science curriculum available.

Again, the library can be a great resource. Books such as *More Great Experiments Than Anyone Could Use in a Lifetime* crowd library shelves, just waiting for you to snatch them up.

- **Teach-nology:** (Internet: `www.teachnology.com/teachers/lesson_plans/science`) A technology resource for teachers, this site really *does* provide more lesson plans than you could use in a lifetime. Most are identified by general grade level, so whether you want to introduce polymers to your second grader (and create some way-cool slime in the process) or explore how businesses include science and technology as a twelfth grader, Teach-nology gives you the tools.

- *Handbook of Nature Study:* Published by Cornell University Press and written by Anna Botsford Comstock in 1911, this book gives you more than 850 pages of information on nature science. Originally written for elementary school teachers and updated where necessary, this volume gives you years' worth of nature information. It also covers what most people consider the basis of an elementary science curriculum: animals, insects, plants, earth, and sky. Throw in a few simple machines experiments and an anatomy review and you're pretty much there. Now . . . where did we put those LEGOs?

- **Exploring Creation Science:** (Apologia Educational Ministries, Internet: `www.highschoolscience.com`; Phone: 888-524-4724) Unique in that it's a lab-oriented science curriculum designed exclusively for homeschoolers. Written by a nuclear scientist and former university professor, this series starts beyond elementary school and covers general science, physical science, biology, chemistry, and physics. These books are written from a Christian perspective.

Unit studies work well for science if you enjoy getting your hands dirty. Check your local educational store for science kits and books that cover individual topics, such as birds, volcanoes, or the ultra popular *Birds and Volcanoes Together.* Or dip into Chapter 13 for a list of unit study publishers.

Social studies and geography

One of the joys of homeschooling is that you can separate learning from textbooks. Both social studies and geography work well when you study cultures and areas of the world with books written specifically about those lands. Begin with your own area, if you like, and branch out from there. Another suggestion is to concentrate on a part of the world that intrigues your child and move around the world from that point.

We spend some time each year covering actual United States and world geography and map skills, but much of the kids' modern cultural awareness comes from their independent reading. I keep a shelf of books about the world and its people, and occasionally point them toward one in answer to a question or to broaden our knowledge of a particular area of the world that comes up during other subjects.

Visit your local library for books that highlight various countries. The library provides easy access to books about all parts of the world. If you want to begin building your own home social studies collection, use the library as a starting point and purchase the books you really like.

A few of the available social studies resources include

- **Mapping the World By Heart:** (Tom Snyder Productions, Internet: www.mapping.com; Phone: 800-342-0236) This is a curriculum that teaches children to actually draw international maps from memory. Children learn about world geography as they draw in rivers, cities, boundaries, and much more. Used and loved by homeschoolers for years, this curriculum is designed for fifth grade students and older.

- ***The Complete Book of Maps and Geography Skills:*** American Education Publishing, Inc. This *consumable* book (meaning that you write on the pages) covers the basics of maps, directions, and world and U.S. geography in a little more than 300 pages. It took us about a year and a half to work through this book, and the kids learned much more about geography than I ever dreamed they would.

- **Geography Songs Kit:** (Audio Memory, Internet: www.audiomemory.com; Phone: 800-365-7464) Learn the names of every country by memorizing and singing songs. It may sound a little odd, but it works! This company also produces a States & Capitals Songs and a History Songs Kit that teaches dates and people in the history of the United States.

History

History hits me right in the pocketbook. A quick survey of our homeschool library shows that history books far outrank any other subject at our house. We don't browse through the bookstore looking for extra math books to read before bed, but a new history title always catches our attention and usually ends up in the bag (after the required visit to the checkout clerk).

The best way to learn about history is to actually live it. Short of spending your entire summer as a docent guide at Williamsburg, reading about it is a close — and less expensive — second. To explore a time period, use reprints from books written at the time you're studying, biographies of men and women who made a difference in their societies, and descriptive volumes that show a glimpse of the age.

You can approach teaching history in one of two ways:

- ✔ **Timeline:** Parents who choose the timeline approach begin at the beginning. Then, as they move up the timeline (or down, depending on your perspective), they add in various civilizations where they fit. Teaching your child the history of civilizations as they come along offers one distinct advantage. Your child doesn't wonder which came first, the Aztecs or the Egyptians. If you teach each civilization in turn as it arises, your child *knows* which culture appeared before the other.

  In much the same way, when you get to the history of the United States, your learner has a framework that she can hang all her new information on. She doesn't wonder what came before 1492; she knows.

- ✔ **Segments:** Teaching history segment by segment, on the other hand, allows you to concentrate on various cultures at different times of your child's schooling. If you want to hit American history each year for twelve years, you can do that. And because this is your course, "American" can also mean a year of intensive Canadian history, Mexican history, and so on. Let your desires for your child's learning guide you.

When you assemble your history tools, take a look at some of these resources:

- ✔ **Childhood of Famous Americans series and Step into Reading:** Random House publishes these biographies that bring a time period to life. For young children ages 8 to about 12, these series introduce readers to times and people long ago. More experienced readers may devour the Landmark history books, also from Random House.

- ✔ **A History of the United States:** Oxford University Press published after a mom got fed up with her child's history curriculum at school. Author Joy Hakim sat down and wrote a ten-volume history of the United States that you can use for students anywhere from sixth through about eighth grade. Each book is divided into 40 or more easy-to-read chapters, so you may read a chapter a day and get through the series in a couple years.

 ✔ *The Timetables of History: A Horizontal Linkage of People and Events:* Simon and Schuster publishes this book that shows historical events year by year. Want to know the exact year of the polio vaccine discovery? It's in here. With this one volume you can look at politics, science, art, religion, and invention. Although this is a great resource to keep you on track if you want to teach events as they occurred, you can also use it as an idea starter for further exploration. Find an event from the time period you're studying and go from there. (You say outhouses were invented when?)

 ✔ **The Writer's Guides To Everyday Life:** Writer's Digest Books, Internet: www.writersdigest.com/catalog. Think of this series as crib notes to history. Individual volumes cover the American Indians, the Civil War, the 1800s, the Middle Ages, Colonial America, Regency and Victorian England, Renaissance England, and the Wild West. Each volume gives you an introduction to life, economy, society, war, famous personages, and more.

Stories of inventors, cultures, civilizations, and military organizations may add interest to your study. These aspects add depth to your history curriculum and also capture the heart and interest of a less-than-interested history scholar if you happen to match your child's current passion with a period in history.

World War II didn't particularly interest my 10-year-old son. At least, he cared little until he got an old copy of a book called *The War Magician*. This book tells the story of Jasper Maskelyne, a British stage magician, and his experiences applying the fundamentals of stage magic to wartime efforts. Maskelyne made cities "disappear" so that bombers missed the settlements and dropped bombs in the middle of the desert, hid a group of tanks with nothing more than camel dung and rancid flour, and performed wartime feats that provide exciting reading today and earned him the admiration of the British army then. Now, my son still knows little about dates and strategies, but he talks for hours about the wonders of Maskelyne and his band. My son is absolutely fascinated by stage magic, and this book opened the door to a topic that he may never explore on his own.

Electives: Music and art

Whether you include subjects such as music and art in your curriculum depends on your state requirements as well as your own devotion to the subjects. Keep in mind, as you plan, that you don't have to teach these lessons yourself. Virtually any community offers a local music teacher for piano, guitar or flute, and many offer art classes as well.

So breathe a sigh of relief because you may be off the hook. If you're not, or if *you* happen to be the local music or art teacher, then I offer a few options that you may like:

✔ **Music Ace 1 and 2:** (Harmonic Vision, Internet: www.harmonicvision.com; Phone: 800-474-0903) Although these computer programs really aren't designed to provide a full music program, they do give you a good start at theory, note reading, and keyboard introduction. Plus, they come with a loose-leaf notebook that includes worksheets that you can copy for further practice.

✔ **The Classical Kids Collection:** (Internet: www.childrensgroup.com/sections/classical) Who can resist titles such as *Beethoven Lives Upstairs* or *Vivaldi's Ring of Mystery?* Each cassette or CD weaves one composer's music throughout an adventure tale that tells about the composer's life or works at the same time that you listen to his music. After hearing this series, my children could identify music from Beethoven, Bach, Vivaldi, Mozart, Handel, and Tchaikovsky when they heard it.

✔ **KidsArt Art:** (Internet: www.kidsart.com; Phone: 530-926-5076) Each small sixteen-page booklet in the Skills and History collections concentrates on a different skill or history period. Titles include Celtic Ireland, Arts of Africa, Arts of the Orient, Chalk & Charcoal, and Drawing People, to name a few.

✔ **How Great Thou Art.** (How Great Thou Art Publications, Internet: www.howgreatthouart.com; Phone: 800-982-DRAW) Designed primarily for the Christian family, this program teaches drawing, painting, colored pencils, and marker art for kindergarten children through adult. Artist and former teacher Barry Stebbing designed this curriculum to be self-teaching; each page presents a concept and then gives the learner an opportunity to practice it.

Writing A Curriculum from Scratch: The Diehard Approach

Some courageous souls embark on the write-your-own-curriculum journey. With a *scope and sequence* (a list that tells them what each grade level covers) in hand, along with plenty of available time, they create each subject's content for the entire school year. Then, I suppose, they disappear to the nearest Residence Inn for a month's rest and relaxation. I know that I would.

Although designing your own curriculum takes a huge amount of effort on your part, it does have one great benefit. If you create lessons that present information the way your child learns, then your curriculum should help your child amass information in a way that few purchased curriculums can.

Most homeschoolers who end up writing their own curriculums do so because they can't locate a prepared guide for one particular subject that they want to teach their children. For instance, I teach business theory to my children each week and have for the past several years. Because I have yet to find an elementary business theory curriculum, I assemble library books and combine business history with vocabulary, personal experience, and biographies to create my curriculum. We talk about sole proprietorships and corporations, the advent of products, such as Kleenex tissues and Hershey chocolate, and the women and men who made it all happen.

If you elect to write your own curriculum, you certainly aren't alone. Parents who were skilled at the subject they tackled wrote many of the single-subject curriculums available to homeschoolers. When they attempted to locate a curriculum to use with their own children, these parents failed to unearth any prewritten curriculums for their specialty because none lurked in the back of the homeschool catalog waiting for discovery. So they sat down and wrote their own.

To write your own curriculum, you need some kind of document that tells you what children learn at each grade level. In edu-speak this information is a *scope and sequence.* Any of these resources work for your purposes:

- ✔ *The Educated Child: A Parent's Guide from Preschool through Eighth Grade:* The Free Press publishes this book that covers what students should be learning at each grade level. Actually written for parents whose children attend public or private schools, this book is useful to homeschooler who can use this information to their advantage. The book gives you guidelines for English, mathematics, science, history, geography, art, and music.

- ✔ **World Book Typical Course of Study:** (Internet: `www.worldbook.com/ptrc/html/curr.htm`) Lists actual skills that students need to master for each grade level. One of the easiest sites to use that gives you real information, you can print out the entire study recommendations for each grade level that you need. The site tells you what the students need to know in real English, so you can design your curriculum point by point for social studies, language arts, mathematics, and science.

- ✔ **U.S. Curriculum Standards:** (Internet: `www.worldbook.com/ptrc/html/us_curr.htm#subject`) Organized by subject and by individual state, so you can look up your state's minimum requirements if you want. Or stick with the national standards links, which give information on almost any subject that you could be interested in, including the National Standards for Theatre Education.

If you're not using *my* curriculum, you're clueless — NOT!

Homeschoolers tend to be a self-confident lot, and sometimes they go a bit overboard. I've actually had people tell me that I didn't know what I was doing because I neglected to jump up and down at their curriculum choices and run out to buy them myself. Did they know that I have a special-needs learner at my house? No. They didn't ask. They didn't care. They simply wanted to push their choices down my throat.

Don't fall for this kind of attitude. Nobody knows your child as well as you do. Although everyone makes mistakes once in a while, you will know if you happen to buy the wrong curriculum one year. You'll probably figure it out before the end of October.

Asking for other people's opinion is great — in fact, talking to people I trust saves me money every year as I think about introducing this publisher or dropping that one from my yearly lineup. But I try to talk to other homeschoolers who know my children. After they know my kids, they have a better idea what may work well. Thanks to other parents' suggestions, I've taken the time to look at many different textbooks that I didn't know about otherwise or didn't plan to take the time. It's kind of like a new coffee mocha brand — you may be leery to try it on your own, but when a friend raves, you just have to check it out for yourself.

Keeping other people's opinions in mind — or dismissing them — the books you buy for your child ultimately depend on what you know about your learner. If you think a particular approach will work with your child, then it probably will. You know plenty about your own child that you never took the time to put into words. Mothers usually call this their "instinct."

Go with your instincts, mom or dad. You know. You really do.

Most of the resources are Internet sites. Although you may locate print versions of U.S. Curriculum Standards in individual subjects, a complete set of K to 12 standards for *one* subject volume can cost as much as $99, which is too expensive for most families to purchase (including mine)!

Check your local library for curriculum standards or a printed scope and sequence if you don't have Internet access. While you're there, you may want to take a look at the Core Curriculum Series, edited by E. D. Hirsch. You may know of them as the What Your Child Needs To Know in X Grade series. Although these books don't include complete curriculum suggestions, they provide a good starting point if you want some general ideas for various grade levels.

With standards or scope and sequence in hand, list the skills you need to teach a particular grade and then put your creativity cap on. Take another trip to the library (if you're not there already) to see what resources you can find that fit your list of skills. For subjects such as math, you may be able to follow the standards suggestions by creating resources as you need them, but a subject such as science or history generally needs some backup materials.

Standards language can be incredibly confusing when you try to apply them to something useful, such as a particular project or book. You may decide before you get too far into this that an extra resource would help. *Home Learning Year by Year; How to Design a Homeschool Curriculum from Preschool Through High School* by Rebecca Rupp shows you how to take the standards that you collect and create a useful curriculum from them no matter what grade you need to teach.

Chapter 16

Special Concerns for Special Students

*W*hen you have a child who carries a "special needs" label to school every day, the thought of teaching him or her at home gives you an additional measure of stress — whether the label happens to be a learning disability, gifted and talented, or something else. Yet these children, perhaps more than any others, respond incredibly well to one-on-one tutoring — which is basically what you do in a homeschool situation.

You may need to adapt your curriculum, change your school year, or alter your expectations for a special needs student. Maybe you need to buy M&Ms by the case. When you bring your child home after attending public school, and you give them a month or two to "detox" and get used to staying at home, you may be surprised at how much and how quickly they learn. Sometimes, the act of re-introducing your child to a daylong environment where they feel loved and cared for does wonders, especially if the school experience was less than stellar.

Considering Yourself Capable

No matter what kind of challenges you and your special needs child face during your homeschooling time, your homeschooling success depends on a few intrinsic basics:

✔ **Exhibiting patience:** Homeschooling a special needs child requires more patience, perhaps, than teaching a child without special needs. If you live with that child day in and day out, however, you already have that patience. If you didn't have it when you first laid eyes on him, you certainly learned it through the intervening years.

✔ **Knowing your child:** You know how to communicate with this child, when he hurts, and when he understands and when he does not. If you really stop to think about it, you know much more about him than a school would. And because this little one belongs to you, his learning success means the world to you.

✔ **Providing a steady environment:** When you teach your child at home, surroundings remain constant, so changing faces and environments don't upset your youngster. This is a great advantage for all special needs children, but for some children this is *very* important.

My son, for instance, freaked out when he saw toys and other items scattered on the floor in our *home*. The disarray bothered him severely. Sending this child to a school where other children sometimes act in surprising ways and adults expect him to move from room to room throughout the day would have definite negative emotional effects. He would be an emotional wreck by the end of the week or completely withdraw from the people around him because of the activity.

Although you need to structure the environment so that your child learns, you don't want to structure it so much that it actually hampers her growth as a person. Standing back and building independence is one of the hardest things some parents need to learn when they homeschool a special needs learner. The oh-I'll-get-it-for-you-honey tendency, if left uncurbed, stifles your child's growth instead of helping it. No one wants to watch a child struggle! Watching my son become frustrated enough to throw tantrums when he was learning to talk again was hard for me, but I knew, as a former educator, that I only had until he reached five years of age to utilize the open doorway of speech development. So we worked on it day after day until he got it. Each day's progress brought hugs and glasses of grape Kool-Aid for him and moist eyes for me as I watched him ever so slowly reach his communication goals.

Your child can become more independent than he is now. Maybe that means bending or reshaping a spoon so he can hold it and eat by himself. Perhaps it means researching and trying every method that you can think of until you unlock the mysteries of the written word and he begins to read. But he *can* do it — especially if you stand behind him and cheer at every step.

AT OUR HOUSE

Fueling future homeschooling

When we first thought about homeschooling, my son was completely nonverbal and showed signs of intense frustration. The local school system tested him for a special needs preschool class, but he did not qualify because he tested within a normal IQ range. So *in spite of the fact* that he could no longer talk to me, the local schools had nowhere for this child to go.

The thought of teaching him at home terrified me at first. Yet I looked back over the past year we'd just completed — through modified sign language, a communication board I created all over the refrigerator door, and day-in-day-out language practice, I was able to reach this child. The first day he said "Mama" again, the tears rolled down my cheeks.

Guiding the Gifted

If your child puts in a good day of homeschool by completing third or fourth grade math, assigned reading, an art project, and reciting the Greek alphabet for fun — all before lunch — then follows you around the rest of the day saying things such as, "Hey Mom! Come watch me reenact the Battle of Yorktown," then there's a good chance that you have a gifted learner on your hands. Especially if the child is age five or six, as this one was when that day occurred. (Honest! I was there.)

Gifted children qualify as special needs learners because they don't learn the same way that the average child does. They process differently, learn information outside the norm (both in content and in speed), and generally keep you on your toes as a homeschooling parent. Because they learn differently than normal, the books and materials sold for general homeschooling often fail to meet the needs of these children, but unlike the homeschoolers of twenty years ago, today's families have access to programs and books that actually work.

Taking different paths

Gifted learners take in information differently. They don't amass details and data faster than usual as much as they take a whole different route to get there. Remember the Family Circus cartoons of Billy's adventures? When his dad called him, instead of walking down the path from the swing set to his dad, Billy jumped off the picnic table, ran around the bird feeder a couple times, touched all the tree trunks, and *then* ran to see his dad.

That's kind of how gifted learners learn. The interesting (and sometimes frustrating) thing about this is that one moment you may be talking about dinosaurs. Then their brains kick in and you end up talking about the similarities between ancient Rome and recent attempts to colonize in space. How did you get there? If you ask them, they outline jump after jump, and map their mental journey for you — but you still may end up shaking your head at the end of the explanation.

They pick up skills that way, too. With absolutely no previous training, he child I mentioned earlier in this chapter who loved Yorktown multiplied in his head by the time he was four. He loved numbers and figured it out. Of course, this leads to some interesting questions later, when you think he knows something that he missed. It goes something like this: How in the world can you multiply and divide decimals and fractions, but you never learned how to *subtract* double-digit numbers? Obviously a day of review is in order.

Because of the way gifted students learn, most general textbook and workbook programs won't work with the gifted unless you want to add much to the material, such as hands-on projects. You can try (goodness knows I did), but don't be disappointed if your children say they're bored.

Like all special needs students, one-on-one tutoring works best with these learners, especially if they test extremely gifted or profoundly gifted. (Extremely gifted students fall within the 160 to 180 IQ range, and the profoundly gifted score 180 and higher). Because most education is developed for the normal student range, these kids usually learn best when taught with creative methods — just like *all* their special needs counterparts.

If all this is new to you, and you hear bells ringing in your head as you read about gifted learners, you may want to read an essay titled *Is It A Cheetah?* by Stephanie Tolan. You can find it at the GT World Web site (`www.gtworld.org/cheetah.html`). Stephanie does a wonderful job explaining how gifted learners react to their world.

Rounding up gifted education resources

You may need to hunt doggedly and upturn an occasional stone, but many resources exist for parents of gifted children — especially on the Internet. Some publishers produce unit studies for gifted learners, and others create curriculum that just works well with them without actually being designed that way.

Is your child ADD/ADHD?

Although some children who live under an Attention Deficit Disorder or Attention Deficit Hyperactive Disorder (ADD and ADHD) classification may actually have an internal chemical problem, most ADD students that I've seen are incredibly bright and underchallenged children.

These kids learn best with structure that they don't find in a normal school setting. They also function as outside-the-box learners — students who may not be interested in the particular subject at hand. And if a subject fails to interest them, they generally don't care if they learn it or not.

If you want to know more about attention deficit and homeschooling, *Home Education Magazine* posts a terrific set of resources on their Web site. In one of the magazine's online feature sections, you can find articles by successful homeschoolers, book recommendations, and more. Go online and check out www.home-ed-magazine.com/INF/SPCL/spcl_add.indx.html.

One distance (*satellite*) school specializes in gifted learners. If you want more structure than selecting your curriculum and flying by the seat of your pants — which is what most parents of gifted learners do for the first few years — you may want to check into The Westbridge Academy (Internet: http://home.flash.net/~wx3o/westbridge) and its offerings. They offer completely individualized programs for Kindergarten through grade twelve. Contact information for the Academy is 1610 West Highland Ave. #228, Chicago, IL 60660; Phone: 773-743-3312.

You may want to look at the following list of available resources, too.

- **The classical curriculum:** A classical education appeals to gifted students because of its depth. Many of these learners like to get their hands around concepts, so they thrive with a curriculum that explores the questions of the ages. See Chapter 12 for more information about the classical approach to homeschooling.

- **Teacher-created materials:** (Internet: www.teachercreated.com; Phone: 800-662-4321) Teacher-created develops many unit studies at the "challenging" level, with titles such as Archaeology, Chocolate, and Freedom.

- **Britesparks:** An Australian Web site (www.britesparks.com) devoted to gifted learners. Areas include a section for kids, one for teens, and resources and articles (including articles on homeschooling gifted learners).

Teaching the Medically Fragile

Children with medical problems spend so much time in and out of doctor's offices, and sometimes even in and out of the hospital, that regular school attendance becomes a hazy fantasy rather than the norm that most children experience. Between doctor visits, scheduled tests and operations, and medical devices ranging from braces to heart monitors, families juggle many more plates than those who simply get a child to school in the morning and soccer practice afterwards.

Homeschool provides a haven and some calm in the storm. You can teach on the good days — those days that you spend at home with an alert learner. Some families take reading or history to the doctor's waiting room and work until the appointment time. When you spend as much time in the doctor's office as these families do, you notice the week the magazines change on the table! After awhile, the office begins to look as much like home as your own living room, and life takes on a whole different timing.

Making your child comfortable as possible and keeping your child alive function as your two top priorities. Continuing to function as a family quickly becomes a third priority, especially if your child becomes medically fragile as she grows older. Somewhere after that comes schoolwork and intellectual learning.

If your hackles rise at this priority list, then you don't have a medically fragile child at your house. The good news is that with homeschooling, your child gets in more useful days during the year than she would otherwise because you're on the watch and can teach each good day. Or if she consistently shows more energy during a specific two hour period of the day, as a homeschooler you can declare that your prime teaching time.

Getting the Goods You Need

Special learners sometimes need special stuff. For one thing, they often don't learn in the same way as other children. Notice that I didn't say *as well* . . . I said *in the same way*. To teach the same information to a special needs child, you often need to let the creative juices flow. The need to present abstract concepts with concrete manipulatives, for example, may keep you pondering for a few weeks. After you figure it out, though, and your learner *gets it,* all the effort suddenly becomes worthwhile and you have the energy to do it again with the next topic.

Special equipment and services

Although not always the case, special needs learners sometimes need specialized equipment and services. Speech therapy, physical therapy, and adaptive devices all lend a hand toward your child's independence. Although medical insurance (if you have it) may cover some of these things, it doesn't cover others. Check with your insurance carrier to see what they cover *before* you seek out costly assistance or devices. A little advance planning can spare you the shock of what it can cost later.

You also may be able to get assistance from your school system. It depends on your state and your local school officials. Some school systems provide speech therapy, physical therapy, and occupational therapy to families regardless of whether they homeschool, yet others withhold these services from homeschoolers. Your local school official in charge of the district's special needs services should tell you whether such services are available in your area.

One option, especially with physical therapy, is to schedule a "training session" with your favorite physical therapist (PT). Especially if your child needs daily stretching exercises that remain the same for years on end, or strengthening exercises that don't change until the muscles change, your local PT may be willing to show you how to do those exercises yourself with your child. First, this allows you to exercise your child in the comfort of your home and on your schedule. Second, this frees the physical therapist — the school PTs that I've worked with in the past all had way too many cases for the available hours of the day.

Your child may not need any of these services. Many special needs homeschoolers don't. You also may experience time periods when you need assistance as I did, and times when you do fine on your own. Go with what you need. If your frustration level rises with no abatement, and you can't see the end of the tunnel for the obstacles, check out some of the resources in this chapter and get some help for your child and for you.

Individualized Education Program

Schools use an Individualized Education Program (usually known as an IEP) for two reasons. First, the IEP lists point by point what a student is supposed to learn in a year's time. Second, it covers the educational establishment's posterior regions by proving that the learner learned *something* the previous year. A well-written IEP gives a classroom teacher a blueprint for the year. They take a long time to craft, especially if you want to actually document a student's needs and progress.

Most homeschoolers don't need to create an IEP for their own children unless they want to document progress and service needs. If you live in a state that requires a yearly portfolio, you may need to file an IEP for a special needs child. Your law (or state homeschool support group) should tell you for sure.

If you decide you need an IEP and don't have the foggiest idea where to begin, the U.S. Department of Education offers a Web site devoted to IEPs. Visit online at www.ed.gov/offices/OSERS/OSEP/IEP_Guide for the ins and outs of the IEP. This site is designed for students actively in their school systems, so your requirements may be a little different. But it gives you a good start. The site also offers a sample IEP form that you can copy and use as a basis for your own.

Information

If you have a special needs homeschooler, then please don't flounder for lack of information! Certain companies devote much of their time and money to the challenge of special learners. From adaptive learning devices to specialized curriculum, it's all out there if you only know where to look.

Ahhhhhhchooo! Allergies

Doesn't everyone suffer with allergies at one time or another? Although almost every adult remembers a reaction to pollen, poison ivy, or even chocolate, some children live with allergies that can be debilitating. Children who generally enjoy school, but who spend two weeks or more at home each month during fall and spring because they have the "flu", or who walk around looking like raccoons due to the black circles under their eyes, fight to maintain their concentration during these down times.

These kids, although not sick enough for hospitalization, live through long stretches where they just don't *feel* well. Depending on an allergy's severity, prescribed medication may lessen the symptoms but not eradicate them entirely. Various and sundry chemicals, building materials, and office supplies found in a normal school setting do nothing to help this child's situation.

If your child experiences mood swings and you think they could be allergy related, you may want to take a look at a book called *Is This Your Child?: Discovering and Treating Unrecognized Allergies in Children and Adults* by Doris Rapp, M.D. Dr. Rapp describes possible food, chemical, and environmental allergies, and she also explains the emotional behaviors and physical symptoms that accompany said allergies. It's a big one — 626 pages of information — but some families found it life changing — especially if they found that their children were wrongly diagnosed as ADD/ADHD.

Individual attention

All too often, the special needs child becomes lost in a classroom situation. She's ready to move on and others don't get the concepts yet, or she doesn't understand and the teacher can't see for the other faces in the room that need help, too. Both extremes lead to a child whose needs aren't being met.

Homeschooling shines as an alternative for these learners. With individual attention, also known through the ages as *tutoring,* these kids progress at their own rate. If they miss something along the way, you take the time to re-teach it. And best of all, when they don't understand because the presentation doesn't click with them, you have the freedom to be creative. Use M&Ms, strips of paper, papier mâché, crayons, a tape recorder, computer software, or whatever it takes.

Conversely, when your learner gets a concept on the first try, she doesn't sit through the presentation three or four more times while you attempt to reach the other students in the room. Here, homeschooling gives you the freedom to move on when she's ready. Then slow down if she requires it later.

Because your child is one of ... well ... one, and not one of twenty or thirty, you also have the opportunity to add extras into your school day. If your learner loves to dabble in paint, take the time to use paint while you explore history. Recreate various painting styles — or even pictures — of the time period. Who cares if you do the whole thing in finger paint?

On the other hand, customizing your learner's program also means that you don't need to force him to do the things that he hates to do. Some students (mine included) absolutely *hate* papier-mâché. The consistency turns their stomachs. Last I heard, papier-mâché proficiency wasn't included in *any* state's list of competent life skills.

If your child hates it and he doesn't need it, why do it? Redirect that energy into something he *does* enjoy. Maybe papier mâché and glue are yucky at your house, but gummed paper (sheets that you cut shapes from and lick to stick onto other paper and things) qualifies as cool. Use what works.

A few of the resources I amassed while working with special needs learners during the past several years follow. Take this information as a starting point. Due to page restraints, there is no way I could list all the available resources, but these links address learning disabilities and special needs of all types:

- ✔ **Don Johnston Incorporated:** (Internet: www.donjohnston.com; Phone: 800-999-4660) Carries adaptive devices, speaking word processors, and highly structured reading and writing software for students who need it.

- ✔ **Intellitools:** (Internet: www.intellitools.com; Phone: 800-899-6687) Markets a large touch pad that you activate with computer software. For physically involved students ranging from those who simply need a keyboard guide to students who require more physical assistance to answer questions, this company sells (and develops, if you have a need they have yet to address) reading and math special needs curriculum.

✔ **ParentPals.com:** (Internet: `www.parentpals.com`) Provides information and links for parents of students with ADHD, autism, deaf and hard of hearing, emotionally disturbed, gifted, learning disabled, mental retardation, health impaired, speech and language, traumatic brain injury, and visually impaired. This is a good starting point if you find yourself at the beginning of the journey.

✔ **Family Education.com:** (Internet: `www.familyeducation.com`.) The special needs link takes you to a page devoted to ADD/ADHD, learning disabilities, and gifted and talented. Each section contains basic information, articles, advice, and a message board where you can meet (or vent) with other parents.

Chapter 17

Finding the Sources You Need

In This Chapter

▶ Surfing the Net to save time, energy, and gasoline

▶ Ordering through the mail from homeschool catalogs

▶ Examining programs up close: Homeschool conferences

▶ Spreading the news by word-of-mouth

*Y*our mind full of rosy possibilities, you set forth to collect all the home education goodies that you can for this year's learning extravaganza. Your homeschool reference file bulges with ideas. You settle on a curriculum or education method after weighing the available options, create a list of must-haves and optional extras for the year, and you're ready to go.

Now you face a wall. You know what you want (or kind of what you want, anyway). Where do you get it? Homeschool supply stores don't sit on every corner waiting for the hordes to enter. Homeschool supply stores would be nice — especially on those days that you'd really like to try something new — but it's not reality.

Throughout this book, when I mention a product, I also list the Web site and/ or the phone number. You can use these to begin with or turn to Appendix A for more options.

Turn to this chapter when you exhaust the library, your local educational store, or you're looking for something esoteric. (If it's too esoteric, then *nobody* carries it.) Sometimes you need to be creative in tracking these items down.

Getting the Good Stuff with Curriculum Guides

Curriculum guides are huge books or Web sites that point you to *everything* that's available for homeschool. At the dawn of homeschooling, when only a few publishers produced curriculum that homeschoolers wanted to use, the job was much easier. Now, so many products flood the homeschool store shelves that covering them all is impossible for one author.

- ✔ *The Complete Home Learning Source Book: The Essential Resource Guide for Homeschoolers, Parents, and Educators:* Compiled by homeschooler Rebecca Rupp in the spirit of giving complete coverage a good try. In merely 752 pages, she reviews more products than anyone could possibly use in a lifetime (published by Three Rivers Press).

- ✔ *Christian Home Educator's Curriculum Manual:* Cathy Duffy's curriculum guide specifically designed for Christian homeschoolers, this book also gives you a huge number of recommendations in 504 pages. Christian homeschoolers who teach at home for religious reasons can find recommendations for products that do not contradict their faith (published by Grove Publishing).

- ✔ **The Education Connection:** (Internet: www.educationconnection.com) Part store and part review Web site, The Education Connection writes up each item they sell so you know exactly what you're buying before you get it. Although their ultimate goal, of course, is to get you to purchase your supplies from them, The Education Connection does a great job of telling you why their products are good.

TIP

Read those reviews!

When you subscribe to a homeschool magazine, you get a ton of curriculum and software reviews with the package. (Depending on your magazine of choice, I may even be the author of some of those reviews.) As you read the same reviewer month after month, and compare his choices to your preferences, you soon get a feel for those writers who are on your wavelength.

When you find a reviewer or columnist that you like, read their columns with an eye toward your own needs. Looking for a history curriculum? Dig out last year's articles from your magazine stash and glance through for history ideas. Homeschoolers tend to throw little away, as my software-laden office may testify. If you really

need to conserve room, you can always clip your faves and file them before you toss the magazine.

Curriculum providers and software manufacturers release their wares to writers for review so that these journalists can spread the word, so to speak. A good review writer turns up materials that you never knew existed because that's her job. And a balanced review writer gushes over the good stuff, warns you against the bad stuff, and introduces you to a whole truckload of it-gets-the-job-done stuff. (Ask me about Edmark's ThemeWeavers early elementary software sometime . . . I could gush for twelve pages!)

Although magazines don't classify as a pure curriculum guide, your favorite homeschool magazine spends plenty of time looking at products, trends, what works, and what doesn't. Over a couple years, a homeschooling magazine mentions enough new products and old favorites to count as a great resource. And don't overlook the ads throughout the magazine. Manufacturers place ads that they think can catch the eye of home educators; if you see something you like, give the manufacturer a call and ask for more information.

Looking at Your Local Store

Sometimes the best educational materials sit right in your own community. A peek into the local phone book under *Educational Supplies* or *Teacher Supplies* may reveal a small goldmine of educational stores. These shops come in all sizes and carry a wide variety of materials.

Although you probably won't find complete subject textbooks in one of these stores (such as Shurley Method or Glencoe Science), this is where you turn for unit studies, workbooks, all-in-one curriculums, such as McGraw Hill's Learn at Home series and much more. These stores also carry items such as construction paper, glue, tempera paints, recorders (as in musical instruments), puzzles, math manipulatives, components for science experiments, and foreign language supplements.

Locating an educational store in your own community gives you the advantage of a nearby store that you can visit when you want to supplement a class or two without waiting for mail orders to arrive. You also have the opportunity to see the books in real life and flip through them before you purchase them. The flip test can tell you plenty — whether the book's text looks like it's at your child's reading level, if the page layout includes too many or too few blank lines, questions or paragraphs for your liking, and so forth. (Because few homeschool children actually enjoy a trip to the educational store, it's also one of the few places that you can escape to browse without a chorus of helpful, hopeful voices wanting to accompany you.)

Avoiding the Malls: Ordering via Mail

When you comb every educational store in town and you still can't find what you're looking for, it's time to turn to the mail-order catalogs. For the cost of shipping, these companies mail their products to your door, which saves you from braving three feet of snow or blinding sunshine to procure them yourself.

Searching the Web for supplies

With an Internet connection and a credit card in hand, you're more than halfway to easy-school-supply acquisition. Most of the home-school vendors operate online stores. Early on, these vendors realized that the Web was a boundaries-free way to reach a scattered buying public. Although some vendors still require you to print and mail an order form and a personal check, now most take credit cards over the Net.

Lest you begin to quiver at the thought of sub-mitting your credit-card number to a computer, let me reassure you. I've purchased thousands of items over the Net in the past ten years, and have *never* been a victim of credit card fraud. I did send a personal check once, however, and received nothing for my $60, but that wasn't a homeschooling purchase.

If you don't receive your online order within a reasonable amount of time — a couple weeks — you may give the vendor a call to ensure that he received your order in the first place. Sometimes glitches happen, and orders placed don't actually make it to the fulfillment house. My orders did not go through all of three times during the past ten years, so you can see it doesn't happen often. But it does occur.

Sometimes purchasing materials online directly from the manufacturer is the only way you can get them. This is the reason that I buy online so often. Spending an hour or so with an Internet search engine saves you a ton of petrol, and you can even compare prices and products from vendor to vendor while you view their sites on screen.

When you search for homeschool supplies, as with all Internet searches, the keywords that you type into the search field determine what you see. Searching a term, such as **homeschool supplies,** on the Internet brings up vendors such as www.mommyschool.com, a Web site that features homeschool books in a dizzying array of subjects. Searching **homeschooling,** on the other hand, is a term that brings up an entirely different collection of sites. **Home-school curriculum** and **homeschool book** give you yet more options.

For a well-rounded list of several thousand pos-sible sites per search, hop on over to the Google Internet search engine (www.google.com). Although not everything appears when you use Google, it certainly beats using some of the smaller engines and wracking your brain for the esoteric search term that can lead you to your goal. Google prefers that you spell *homeschool* as one word, as in *homeschool* or *home-schooling.* The search engine gets a little testy if you continually search for items under *home school* instead of *homeschool.*

With Google, you can also specify what you *don't* want to see in results; if, for example, you want only homeschool supplies and not general teaching materials, type **– teacher** in the search text box along with your search term(s), and Google does its best to give you sites that omit the word *teacher.* (Be sure to put a space before the minus sign, though, or it doesn't work.)

The first year that you homeschool, unearthing the catalogs themselves may prove to be difficult. After you've been at this for a while, however, your mail-box overflows with print offers from every company imaginable. Are you inter-ested in an honest-to-goodness home wheat grinder? Wait a couple of years, and this company will track you down through homeschool mailing lists.

A few catalogs deserve a place on the best-loved stack. These are the books you pull out year after year because you love their products, their promptness, or both. Some catalogs are so big that *not* finding what you need is difficult, and other niche catalogs earn a place in your heart because the company owners think like you do, and you find every item fascinating.

Although these catalogs don't sell every product available to homeschoolers, they provide a good starting point:

- **Christian Book Distributors Homeschool:** (Internet: `www.christian book.com`; Phone: 800-247-4784) This catalog carries an amazing assortment of curriculum and supplements for Christian homeschoolers. Although all their products are not specifically Christian, all are acceptable to people who follow the Christian faith.

- **Nasco:** (Internet: `www.nascofa.com/prod/Home`; Phone: 800-558-9595) This company sells so many educational materials that they create twenty catalogs to showcase it all. Their arts and crafts, science, math manipulatives, and physical education supply catalogs would interest most homeschoolers. Nasco also released a special needs catalog recently. Nasco's primary customer is the public school or teacher.

- **The Learning Source:** (Internet: `www.learning-source.com`; Phone: 937-339-9656) This is like an educational store in a catalog. Look here for the products that you find in any general educational store: Teacher-Created Materials unit studies, Instructional Fair math manipulatives, and Steck-Vaughn science books, to name just a few. The Learning Source also offers a ten percent discount and free shipping to homeschoolers who place an order over $100.

These companies sell a little bit of *everything*. Look for other vendors throughout this book; you can find them listed with information on the subjects they specialize in (for example, I talk about the Great Books Academy online store in Chapter 12). Appendix A points you to even more curriculum and resources.

Attending a Homeschool Conference

Every state has one. Even the most diehard homeschoolers often miss them because they forget to mark them on the calendar. But if you're on top of things, and don't mark the information on the sticky note that gets swept underneath the refrigerator until *next* June, you'll be ahead of the game.

Some states throw large conferences, and others host smaller ones. Check with your state or local homeschool organization for a list of conferences in your area, and their dates. Sometimes various cities within a state hold conferences in the course of a year. No matter how far or near the conference is to your home, homeschooling conferences all have one thing in common — no, not food — vendors. They all offer a *vendor room,* which is usually filled with individual booths and/or tables where each vendor advertises and displays their products. You can look over curriculum, feel the bindings, ruffle the pages, read the words, pose questions directly to the sales representative standing inside the booth, and decide whether it's a program that you want to implement at your house.

The reigning argument for attending conferences and buying from the vendors on-site is that you don't have to pay shipping. Although that can be a biggie, getting to see those books up close and personal is even more important.

If the state next to yours has the reputation for holding a really great conference, you may want to set aside the time and visit the out-of-state conference as well as your own. The convention in my state, for instance, pulls homeschoolers from the surrounding four or five states. They attend their own conferences, and then carpool to this one. Appendix B lists the various homeschool associations by state: Call one of these associations and a staff member will happily tell you when the next homeschool convention comes to your state.

Hearing It from the Horse's Mouth

Your best friend Jose just told you about this great phonics program that he bought for his first grader. Best of all, he told you what company publishes the program and provided you with the company phone number! Your tracking job is almost done. You pick up the phone, order the program, and it wings its way to you.

Sometimes finding what you need really is that easy. A friend finds a curriculum or supplemental product that really works for her, and she passes along the information to you (and every other homeschooler she knows, hopefully). Word really does get around in the homeschool world — especially if you belong to an area support group, subscribe to an Internet mailing list, or gather with other homeschoolers for play days. Just like good recommendations tend to spur sales, bad ones steer you away from the questionable stuff.

Part IV

Nailing Down the Details

The 5th Wave   By Rich Tennant

THE REFRIGERATOR MAGNET MUSEUM OF ART

In this part . . .

Details that keep on moving around while you're trying to hammer them into place are no fun. But that's the way it goes some times — details lie everywhere, and when you grab one to fasten it down, the rest of them scatter. Welcome to the life of a new homeschooler.

You decide to homeschool, your curriculum arrives, and you feel overwhelmed. Book stacks cover the dining-room table that you planned to use for dinner this evening. You realize that you already spent a little over the planned budget and still have two children to buy for. You feel a bit out of your comfort zone.

This is the part to visit when a day like this becomes part of your reality. The chapters in this section help you define what you call your school space, organize the books that too easily cause chaos, and keep a lid on the yearly costs. Also, browse through this part for information on using the home (school) computer for more than a huge bookend and the ins and outs of grading. Lest you feel lonely, this part also talks about meeting other homeschool families and gathering together for learning and fun.

So sweep the books off the table — tucking them into the nearest empty kitchen cabinet will do for now. Fix yourself a cup of tea and snuggle down in the now clutter-free dining room to cover the details of homeschool organization and the other realities of the educational life.

Chapter 18

Defining Your School Space

*V*isions of the perfect schoolroom dance in your head. Blackboard-covered walls, begging to be decorated with colored chalk, beckon. Seasonal trimming sparkles invitingly on brightly festooned bulletin boards. Around the corner, computers beep as children investigate the latest software in the lab. Then you wake up.

Thankful that it was all a dream, you look around at your home, and the following question nags at the back of your mind: Do I have enough extra room and equipment to embark on this homeschool adventure?

In school or out of it, the fantasy schoolroom described is just that — a fantasy. No one has the time or materials to do it all perfectly every time. One of the beauties of homeschooling is that you can start where you are and use what's available to you. Then, if you like, you can add to your stash as time goes on.

Making Room for Chalk

At some homeschools that I know and love, learning materials bulge from every closet. These moms and dads, marking every tub, tin, and bookcase so they know exactly what they have and where it is, collect from used curriculum and garage sales. Then, when they need the Hebrew version of Scrabble, they drag it out from under the bed for the day's lesson. The whole house functions as a schoolroom and a storage place for homeschool paraphernalia.

Other families set aside one corner or a bookshelf and small, covered crate to hold all their supplies, and they're set for the year. They function quite well with a minimum of extras, still get the job done, and have room under the bed to store off-season clothes instead of blank sheets of poster board. These homeschoolers, though, are part of a pretty rare breed.

Most homeschool families fall somewhere in the middle. They don't collect every educational doodad that they see, but they do set aside a closet shelf and maybe a bookcase or two to hold books and supplies. This keeps everything together with a minimum of allocated space.

Setting aside the optimal amount of space

When do you decide enough is enough? When all the room under the beds boast of homeschooling supplies? When you find yourself adding a fourth bookcase to the family room? When you're calling the builders to add an extra room onto the house? When you crowd the new computer into the kitchen?

If you guard the door against the Homeschool Stuff Collectors Society while I share, then I'll tell you a secret: You only need to collect as much stuff as you feel comfortable using.

If you enjoy amassing large quantities of things, then homeschooling will quickly move to the top of your shopping list. You can find *so many* things to buy for your homeschool! Some of it classifies as useful, although other objects can only be considered froufrou.

If you have a library card and the books in hand that you need to cover the current year's subjects, then you're probably set as far as the absolute necessities go. One good, kitchen-cabinet shelf or bookcase shelf, or a couple of those pseudo-milk crates that you can buy at discount stores should work as storage space. Then you can create your school space virtually anywhere that you find comfortable. When you begin to collect extra goodies, however, you require more storage space. That's where the beds come in.

Buying too far in advance increases storage needs

After you assemble the basics that appear on every public school to-buy list — paper, pencils, crayons or markers, glue, and the like — the rest is gravy. Construction paper is nice; scissors and glue see plenty of use with the younger set. If you see a science project that would work well with your current year, by all means buy it if you have the extra cash and you think the brood would enjoy the experience.

Buying this year for seven years down the road, however, tends to be a waste of money in the long run. If you happen to use a good number of out-of-print reading books in your homeschool, that's one thing, but purchasing most items because they're available and they look good for several years in the future generally fills your supply closet with an abundance of useless stuff.

For one thing, you have no idea what will interest your second grader when he reaches high school. Several years of development and refinement lay between second grade and the senior year; your little one may find a completely different set of fascinations by the time he's a teen. In addition, the curriculum that looks so good now may lose its luster in a few years when the new edition hits the bookstore shelves.

Like all rules, the caveats for advance-curriculum purchasing also have their exceptions. However, you may want to go ahead and buy for the next couple years so you have it on hand if

- ✔ **The publisher announces a major revision of a particular curriculum that you're in love with and are sure to follow for the next several years.**

- ✔ **You don't follow the traditional calendar year.** You teach all year round and take a vacation when you need it instead of when your area schools declare time off.

- ✔ **You follow one particular curriculum year after year, but you aren't sure when you'll finish the current installment.** In this case, you may want to plan ahead and purchase the next book or two in the series.

We do this with history. Our history curriculum, although not actually set in stone, follows a logical historical progression. My children know that as soon as we finish the study of Viking culture, play a few, way cool Viking games, and create some faux Viking projects, that we're off to study the Middle Ages. Because I know that we'll cover the Middle Ages and then move into the Renaissance, I purchase books a year or two ahead to be sure they'll be handy when I need them. Spending half a year or two years on the Middle Ages doesn't matter — I can pull the next book off the shelf and keep going.

When you think about how to fill *your* homeschool supply closet, try to purchase only the whizbang extras that you'll really use. A closet stuffed with educational items that you never get around to using means that

- ✔ You have a closet that's useless for anything else because it's full.

- ✔ The kids never get the educational benefit from the products because they sit idle.

Once or twice a year, I go through my school closet and pull the items that I want to use before the end of the current semester to ensure that I actually incorporate certain activities into my teaching day. If I didn't, my home would turn into a collection of educational box art.

Deciding between the Den, the Dining Room, or the Whole Darn Place

When you look for a place in your home that would be suitable for a school space, the goal is to find a spot where everyone feels comfortable congregating each day. Although the back porch may be good during spring and early fall, too many rainy days can depress scholars and force them to find another schooling spot. Save the back porch for really beautiful days and try to locate a space inside the house for daily lesson and reading time. Your raindrop-free textbooks will thank you.

You can also use a multipurpose room for a homeschooling classroom. The living-room floor and chairs make a nice place to work if you object to hard chairs in the kitchen or dining room, especially if your children stay awake on the sofa. The parental bedroom, although not optimal all the time, provides a soft, cushy bed for reading and a space big enough that everyone can pile onto it if they're careful with toes and noses.

Even the corner of a room works great as a school space if that's what speaks to you. Setting up a bookcase, a table, and a storage area with paper, pencils, and extras keeps everything in one place and within reach. If you have a toddler or preschooler at home, teaching the other children in one portion of a larger room allows the youngest family members room to roam and play.

Like everything else in the homeschooling universe, you work with what you can to fit your needs. Do your children need absolute quiet when they work? Take that into consideration when deciding on a school space. Must you complete other tasks as you teach? Then situate them close to where you'll be working.

Gathering around the kitchen table

For some families, the absolute best place for a homeschooling class is the kitchen table. For one thing, it provides a warm, comforting atmosphere that's hard to beat. Who can feel poopy when they wander to the room where hot soup, bread, and cereal regularly make their appearance?

The kitchen also provides a ready-made table or counter, along with chairs, benches, or stools to sit on while you work. Although the living room couch may look inviting, it's also so cozy that you awaken an hour later wondering where your time and that chapter went. A more pedestrian reason for working at the kitchen table is that it gives the Educating Parental Unit (that would be you) time to work on breakfast, lunch and dinner while still overseeing school activities. And if you're used to fixing three meals a day for an entire family, you know how much time it takes! Having everyone together in the kitchen while you chop, puree, and sauté relieves some of the daily get-it-on-the-table stress.

Setting aside a special room

If you're fortunate enough that your home contains a room that you don't currently use, you can always transform it into a schoolroom. Using one specific room allows you to assemble all (or most) of your school supplies in one space. This cuts down on clutter in the long run. Not having to search through two different floors of your home for the red construction paper can streamline your school day.

At our house, the schoolroom was always the last area to be cleaned because we used it so much. Designating a whole room as your schoolroom gives you the option to shut the door when you have guests. Closing the door keeps a lid on the clutter that seeps out of the room at the same time that it keeps visiting little fingers from rifling through your school stuff. If you have many small or inquisitive children visit your home, your children probably won't take the results of their busy fingers with the best grace. (I know that mine don't!)

Another benefit to using an entire room for your school space is that you have definite *on* and *off* times. If you're in a room that has been designated for school, then children may come to associate paying attention and getting down to business with being in that room during school hours. At other times of the day when they're out of the schoolroom, children feel free to participate in activities that don't involve grammar or numbers.

This approach may be most effective with younger children. By the time a child is ten or eleven, she *knows* when school time falls and when she is free to pursue her own interests. With children between 5 and 8 years old, however, those lines sometimes blur a bit.

Just because you have the room available doesn't mean that you need to set it aside as a full-time schoolroom. If incorporating your school space area into a larger room of your house, such as the kitchen or living room, fits your family style, then do it. Some homeschooling families find that separating school from the rest of life adds nothing to their standard of living.

The perils of your own place

The first five years that we homeschooled, we designated the spare bedroom as our schoolroom. Complete with computers and primary school desks, this tiny work of art functioned as our school away from school. The kids had a special room to store crayons and pencils, paper and workbooks.

During those five years, almost every day that dawned on our schoolroom illuminated an area that was messy beyond belief. The floor bore the constant remains of the yesterday-after-school-construction-paper project. We-luv-you-mommy messages were scrawled on the whiteboard more often than Greek nouns and verbs. Not that *We luv you* is bad — it just didn't match the whiteboard's originally intended purpose.

Books littered the floor from the bedtime reading scramble the evening before. Some days, the first hour of our school day became a clean-the-pit exercise. The little desks and white board were nice, but they quickly lost their appeal.

In addition, our schoolroom was on the second floor, and my husband and I maintained offices on the first floor. This made checking e-mail during independent reading time less than handy. I found myself running upstairs and down all morning long — greeting the delivery person right in the middle of a science lesson, grabbing a history resource I mistakenly left in my office, or printing an occasional lesson supplement from the computer that I needed before beginning the next subject.

When we moved into our present home, I proposed a radical lifestyle change — no more schoolroom. Instead, the children work at a long conference table set up in the basement right outside mom and dad's shared office. The table is big enough to spread out their work if they need to, yet small enough that they can clean the area before they trash it again. (That, at least, is the goal.)

Many homeschoolers dream of having a whole room for their school space, and some set aside space for a schoolroom and love it. For us, though, designating a whole room for school definitely put a strain on our lifestyle instead of enhancing it. Our schoolroom had to go.

LEGOs in the living room and homework in the hall

Some families live in and use the whole house as a school space. Yours may be one of them. Regardless of a room's intended purpose, the children in these families expand to fill their allotted space and move from room to room throughout the day. These homeschooling families deserve credit for actually using every square inch of their home space and *living* there.

Although the home that uses all of its space for living in as well as home-schooling may look like chaos reigns supreme, any child from the household can report the exact progress of almost every activity in the home, "That? Oh, yeah. That's Antoine's LEGO tower. He wants it to reach the ceiling by Monday." A little awed, you leave said tower where it stands and move on to another room.

If your books and supplies stay in a place where they're accessible, you don't actually *need* a specific place to sit and work. If you want, you can spread out throughout your home, read in the bedrooms, and sculpt on the kitchen floor. Children must feel comfortable on the floor; they spend plenty of time there. If it doesn't bother you and it doesn't bother them, why change it?

Most adults and some children feel more secure if the school space is a specific area. If your family members feel differently, then go with the flow and see how it works. Maybe your daughter's creativity only flows when she sits underneath the family room table. I find my girl there quite often. You could always help her out and install a portable light that hangs beneath the table so she actually sees the words she reads.

Let *your* needs determine *your* space

When you look at your home to figure out where you want to spend time during school hours, try what seems good to you. Who cares if you have three empty rooms upstairs and you prefer to work at the kitchen table? I won't tell anyone if you don't.

And if you decide to move the girls into one bedroom so you can change the empty room into a dedicated schoolroom, go for it. Of course, it helps if the girls happen to be friends to begin with, but it's your house, your children, and your school. Do what seems best to you.

The moral is that you are in charge here. If you homeschool, you do so because homeschooling is the best decision for your family right now. Take that freedom and look at your home. The same standards apply. No matter where you decide to do school at your house, it needs to be the best decision for your family today.

If you find that your organization needs to change next month or next year, then change it.

During our schoolroom years, I moved those little desks all over the room trying to determine the best fit for the way that I explain information and the way that my little scholars internalize it. No one will say a word if you decide to move your school space from the basement to the living room. At least, no one *should* say anything — I know everybody has an opinion these days, but where you put your school space is your decision.

I have a homeschool friend who I've known for several years. In that time, I've seen her move the school space all over the house. School started in her basement. Then it moved to the dining room. After that, migrating to the family room off the kitchen for more comfort, she held classes in the kitchen for a long while. Now she has designated a room that sits above her garage: It's perfect for her. Finding the ultimate space took some time. It may mean a couple of migrations for you, too, but you'll get there.

If your son feels better in the hallway when he snips those construction paper creations and it doesn't bother you, then why not leave him there? Little pieces of construction paper come up much more easily with the vacuum than they do when helpful hands try to pick them up and swipe them off the table onto the floor. You need the sweeper then anyway. Why not start on the floor from the beginning?

Sometimes you do need to practice perfect posture and sit still. Penmanship and pencil drawing, for example, really do work best when your child sits in a chair at the table. (Believe me, we've tried all kinds of ways to do handwriting, and the most legible results come from table and chair. Underneath the table does *not* do it for me.) Building projects, however, really don't require a table any more than dolls or cars do. Your child can pretend and create just about anywhere. Use what works for you.

Chapter 19

Keeping the Costs Down

In This Chapter

▶ Cutting your expenses

▶ Visiting the library

▶ Buying used curriculum

▶ Writing your own curriculum

*R*emember the story that circulated a few years ago about the Gourmet cookie recipe? You know the one — a friend of a friend of a friend inadvertently pays an outlandish price for a well-known corporation's cookie recipe and then sends the recipe out to everyone in the known universe so that she feels better about the hundreds of dollars she paid. I hate to break the news to you if you haven't heard it somewhere before now, but the story isn't true. Known as an *urban legend,* it's a tale that sounds like it should be true or could be true, so people believe it.

The costs of homeschooling fit neatly into the *urban legend* category. You hear horror stories from the media about the "true" cost of homeschooling. Fear begins to gnaw at you, and you wonder if you can do this homeschooling thing after all if it's going to be *that* expensive. To dispel at least one urban legend from your life, let me tell you the truth: Homeschooling doesn't have to cost an arm and a leg. It's as inexpensive or as costly as you want to make it.

Although a few families gleefully spend thousands of dollars on homeschooling each year, most people simply want to reach the end of the year with a little left in the homeschool fund. Spending $300 or less per child per year is not unusual. Some families even manage to spend under $300 per *family* per year and still do a great job teaching their young ones.

Slashing Curriculum Prices

You can provide your children with a good, solid education without spending money like water. A textbook or program's high price tag is no indicator of its usefulness to your children's educational needs. The goal is to locate resources that work for your kids and to help them learn what they need to know. Keeping your goal in mind while you shop for curriculum (those books that help you teach particular subjects such as math or science) may save you money all by itself.

Many homeschoolers find that their needs for inexpensive curriculum vary with the years: Some years, you find yourself with a tight budget and realize that you need to cut expenses. This sounds like you? The following tips help.

On the other hand, if this is the year that you want an expensive educational device (such as a good-quality microscope for high school science) and you need to cut the costs of educational books and supplies to afford the equipment, then you may glean an idea or two that you can use here.

Choosing an inexpensive curriculum

One of the easiest ways to keep a lid on costs is to select one of the more inexpensive curriculums out there. If you have your heart set on a science book that costs $80, a math book that sets you back $60, and $130 in miscellaneous history books for the year, you've already spent over $250 for one child, and you need textbooks for other subjects! Looking at one expensive textbook may not be so bad, but when you throw two or three more into the pile, the numbers add up frighteningly fast.

An easy way to guard against this curriculum overload is to set a maximum annual budget for each child. If your yearly budget for each child is $200, for example, you may need to use some creativity to fit everything into that, but it's certainly doable. A set budget means that you can't run out and buy the neatest, coolest curriculum that you see this week *unless* it happens to fit within your price range. Price range limits may not be loads of fun, but they are part of living.

Sitting down with your child, your budget, and your curriculum ideas may be a good exercise in economics. This gives you a great opportunity to explain why money really doesn't grow on trees and to drive home the concept of *opportunity cost* — that when you purchase one item, the money is gone and you lose the opportunity to buy something else. (Quick! Jot it down as a math or business lesson! That golden moment you just shared counts as class time.)

Another option is to start with a prepackaged curriculum-in-a-book that covers most of what you need for the year and fills in the extras as you need them. Several publishers market whole grade-level curriculum books for preschool through eighth-grade learners. Each book covers everything that you absolutely need to homeschool, and they all retail for about $20 to $45. Not bad for a year of learning! Realistically, you need to supplement these books with reading books from your home or local library. Some of the available options are

✔ **Basic Skills Curriculum:** From McGraw Hill (Internet: www.mkkids.com), the Basic Skills Curriculum covers reading, writing, math, vocabulary, testing skills, and it includes a CD-ROM that you can use in addition to the book. (The CD adds some educational content, usually math, but is not required to use the book. It's a freebie.) Although this hefty book comprises 600 pages, you still need to locate science, social studies, and probably spelling to create a complete curriculum. These books are for scholars ranging from grade one through grade eight.

✔ **Comprehensive Curriculum of Basic Skills:** This curriculum comes from American Education Publishing, a division of McGraw Hill Publishing (Internet: www.mhkids.com). Also specializing in reading, writing, and math, the Comprehensive Curriculum series includes English, science, some history, citizenship (depending on grade level) and study skills. The back of the book contains some teaching ideas and a complete answer key. Although the front of the book lists no science and no social studies, the reading selections concentrate on these subjects and geography. You could easily use the reading selections as starting points for further study. At the Web site, search the online catalog with the keywords **comprehensive curriculum** to locate the books.

✔ **Home Education Curriculum:** (Instructional Fair, Internet: www.instructionalfair.com/cgi-bin/IFG_US.storefront) In one book, you get 36 weeks of lesson plans that address each subject: math, reading, grammar, writing, spelling, social studies, and science. After the plans you get a set of teaching suggestions for each week's subjects. The last half of the book is devoted to worksheets you can use to help teach the concepts in the lesson plans. Many of the plans require common reading books (such as *Mr. Popper's Penguins* and *Anno's Journey*) that you can find at the library.

✔ **Learn At Home series:** Available for grades one through six, this book also comes from American Education Publishing (Internet: www.mhkids.com). This is one of the curriculum sets truly designed for homeschool use. One of the median-price options, at $29.95 retail, the book includes 36 weeks of lesson plans ready-made for the homeschool teacher, 36 weeks of teaching suggestions and activities, and worksheets for the student to complete. And it covers reading, language, spelling, math, science, and social studies.

Finding used curriculum

Unlike chocolate-chip cookies, you can use textbooks more than once and still get the same result. The easiest way to reuse curriculum, of course, is to pass books down the line in your own household. You buy them once and each year that you reuse them gives you a bonus.

If you have more than a couple children at your house, and you find curriculum you really like, using it with more than one child helps to justify the cost of a hardbound textbook. It also saves you time the second or third time you teach from the same book. You open it, think "Oh. I remember this." And off you go.

Short of passing books down the line, you can track down used curriculum in a wealth of places. Some homeschoolers give their used books to other families who need them or sell them to other homeschoolers at a more-than-fair price. (I've been on a long-term-swapping binge with several families for a number of years, and pick up titles I think they'll like if I see them at a really good price. Because I only spend an extra dollar or two at a time, it becomes more of a game than a burden. You can read more about sharing with other homeschoolers later in this chapter in the "Tapping the Fountain of Fellow Homeschoolers" section.)

Once or twice a year, most areas gather their homeschoolers together and hold a used-curriculum fair. The idea is that you sell what you no longer need for a few dollars, and you buy what you do need. Of course, what you buy depends on what other homeschoolers offer for sale, but you can really cut your costs if you live in an area with a good, used-curriculum fair. Keep in mind that *good* is a relative term. You probably won't find as many high school level science books at a used book fair as you will resources for kindergarten through fourth grade. Whether you turn up great stuff depends on what you need to begin with.

✔ **The Back Pack:** (Internet: www.thebackpack.com) Unlike many curriculum vendors, this company sells textbooks that the schools currently use or used in the past. If you're looking for a book from a school publisher, such as Heath, Silver Burdette, or Holt, check out The Back Pack.

✔ **The Educator's Exchange:** (Internet: www.edexbooks.com) This vendor carries all kinds of stuff, from math manipulatives to music curriculum. If you find yourself looking for something out of the ordinary, The Educator's Exchange may well become one of your favorite stops.

✔ **Homeschooling Daily Used Curriculum Vendors:** (Internet: my.ohio.voyager.net/~baugust/oldbooks.html.) This site lists a number of used curriculum destinations. Out of the 100 vendors listed at this site, you should find a favorite or two.

✔ **VegSource:** (Internet: www.vegsource.com/homeschool) Although started as a resource board for vegetarians, this is one of the hottest curriculum sites on the Web. The Swap boards list new items daily, and the items tend to go fast, so if you see something you like, you need to hop on the Internet.

Writing your own curriculum

Writing your own curriculum always saves you money because you don't have to purchase anyone else's textbooks. When you embark on an adventure like home-curriculum production, however, you trade time and energy for money. Creating your own curriculum year by year from scratch takes an enormous amount of time. You need to look at each year's expectations and then design a curriculum around that.

Designing a curriculum from scratch with the help of library books isn't impossible — far from it. Many homeschoolers do it every year. Some write their own curriculum to save money, and others do it for the creative outlet. A few homeschoolers create curriculum because nothing yet exists that meets the needs of their children.

For an in-depth look at writing your own curriculum and what it entails, take a look at Chapter 15. I suggest resources to help you in your task as well as an approach or two that makes the job a little more manageable.

If saving money is your main reason for writing your own curriculum, you may be better off pursuing some of the other ideas in this chapter. Buying one or two books that you plan to use for several children and utilizing the library for the rest isn't that expensive, and it would certainly save you the time that you'd spend on creating your own curriculum.

Tapping the Fountain of Fellow Homeschoolers

Belonging to a local support group or bumming around with a group of like-minded homeschoolers offers more benefits than monthly sanity dinners. Fellow homeschoolers often work together to keep the cost of homeschooling to a reasonable level: loaning books to one another, stocking a textbook loaner library for member families and new homeschoolers who are just beginning.

Check with your local support group to see if it offers any cost-cutting perks. To locate a support group in your area, short of hanging out in the library at all hours of the day, contact your state homeschool association. Appendix B lists homeschool organizations by state, in case you don't have your local group's phone number memorized.

Borrowing books long term

Many homeschool groups operate a cooperative homeschool library. You visit the library at the beginning of the year, check out the books that you need for that school year, and return them in the spring (or sooner, if you're finished with them) so another homeschool family can take them home. Homeschoolers stock the library by donating their books as they finish with them rather than reselling them at a used-curriculum sale.

If everybody pitches in to help, the cooperative library can be a great local resource. One possible downer is that other families may not donate what you need this year, and you end up having to purchase a few books on your own. Your other alternative, of course, is to take what you can get and run with it. It makes for a rather haphazard curriculum but certainly a doable one if it's your best alternative during a term or two.

Sometimes groups of families get together informally and swap books around. I did that for several years when a group of us were in our first few years of homeschooling, and it worked great! We actually saw what other families used in their homeschools, borrowed an occasional science or health text if we needed one, and examined other texts on a long-term basis while we decided whether we wanted to purchase a copy for ourselves.

If you borrow or lend books to other homeschoolers, you always run the risk that one of you will never see the book again. Not many people keep books intentionally, of course, but texts tend to get grouped together if you're not careful, and before you know it the book you borrowed is lost somewhere in your personal library. At that point, the only thing to do is fix yourself a nice cup of chocolate or tea and sit down to rifle through the books until you locate the animal. Your best bet is to keep one sacred loaner shelf somewhere in the house so you can immediately identify the books that don't actually belong to you.

On the other side of the equation, if you loan a book out for a long time, try to ensure that it's one that you won't need for awhile . . . if ever. I've loaned items to co-op members who dropped off the face of the earth, quit homeschooling, and I never saw them again. (Come to think of it, one of those families still has my baby stroller.) When that happens, you hope the book is still in print if you really need it, and you buy another one or chalk the whole experience up as a lesson learned.

If you want to go into the long-term loaning practice, make sure that you keep a good, current list of what you loan, who you give it to, and the person's current phone number.

Buying as a group

Get together with other homeschoolers and purchase things in bulk. Although this may not be the rule for everything, various items cost less when you buy a whole truckload of them (or at least ten or so). Of course, before you go out and purchase 100 of something, you need to be sure that the homeschoolers in your community or co-op are interested in taking one off your hands! Otherwise your research and savings are for naught.

If your local live theater group offers daytime performances, give them a call and ask about educational pricing. Educational ticket pricing may mean that everybody's passes cost less, or the theater may offer a free teacher/chaperone ticket for so many student tickets sold. Either way, when you're the teacher and you're paying for a good number of the tickets, you save.

Sometimes educational software vendors offer a deal on various software titles. If you purchase multiples of a particular title, you get it at a significant savings. Generally, they want you to buy ten or more copies of the software, and that's where your buddy homeschoolers come in. If a significant number of them are interested in software, they may go in with you to purchase the disks.

News magazines and books, such as *Weekly Reader*, *God's World News* (a Christian version of Weekly Reader magazine), and the celebrated Scholastic Book and Software Clubs offer deals to homeschoolers who pool their orders. The weekly news magazines ship to one address at a significant discount, and the book and software clubs give you points that you can use towards educational materials or books for your cooperative homeschool lending library or support group.

Asking for the Discount

When you shop for homeschool supplies and books, ask the store if it offers a teacher's discount. Many bookstores and educational supply stores offer discounts to homeschoolers these days. A store may ask for some proof that you homeschool, depending on your state of residence and the store management's rules.

If the store needs proof that you homeschool, and you use a full curriculum from a private school or register with an independent study program, then those documentations may work as proof for the merchant. Your local homeschool support group may also give you a membership card. If you have one, use it as proof of homeschooling when applying for educational discounts. If you have any type of documentation from your state of residence that you can show, it's a foolproof way to get the homeschool discount. Not many shops argue with the State Department of Education.

Making the most of the Net

From its scholarly and somewhat nerdy beginnings, the Internet has become a huge boon to the homeschooler. On any particular day, homeschoolers unearth free unit studies, supplemental lessons to augment what the textbook suggests, and culture galore. Chapter 22 tells you more about the Internet and how to unearth these treasures. If you're willing to spend a little time poking around, an Internet connection definitely qualifies as a money saver in the long run.

Perhaps you've been holding out because you're uncertain whether a computer would be a good addition to your homeschool experience. A computer definitely functions as a useful homeschool tool if you use it rather than dust it. However, a computer that you only dust and turn on once in a blue moon exists as an extremely expensive paperweight rather than the educational tool it can become.

Putting money toward a computer that will truly be used for education is easier to justify as opposed to the machine that you thought about getting back when the kids were in school. With the cost of reconditioned computers these days, you can find a machine in the $500 range that arrives with a full warranty, a decent supply of software (such as Microsoft Word, Excel, and maybe PowerPoint), and an internal modem that you can use to connect to the Internet. That $500 goes a long way when you think about the computer's possibility as a keyboarding (typing) tutor, finder of free educational materials (via the Internet), research tool (via the Internet) and writing tool. And that's only the beginning. With the addition of some well-chosen software, that computer can teach or reinforce skills at any grade level. You can find out more about computers in *Macs For Dummies,* 7th Ed. by David Pogue, *PCs For Dummies,* 8th Ed. and *Buying a Computer For Dummies,* 2nd Ed. by Dan Gookin (all published by Hungry Minds, Inc.).

Breaking Out the Library Card

Repeat after me: "The library is my friend. The library is my friend . . . !" There you go — you're getting the hang of it!

The local library really is the homeschooler's friend. Where else can you find videos, computer software, books, periodicals, newspapers, and music, all for free? Of course, you have to return them sooner or later, but some libraries let you keep resources for up to a month.

Libraries hold books on virtually every subject from philosophy to history, and some libraries offer a startling range of choices for any particular topic. Best of all, you can use the library's collection to supplement your lessons as you need them. This cuts down on the number of books that you need to purchase for your home library, and it also drastically reduces the amount of storage space that you need for books.

While you browse the book stacks, be sure to check out the library's other offerings. You may be able to check out a video, computer software, or music to enhance your study. Periodically, I browse the video shelves looking for historical videos or documentaries that parallel the current history topic that I'm teaching. This lets me add some extra interest to the subject along with additional information that may not be in the books I use.

If you know what you want to cover during the year, your best bet is to spend an afternoon or two in the library and note what sits on the shelves at your branch. If you want a resource that your library doesn't have, you can always try to get them from a main branch. Short of that, if you know exactly what you want, libraries participate in a program known as interlibrary loan. Your library can request any book that you want from another library and have it sent to your local branch for you to check out.

Sometimes you want the same books as every other homeschooler in your town. When that becomes an issue or on those days when you simply want the book to be there when you go to pick it up, you can use the library's reserve service. This grabs the book off the shelf and holds it for a few days until you arrive to borrow it. Usually people reserve the latest-and-greatest release — your librarian may look at you funny the first time that you reserve *Great Deeds of Egyptian Engineers,* but he'll get used to it in time. If you have access to the Internet, you may even be able to reserve books online. More and more libraries allow you to virtually browse the stacks, request a hold for titles that you want, and then pick them up at your nearest branch a couple of days later. Not only does this save you time, but also you can browse the catalog 24 hours a day without leaving the comfort of your computer chair.

Libraries tend to limit the number of books that you can check out during certain times of the year. Holidays especially put a crimp in unlimited book borrowing. If you plan to do a lesson on Valentine's Day, for example, you may want to take a look at the books in late December or early January to ensure that you see them.

And keep an eye on that calendar! Twenty-five books a week overdue can really put a crimp in your cost-cutting plan. With few exceptions, you can always extend the borrowing period if you catch it *before* you owe money.

Understanding Copyright: What Is Fair Educational Use?

Copyright is a fairly fuzzy subject, but one that touches homeschoolers where it hurts — in the pocketbook. What can you legally copy as you teach your children, and when do you need to purchase multiple copies? On the one hand, purchasing individual copies for all students seems silly, but then again, you don't want to break the law.

To begin with, any teaching materials that you purchase that contain black-and-white pages *and* the notice "Reproducible for classroom use" is fair game — you can reproduce the book's pages for your whole cadre of children. If you have older children to teach now and plan to hold onto the book for your younger ones later, that's fine, too. Unit studies, some educational coloring books, and books with worksheets often carry the permission-to-reproduce statement.

What the permission-to-reproduce statement does *not* grant you, however, is permission to buy one book and reproduce it for every homeschooler in your town. If you find yourself teaching a course to a small group of homeschool children and you want to use your book as part of the class, then that group qualifies as your "class" as long as you teach the course.

Be sure to take a moment and look for the permission-to-reproduce statement before you purchase educational materials. Look for it on the title page or on the table-of-contents page. I sometimes purchase more copies of a book than I need to because I don't see the notice.

When you copy books for educational use, you can make a copy for every student in your class. Usually, this means one copy for each of your children. The basic dos and don'ts of educational copyright use are

- ✔ **All copying done for the purpose of selling the copies to make money is an infringement of copyrights.** If you plan to do that, everything else in this section is irrelevant, and you're breaking the law.

- ✔ **You can copy one chapter of a book as long as it's less than 1,000 words or ten percent of the entire book (whichever is less).** So, if you only want to cover Chaucer's "Prologue" to *The Canterbury Tales,* you really don't need to buy the whole thing.

- ✔ **You can copy an article from a magazine or newspaper.**

- ✔ **Copying a short poem (less than 250 words) is okay.**

- ✔ You can copy a chart, drawing, or cartoon from a book, periodical, or newspaper.

- ✔ **Copying a whole book instead of purchasing a copy for your own use is a big no-no.** Save your pennies and buy the paperback or check it out from the library.

- ✔ Copying from a workbook that's intended to be filled in is also a no-no, unless it carries the permission-to-reproduce statement.

- ✔ Each copy that you make needs to show who owns the copyright and where you got the information — usually that information appears at the bottom of an individual workbook or on copyable pages, so you merely need to ensure that the entire page gets copied along with the notation at the bottom.

Do I really need the teachers' editions?

When you think about curriculum and saving money, whether to buy the extras becomes a question. Some curriculum manufacturers create textbooks, review books, teacher's guides, and a host of other materials that complement or explain each student text. Do you *really* need all this as a homeschooler?

Whether you need the teacher's edition depends on how comfortable you feel with the subject. For example, I wing through grammar and English on my own, but an upper-level-math text makes my knees weak. If you feel comfortable teaching a course such as second-grade math with the help of a few M&Ms, beans, or counters when you need them, then you probably don't need to add the teacher's guide to your order.

Many teacher editions do little beyond providing the answers to the problems and questions in the student text. If your chapter discusses botany and you can identify the parts of a flower on your own, then the teacher's edition quickly takes its place as a nice doorstop. If you find that you need the answers to streamline your day, however, the teacher's edition becomes an investment rather than a throwaway.

Some teacher's editions offer suggestions for presenting the daily lesson, but if the text isn't designed for the homeschool classroom, these books take a "big group" approach. You find directions for tertiary discussions that add time to the class presentation, programmed, say-this-to-the-students-while-you-write-on-the-board guidelines, and instructions for introducing and wrapping up the lesson. In most subjects, none of this is actually necessary to teach one student.

Save money and try the class on your own without the teacher's guide. You can always order the teacher's edition later if you decide that you need it. If your children give you glassy-eyed stares day after day, either they're experiencing food comas after lunch or they need some extra help to master the material. That's when you fork over the bucks for the teacher edition or toss the entire curriculum and go with something that clicks with your kids.

Find those books for pennies!

You look at the list of books that you want your child to read, and your wallet begins to show withdrawal symptoms. The next time you open it, you find three one-dollar bills cowering in the lower corner, defying you to fish them out. Reassure your money that it has little to fear.

Hanging out at the library with your book list is great, but every now and then it's nice to have the books available at home. For one thing, most homeschoolers don't have the time for radical book research during the day between teaching the children, rustling up meals, and dodging the family dog. Ten p.m. and beyond serves as the favorite research time in many homeschool households, and the only library open at that hour is the one at the local university! (Because, as we all know, college students never sleep.)

One option short of a late-night trip to the college library is to purchase some electronic texts, also known as *e-texts.* Electronic texts on CD-ROM (or from the Internet) enable you to store hundreds of books in a tiny space until you need them. When you want your child to read one of these books, you print it out on your home printer.

All these books are public-domain classics, which means that copyright laws no longer apply and you can print out the entire book for your use. E-texts include authors such as William Shakespeare, Robert Louis Stevenson, and Plato. Many of the titles are written by popular authors of the past, such as Edgar Rice Burroughs, who gave the world *Tarzan.*

Usually you can find an e-text CD ROM for $25 or less. If you want to download all the books yourself, you can do that for free from various Web sites, such as The Internet Library (`www.ipl.org`), the Online Books Page (`digital.library.upenn.edu/books`), and Project Gutenberg (`www.promo.net/pg`). An online search for e-texts reveals sites, such as the Net 1000 Online Texts page, which lists many links for free online electronic texts (`www.net1000.net/arts/literature/online_texts`).

Look for electronic text CDs in the discount bins at your local software retailer. Because these books are in the public domain, the CDs generally don't cost much. But don't be wowed by the number of books that each CD contains. The packages that boast 5,000 titles count individual poems by poets, such as Walt Whitman and James Whitcomb Riley, as individual titles. Most of the time, a good CD-ROM gives you several hundred usable books, which still isn't bad for under $30.

I don't purchase duplicate copies of reading books or textbooks for my children. They're a year apart in grade level, and when I teach something to both of them together, I read aloud from the one copy that I have or tell them they need to read a particular book within the next couple days. They schedule their reading time so they complete the task individually. After everyone finishes reading the book, we go over its contents.

I purchase one math book or workbook, such as a foreign-language text that my scholar marks in, for each of my children. And, once in a while, I purchase duplicates of a book that I actually have permission to copy. For example, I use an art curriculum with my children that I have permission from the author to copy. And the text is relatively expensive. However, I tried giving everyone a photocopy of individual pages, and they didn't seem to enjoy the course. After asking them if they thought it would make a difference, I purchased a second copy of the art book and now everyone is happy.

If you want to read the educational copyright guidelines for yourself, look for them on the Internet at `www4.law.cornell.edu/uscode/17/107.notes.html`.

Chapter 20

Turning Chaos into Organization

• •

In This Chapter

▶ Using homeschool planners

▶ Sorting through the paperwork

▶ Deciding on your school days

▶ Surviving homeschool burnout

• •

"*O*h, hello! Let me dig out of this stack of clippings that I'm filing by subject and step over last year's textbooks. It's nice of you to stop by! Here . . . I'll sweep this owl pellet that the kids dissected last week off the table. After they uncover all the little bird bones, I hate to take it off the kitchen table. The owl ate a sparrow. See? Here's the beak . . ."

If this greeting is part of a scenario that sounds frighteningly familiar with a few substitutions, then you know a disorganized homeschooler or you are one yourself. The homeschool trappings get to us all, but it doesn't have to stay that way. (Goodness knows I need to clear the kitchen table of questionable things now and then so that we can eat in peace.)

Although all may seem cluttered now, there is a way out of the mess that the papers, curriculum, educational toys, and computer software makes, short of setting a match to it. You may be surprised at how little paperwork you really need to make a homeschool function. Posting every scribble that Junior places on a piece of paper is tempting but unnecessary.

Tracking Your Week with a Planner

When it comes to day-by-day scheduling, nothing beats a subject planner. Use a planner to keep track of pages covered, projects started and completed, special extras, such as field trips, and attendance. Although it may seem like organizational overkill at first, a planner really does streamline your life. You can see where you've been and where you're going.

Your planner can be as elaborate or as simple as you like. One family I know uses simple notebook paper with each subject listed down the side for a particular day. Every morning, the kids eat breakfast and open the notebook to see their day's lessons listed beside each subject heading. If you use many workbooks and textbooks and you go from chapter to chapter (even if you skip a few or complete them in some random order), this kind of planner may be all you need. Checking off each subject as you complete it serves as an attendance sheet of sorts; no checkmarks on the page means that school was cancelled for the day. If your planner has loose-leaf notebook paper or punched copy paper, a turn of the page designates a brand new day full of new educational adventures.

Unless your state requires some type of daily documentation for legal home-school compliance, your planning pages don't need to be works of art. In the public and private schools, teachers produce lesson plans that span pages to ensure the administration that they do something all day. Experienced teachers who teach the same level year after year can simply dust off last year's lesson plans and go at it again, refining as they go to reach a new student group.

If you plan to teach a new concept, such as fruit-fly genetics, and you gather a couple of books (or use the year's science text that you bought), maybe a software package that offers hands-on genetics practice, and a couple of fruit flies off the bananas in the kitchen, then you really don't have to spend five pages explaining what you're going to do. Your homeschool lesson plan may look something like

1. Read *Genetics* by Caroline Arnold and *The Code of Life* by Alvin and Virginia Silverstein (both from the local library).

2. Work through BioLab Fly software (Peirian Spring Software).

3. Conduct fruit-fly experiment.

You don't even have to use full sentences if you don't want to. As long as you remember what you did, the barest notations will do. Because most of the books that we read come from our home library bookshelf, I don't even bother to include authors or series titles unless I have several books with similar names.

Since our first day of homeschool, I've used a reproducible planner. I have master pages that I keep in one file, and I use a copier to reproduce the attendance sheets, weekly class schedules, curriculum selection forms, and anything else I need from semester to semester. Because I found a planner that I really like, I don't need to relearn a new record-keeping system each year. My pages carry the same notations from year to year, and a quick glance through past years' filed pages tells me when I covered a particular topic for the first time.

Displaying genius

If your Junior really does great work (even if you're the only one who thinks so), invest in a few inexpensive picture frames. Frame the really good projects and hang them on the walls for all to see. If you like, you can even change out the artwork each year to keep it "fresh" and provide a pictorial presentation of his progress.

Several different companies produce teaching planners and even homeschool planners to track your days. You can use a paper-based system, a computerized system, or something else that fits your needs. (I wouldn't recommend reconstructing your days in clay, however. The kids tend to get into it. Before you know it, that great science experiment becomes a lowly pot.) I've known families who use the little squares on the household calendar as the basis of their homeschool planning system.

Look for regular lesson plan books at your friendly educational store. If you want a system specifically designed for homeschooling, your best bet is to search the Internet or browse through a homeschool catalog or two. You can download several homeschool planners, which include both individual-planning pages and full-scale computerized planners.

For individual pages that you download and use to compile your own home-school planner, try one of the following products:

- ✔ **The Eclectic Homeschool:** (Internet: `http://eho.org/downld.htm`) An attendance sheet, a daily planner, weekly planner, reading list, diploma forms, and more. Also look here for complete yearly calendar pages to download and print out.

- ✔ **The Homeschool Home Portfolio Page collection:** (Internet: `www.home schoolhome.com/PORTFOLIO%20PANTRY.html`) If you live in a state that requires an end-of-the-year portfolio, this site provides you with a table of contents, interest inventory, and interview form, among others. Using these pages, you can organize your portfolio and make it sing.

- ✔ **Microsoft in Education:** (Internet: `www.microsoft.com/education/content/TLDownloads.asp`) A two-CD set with all kinds of templates: attendance forms, grading sheets, lesson plan forms, music staff paper, and much more. Better yet, you can download the entire CD contents directly from the Web for free.

✔ **Young Minds Homeschool Forms:** (Internet: `www.donnayoung.org/`
`forms.htm`) Subject planners, journal sheets, lesson logs, curriculum
sheets, and more are on this home page. With a good printer this could
become a one-stop-form shop for your homeschool. Several of the forms
offer various download choices: Adobe, rich text, Word, and so on.

For complete computerized planning packages, you may want to try one of
those in the following list:

✔ **Classroom Planner:** (Internet: `www.classroomplanner.com`; Phone:
888-778-2111) This software, tracking up to twelve subjects per semester
for as many students as you can handle, gives you more than enough to
keep you organized. Because it's actually designed for classroom teachers, the Classroom Planner contains more components than you need
for homeschooling, but it does offer some great benefits to the homeschool family. The program tracks individual assignments, gives you a
place to design daily-lesson plans for each subject, and then displays
each subject one day or week at a time or it shows you a summary of all
subjects. This planner also helps you keep attendance, track your educational budget, and provides a general calendar that you can use to
enter vacation dates or special events.

✔ **The Eclectic Homeschool:** (Internet: `http://eho.org/downld.htm`) In
addition to single page downloads, the Eclectic Homeschool also hosts a
Customized Weekly Planner that you can download and use. The directions are a little involved because you need to customize, but it's free.

✔ **HomeSchool Easy Records:** (Internet: `http://home.earthlink.`
`net/~vdugar`) Includes a unit studies/course planner that you use to
plan unit studies or overall courses, thus making unit study development
much easier than tracking sticky notes all over the house. Easy Records
also prints curriculum reports, report cards, and high school transcripts.

Resist the I'll-track-it-all-later syndrome that hits so many homeschoolers. If
you don't note what you did *somewhere*, I guarantee that three weeks down the
road on a Tuesday afternoon you won't remember exactly what you did and
you'll be unable to reconstruct your days. If you spent Tuesday afternoon
cleaning the house, that's one thing, but if this was the afternoon that your
daughter discovered a love of engineering concepts, you don't want to forget it.

Seeking the Paperless Society

If your house overflows with paperwork, join the club. Even the neatest homeschoolers struggle with paperwork overload. Between record-keeping pages,
various creative projects (including that way-cool, desert diorama that your
fourth grader constructed three months ago), and completed assignments,
what used to be your home could easily disappear under piles of miscellaneous paper scraps.

If you sit down to analyze the rubbish . . . er . . . um . . . treasures, you'll probably find that the stack falls into two major categories. Alone, each of these piles could easily overtake a kitchen or dining room, but together they're deadly!

✔ Mailings and homeschool information (including homeschool articles and magazines)

✔ Projects and assignments

In an attempt to help both you and I overcome homeschool clutter, I offer the following suggestions. You don't have to incorporate all of them (or any of them for that matter) into your routine but use them as a jumping off point for your own organizational thoughts. You may find a solution that fits your family uniquely, keeps everything together and organized, and the envy of the local homeschool coalition.

To reduce the homeschool clutter:

✔ **Maintain one area for homeschool equipment, supplies, and projects.** The more rooms that you use for school and project presentation, the more clutter that you need to chase around the house. If you restrict homeschool items to one room, one corner, or even a specific table, the amount of paperwork that you need to track is drastically reduced. Of course, convincing your little scholars that they need to keep everything in one place is like trying to herd cats!

✔ **File the year's papers in a cardboard box, and store it in the attic, basement, or garage at the end of the year.** These cardboard filing boxes come three or four to a package. You assemble the box and use it like a tiny filing cabinet. Unless you have a whole collection of children, one box should work for a whole year's worth of untossable goodies.

Yearlong, I use a cardboard box as my working file and then transfer the end-of-year files (such as completed attendance papers) permanently into a metal, filing cabinet. You can keep all your papers in one cardboard box, however, label the box with the year when it's full, and store it in case anybody should ask for its contents down the road.

One nice feature of the filing box is that you can keep all your papers and projects in one place — a must for those homeschoolers who need to file a portfolio at the end of the year.

✔ **Store the year's books and supplies in an upper kitchen cabinet — especially if you decide to work in the kitchen!** This solves the whole clutter question. If it doesn't fit into the cabinet alongside the school-books, then it's history. Decide what to keep as it forces its way into the kitchen cabinet and throw the rest away. For an end-of-the-year portfolio, save the best of the your student's work.

> ✔ **Use a milk-crate-type container for periodicals and catalogs.** They tend to get out of hand unless you have a specific place for them to go. One plastic storage crate holds many periodicals and catalogs, and they stay in one assembled place until you need them again.

Thirty Days Hath September . . .

Deciding when homeschool is in session may be a cut-and-dried decision. Depending where you live, your state may tell you the hard part of the school year. Most states dictate the number of school days that you need in a year, and some even specify that you need to homeschool each day that the public schools are in session. If you want to keep it really simple, get a copy of your local school calendar (most newspapers publish it sometime during the year) and use it as a guideline.

In other states that allow homeschoolers more leeway, you can let your calendar creativity take hold. Generally, homeschoolers need to teach anywhere from 145 to 186 days per year with most states hovering at a 180-day average (your state may vary).

Most schools and the majority of homeschools start in late August or early September and finish in late May or early June. If your family presents a special situation, such as a medically fragile, special-needs homeschooler or parents that travel quite a bit during the winter, you may want to rethink the September-to-June cycle. Unless your state specifically prohibits it, nobody will bother you if you decide to homeschool all summer in the air conditioning and take your vacation when it snows. As far as most states are concerned, the main point is that you teach the required number of days (the required number that your state specifies).

When my kids were little, I found out the hard way that if they took two weeks off from school, they didn't remember how to read or add when they came back to homeschool. In an effort to reduce the stress on all of us, I instituted the year-round school. For the first several years, we took off no more than two weeks at a time, usually breaking for about a week or so. And we did school from January through December with little breaks as we needed them. That way, I didn't need to re-teach skills as often, the kids retained much more, and they got used to the rhythm of morning schoolwork as a lifestyle instead of glancing longingly at the calendar and counting the months (or days) until June 1.

If you want a copy of your state laws, you can probably get one from your state's homeschool association. Appendix B tells you how to contact your state organization; if you want to track down your state guidelines online, look at www.hslda.org/laws, The Homeschool Legal Defense Association Web site, or at www.nhen.org, the National Home Education Network Web site.

Scheduling for Sanity

Take it from someone who tried and failed: You cannot teach fourteen different subjects each day for nine months without burnout. If the children don't lose their patience with the program, then you will. When you decide which classes fall on what days, keep in mind that you and your family members all have physical and mental limitations — you can only do so much in a three-hour period before your brain shuts down for the rest of the day.

I have to take stock in burnout prevention every now and then myself. When I look at everything that I want to teach the kids — partially because I find it so fascinating — I sometimes try to pack too much information into one day. Their eyes glaze over, and I know that I just lost them. There's nothing I can do at that point but send everybody outside for some bicycle-riding recreation while I sit down and try to determine where I tried to do too much.

Remember that you have until your child reaches 18 to fill him full of wonderful skills and data. Although you may feel the crunch of time passing, you really don't need to do it all this year. Some subjects, such as logic and calculus, he may actually be too young for, and others, such as handwriting, he outgrows after sixth grade (or maybe even before if his handwriting suits you as it is).

To keep the continuity going, you probably need to schedule some time for math and language arts every day. Language arts consists of writing, spelling, reading, phonics, grammar, and English. If you spend some time on spelling and vocabulary twice a week or so, set aside a day for reading practice (also known as free time or pleasure reading), and use three days for English grammar or writing. You can get it all in without overloading yourself or your students.

Science class generally occurs once or twice a week in elementary and middle school, and social studies or history happens a couple times a week as well. If you fill in a foreign language four times a week, art once or twice, and a music lesson or two, you suddenly boast a pretty full schedule. You also get everything covered within a week's time, and it creates a minimum of stress on everybody.

If you choose to go the unit studies route, design your unit study (or purchase a ready-made one) to cover one or two weeks at a time. Then you simply teach the unit study and all the subjects fall into place. Wonderful, eh?

In the name of sanity and maintaining interest, if we experience a spark of interest in the week's history lesson, I may cover history every day for two weeks and then pick up the science that I left lying in the dust after the history fever subsides. We still get it all done, and I capitalized on high-interest levels at the same time. (Using my handy-dandy planner sheets to mark down what I teach and when I teach it, I am reminded to go back and hit those science lessons later.)

Keeping Your School Spotless

Unless you're Martha Stewart, you will survive if someone finds a small, dust bunny under the middle of your king-size bed. Although you may find it hard to imagine, most people don't care if your canned goods aren't alphabetized. (Organizing your canned goods on the shelf according to the alphabet does make finding the corn and cranberry sauce much easier, but your organization probably won't raise your housekeeping standards in the eyes of other people.)

If you plan to homeschool, you probably need to resign yourself to a sometimes-messy house. Your home doesn't have to be messy all the time, and it certainly doesn't have to qualify as a constant shambles, but sooner or later you will find projects on the table for more than 24 hours at a time and maybe even textbooks left out.

Finding time to actually clean the house while you homeschool is tough unless you design a schedule that you can live with. One homeschooler that I know takes every morning for housework time before the group settles down to schoolwork. She posts a rotating calendar on the refrigerator so that everybody — parents as well as children — know their daily pick-up and organization jobs, and she remembers to take a look once in a while to ensure that it's getting done.

Other families set aside Friday afternoons or Saturdays for deep cleaning and overlook the messy spots the rest of the week. No matter how you decide to tackle the job, cleaning and cooking qualify as subject matter for Home Economics class. I actually set aside Friday afternoons for cooking class, when we concentrate on the math skills needed to produce an edible dessert.

If the idea of an occasional messy home is completely unacceptable to you, then you may not be a candidate for homeschooling. The sheer several hours per day that it takes to teach your children at home definitely cuts into the productive hours of each 24-hour period.

Feeling the Burnout

Sad to say, every day in the old homeschool isn't all wine and roses. If it were, people would beat at our doors to find out how we do it! Just like the public school teachers, you have days that you don't want to teach school. It's normal. Expect it. And don't let it freak you out when it happens the first time.

You may feel this way because you're simply trying to do too much. The super-homeschool-parent syndrome hits us all at one time or another, and homeschoolers need to shun it. I didn't get it all done perfectly before I began homeschooling, so I don't know why I suddenly expect everything to magically fall into place now that I teach the kids at home.

Maybe the winter doldrums hit you this week. The sky is gray, and you feel gray inside. The last thing that you want to do is gather the troops together for another day of classes. This is the day to do something different. Select something out of the ordinary: Bake gingerbread cookies for *Home Ec Day;* make balloon animals and call it *Art class.*

Perhaps you simply feel overwhelmed, and you need to know that you *are* making progress. Fix yourself a hot cup of your favorite tea and browse through your year's records. Look at everything that you did this year and rejoice that you're on track. If you're behind in something and you don't want to use summer days to catch up, take the time now to figure out how you plan to get to the end of the book by the end of the year.

We always know when the burnout days hit at our house. My husband and I look at each other, sigh, and wonder out loud whether a hired taxi can be there by 8:30 to get the kids to school. In six homeschool terms, I have yet to actually call the taxi, but I admit it's a tempting thought on some mornings — especially those mornings that I wonder whether I have the energy to homeschool one more time.

When the burnout blues hit your home:

- ✔ **Spend the day on some way-cool-art project.** Especially if the outdoors is drab, brighten the inside with construction paper butterflies, a new painting that you can frame, or a holiday wreath. Which holiday? Pick whichever holiday comes up next. Tie small flags to a wreath for Independence Day, shamrocks and gold coins for St. Patrick's Day, or make up a holiday of your own and decorate for it.

- ✔ **Declare a computer day.** We have quite a few programs that have educational content from Sim Safari, where the kids learn about animal management and economics, to Droidworks, where they build robots that complete various tasks. Burnout days are good times to declare computer time. Load the software and let them go for a couple hours while you relax with a cup of tea.

- ✔ **Pull out the educational videos.** If you have videos around the house, surely you have some that you could consider educational. Think for a minute: Even Disney videos can be viewed with an eye toward the animation art (call it *Art class*). If you happen to have a Disney animated feature on DVD, pop it into your DVD player and watch it in Spanish or French so your kids hear the flow of a different language.

✔ **Go to the library.** Maybe it's time to get out of the house. Hit the library and look for good fiction; let the kids browse for nonfiction titles they'd enjoy; then head home for an afternoon of reading. Any nonfiction books they read goes on the planner under the specific subject.

✔ **Take a vacation day.** If your schedule allows it, take a snow day. The schools do it! Sit outside and watch the birds nest. Deep clean the hall closet (some people find that relaxing) or sit and admire the latest LEGO creation.

✔ **Take your books to the park.** Sometimes a change of scenery makes all the difference. Load up the books, a picnic lunch, and hit the park benches. Reading under a tree does wonders for your mood, unless you happen on one of those beetles that bite.

✔ **Call another homeschool family and go to the zoo.** Burnout loves company. Take a trip to the zoo, the park, or simply spend time with another homeschool family. Sharing an afternoon together gives both home educators the mental fortitude to go another round.

Chapter 21

Making the Grade

*T*racking your student's progress, whether it's with letter grades, smiley faces, or complete portfolios, can be a bit unsettling for the beginning homeschooler. It seems like such an unnecessary part of your day when your main objective is to teach skills and you find yourself putting numbers at the top of seemingly endless papers. (Of course, they only seem endless because we . . . er . . . uh . . . let them pile up.)

Whether you're for grades in homeschool, against grades, or you're looking for another alternative entirely, you can look for answers here. Here you can find out about homeschool grades, standardized tests, and portfolios with a few extra options thrown in for good measure.

Deciding Whether to Keep Grades

Whether to collect and post grades in the homeschool is a reasonable question. And plenty of homeschool parents are asking it these days.

Whether you decide to keep grades in your homeschool depends almost entirely on you unless you live in a state that asks to see grades at the end of your school year. (If you don't know whether this applies to you, begin your search in Chapter 4, which talks about the legalities of homeschooling.) As long as you have some system of tracking progress that others can understand if they need to, you're probably all right. If you live in a state that requires portfolios and you submit examples of your student's work with smiley faces on them, then you may not need a percentage grade for the school district official to see that your child is learning.

Some states require that you keep your yearly grades on file. In this case, the law requires you to report some kind of final assessment. You may use the grading system or a detailed description of your child's progress. Your state homeschool association should know what's required and the best way to meet the requirements. Turn to Appendix B for a list of state homeschool organizations.

If grades make you feel better, use them. Because the point is to understand the material enough that the child gets the right answers, my family had a standing do-it-over rule for many years. If the problem or answer is incorrect, we talk about it and then the child does it once more.

Put the pros and cons on the scale. You never know. The concept of grading may seem unsavory in your mind, but grading may turn out a straight-A student.

Pros:

- ✔ Grades give you a concrete measure.
- ✔ Grades tell you how much material the student actually mastered from the information you exposed him to.

Cons:

- ✔ Grading every single scrap of paper becomes overwhelming.
- ✔ Grades assign a number to everything. How can you put a number on effort?

Writing the tests that they take to make the grades that you record in the house that Jack built

Grades give you good information *if* you correctly structure the test or quiz. If you create a quiz that covers subject material that even the dog could pass with flying colors, then all that your student's quiz paper tells you is that he knows as much, or perhaps more than, the dog. Quizzes like this pad a transcript and make the student look good on paper, but they tell *you* absolutely nothing. As the tutor who teaches this stuff to begin with, you should be able to glance over the quizzes and tests and get a good grasp of what your student does and doesn't know.

How can you tell if you're creating a good, sturdy test? Some dos and don'ts:

- ✔ **Only ask for information that has been actually discussed or read.** Asking about the engineering behind the Roman Coliseum when you didn't cover that topic isn't fair.

- ✔ **Ask reasonable questions.** Demanding to know the obscure person's name found on page 294 of the state history text does nothing but infuriate your child.

- ✔ **Include important points about each section or chapter.**

A good guideline, if you're the one creating the test, is to ask your student what you would want to remember after reading a chapter in the text. Then incorporate that information into a variety of question forms. Although simple quizzes can be all true/false or all multiple choices, a good test uses a smattering of both — plus a question or two that requires a written answer for good measure. Requiring older students to put their thoughts into words, rather than simply identifying the correct answer on a page, encourages them to actually think about the material covered. Elementary students may actually do better with oral tests that don't require writing the answers. Talking to the student about what she read or the project she completed and writing down her answers, gives you just as much information (and sometimes even more) without asking her to structure several paragraphs that outline her knowledge. Think of it as an essay in the air.

Some commercial textbooks come with review questions and tests that are deplorable from a testing standpoint. If you read through a test that comes with your textbooks and it makes no sense to you, feel free to skip it or modify it. (If you get your books from a particular school or satellite program that scores all your child's tests and you happen to disagree with the test wording, give your umbrella school a call and talk to them about it. Fly over to Chapter 11 for the more on satellites.)

I have yet to use grades in my homeschool. My children work through their subjects year after year without any numeral or letter assigned to their progress. If they don't understand, then I keep presenting the same material in different ways until the topic clicks. When they do understand, I move to the next topic. We may begin some school terms with one subject a bit behind grade level and then catch up, and at the beginning of other school terms, we begin ahead of where we should be and take it easy for a few weeks in that particular subject. Even without an official grading system in place, my kids can tell you what grade they would be in if they were in the public school system, and their skills match or exceed those of their peers.

Figuring the grade

Grades aren't impossible to figure out with a good calculator or sharp pencil, but plopping percentages onto papers does take a moment or two of concentration. If your student is beyond the smiley-frowny-face-grading method, you probably need to incorporate percentages and letter grades into his life.

One way to figure grades is to keep a calculator handy. Divide the number of problems correct by the total number of problems, and you have a percentage. If your page has 14 problems and your student got 12 right, divide 12 by 14 to get a percentage correct of 86 percent. If your student always gets every problem correct, of course, then she consistently gets 100 percent at the top of her pages with no division necessary. Few of us, however, are fortunate enough to have this problem at our houses.

An easy way to keep grades (unless you have a computerized planner that does all the work for you like the ones discussed in Chapter 20) is to assign quizzes and tests worth a multiple of ten points: 10, 20, 30, and so on through 100. Then you can use the following grading scale:

- ✔ 90 points up to 100 points = A
- ✔ 80 points up to 89 points = B
- ✔ 70 points up to 79 points = C
- ✔ 60 points up to 69 points = D
- ✔ 59 points and below = uh oh

Using the ten-point plan and the percentage division together works something like this:

1. **Your student takes a quiz worth 20 points.** Either the quiz itself has twenty questions on it, each one worth a point apiece, or it has ten questions and each question carries a worth of two points.

2. **She gets 18 of the 20 correct, which gives her 90 percent (a low A).** To find the percentage, divide the total number of available points (in this case 20) into the number of points correct (18), which yields the percentage (90).

3. **You enter that percentage as a 90 in your plan book next to Quiz Chapter Three or whatever you decide to call it.** (You can call it Alpaca Quiz Number One if you want to — this is your school.)

4. **Through the semester, you continue to enter quiz and test results into your planner.** You score and tabulate each quiz or test in exactly the same way.

5. **At the end of the semester, you add up all the percentage scores (90, 70, 100, 85) and divide them by the number of quizzes and tests you offered.** In this case, you'd divide the total by four. The result is your final grade for the semester. You take that percentage, which, in this example, happens to be 86.25, and plug it back into your grading scale. The percentage 86 falls between 80 and 90, so the semester grade is a B.

To make things fair, you may want to count each test score twice (also known as *weighting* the test) so that it actually counts more than your general quizzes. Otherwise, a student who blows a quiz or two yet aces the chapter test may be in trouble when he actually learned the material. Another option is to only construct tests and not use the periodic quiz checkup at all.

Tracking Those Unit Studies

Grading and assessment can become a bit tricky if you teach using unit studies instead of individual subjects. How do you give a letter grade to the life-size catapult in your back yard? Do they get a *B* because they made it, and it almost works, or an *A+* because they refrained from sending that bowling ball through your neighbor's window? Hint: This would probably qualify for an *A+* in citizenship, a *B* in engineering (science), and maybe an *A* for creativity.

If you want to find out more about unit studies, take a gander at Chapter 13. It talks about using unit studies as your full curriculum as well as dipping into themed studies. Even create your own if you want to. Due to their hands-on nature, unit studies don't always lend themselves to letter grades. As long as you keep a good number of individual pages or written assignments incorporated into your topic, you can work with percentages and letter grades in a reasonable way. After you leave the "normal" realm of education and begin experimenting with hands-on projects, creative writing, and other like endeavors, you may need a new measurement tool. Creativity often eludes letter grades. (See the list of grading cons earlier in this chapter.)

That's where the unit-study *portfolio* comes in. Because the main goal is to show that your student spent all those weeks doing something educational and profitable as well as fun, a portfolio documents your student's progress. Not as intensive as the yearly portfolio required by some states, a unit-study portfolio can be thought of as a topical scrapbook. See the following "Keeping a State-Required Portfolio" section for more.

Your student may incorporate photos, poems, stories, descriptions — even a page or two from your student on why he enjoyed (or in some cases, *didn't* enjoy) working with this topic. Photos are great to show large projects, scientific experiments, and other such learning opportunities that refuse to flatten out for storage. (Have you ever tried to shove a test tube into a page protector?)

The scrapbook can be as elaborate or as simple as you want to make it. Perhaps you want to include a few worksheets that your student completed as part of the study. Maybe one page lists the books that she read or the various types of media that you explored as part of your topic: books, CD-ROMs, and videos.

When you include media, be sure to jot down full titles and authors along with publishers or production companies so that you can find these materials again if you want to. With so many books and videos entitled *Ancient Egypt,* you could peruse the library shelves for an hour and still not locate your favorite volume.

If you teach with unit studies all the time, you'll devise your favorite method of record keeping as the years go by. Perhaps you may come up with a better way to track unit-study progress than through a pictorial and written scrapbook. Maybe you want to video snippets of the unit study as it unfolds, edit the video, and burn it onto a CD-ROM as a memory of the adventure. Do whatever works best for you as long as it documents your student's learning in a way that others can understand. (Writing your entire report using what your student learned of the Miami Indian language may be way cool, but it fails to meet the *understandability* requirement of your portfolio unless a measurable number of the people who you know read and write Miami.)

Keeping a State-Required Portfolio

What did your child actually do this year in homeschool? Some states want to know, and they require parents to file a portfolio for each child every year. Although the sound of the word *portfolio* may seem scary, your state probably spells out what the education officials want to see. The goal of a portfolio really isn't to stress you out. Think of your portfolio as a snapshot of your year: what you learned, where you went, and what you created.

States vary on what they want to see included in a yearly portfolio. Check your state law or call your state homeschool association to make sure, but in general, educational officials want to see a combination of these items:

- ✓ **Attendance records:** This ensures that you taught the number of days (or in some cases, hours) that your state law requires.

- ✓ **Record of subjects taught:** The easiest way to show subjects taught is to include a copy of your planning book that includes notations, such as "Science page 15; plants discussion." If your state doesn't require that much detail, you may need to provide a simple list instead.

- ✓ **List of materials or textbooks:** If you put together one of the Skillcraft Visible Horse models as part of science and anatomy this year, it goes on your materials and textbook list. (Anyone who ever took the time to assemble and paint one of these things will be duly impressed.) Also, include any textbooks that you used throughout the year.

✔ **Reading lists:** Did your student read it? Is the book at or above grade level? Then include the book title on your reading list along with the author's name and the date read. I keep a running list of classic children's literature that I want my kids to read. The list is divided into grade levels, and each child has a column next to the title. I jot down the finish date for each book as they read it.

✔ **Creative projects (or photos and descriptions of said creations):** The reproduction of an Egyptian town that your students made last year will *not* fit into a standard portfolio album. However, a good snapshot or two will. Pairing the snapshot with the story of the town's creation and how you came to create it to begin with can add pizzazz to your portfolio.

✔ **Writing samples:** Did your student write a rump-kicking poem this year, or maybe even a set of poems using several different poetic forms? Include those puppies in your portfolio. Along with the actual mechanics of writing, as in handwriting, school officials are also looking at writing samples to prove that your student is learning to think. Short stories, paragraphs, and descriptive narratives all qualify as writing samples in addition to the usual page of sentences or grammatical work.

✔ **Worksheet and workbook samples:** These show that your child is working at grade level. You get to pick the samples so send a few of the best, but the goal is to show that your child follows directions, understands the worksheets, and that they're close to grade level.

✔ **Copies of standardized test results:** Proving that you have them and that your student made progress throughout the year.

✔ **Written yearly evaluation:** How did the student do overall? What goals did she meet? What goals need to be restructured for next year? Where did she excel, and where (if at all) do you need to re-teach at the beginning of the next year?

✔ **Photos and descriptions of activities:** If you went to the zoo to study venomous creatures, include a snapshot or two. Remember to grab your camera before you head to the ice rink for the monthly skating extravaganza. Get a few photos of your child volunteering at the library, the zoo, or the local bakery. These tell school officials that your student has a real life and doesn't spend his whole year preparing his portfolio.

Slipping individual pages into the clear plastic page protectors that scrapbook aficionados use helps to keep your portfolio pages neat, clean, and organized. Slipping pages into the protectors only takes a few minutes, and you can find these protectors at any Wal-Mart, Target, or craft store that sells scrapbooking supplies.

The Homeschool Home Portfolio Page on the Internet at www.homeschool home.com/PORTFOLIO%20PANTRY.html offers a collection of free portfolio-planning forms. The seven pages include a table-of-contents form, writing checklist, reading log, interest inventory, interview page, reflection form (that allows you to attach your own comments to the various projects completed throughout the year) and a parent-response letter. If you need them, you can download these pages freely.

Testing Standardized's Validity

Standardized tests ask a set group of questions to a huge number of students at a particular point in their education. So your standardized test may say "Fourth Grade Fall" or "Spring Second Grade." If you take the third-grade-spring test in the fall of fourth grade, then you'll skew the results and your answers won't correspond with the rest of the students who took the fall test. Your student will know too much. Likewise, students who take the fourth-grade-spring test in the fall of fourth grade won't score as high as they may if they take the test in the spring after a year of fourth-grade learning.

Several companies manufacture standardized tests. The following list shows a few of the tests available.

- **Iowa Test of Basic Skills:** Also known as the Iowa Basics, this test ranks your kindergarten-through-twelfth-grade child on math, language, spelling, social studies, and science. Anyone with a bachelor's degree can administer an Iowa Test of Basic Skills, which is provided by Bob Jones University Press. Call 800-845-5731 or go to www.bjup.com for more information.

- **Stanford Achievement Test:** Stanford offers grade-level tests that test reading, vocabulary, math, spelling, study skills, social studies, science, and a few other areas for kindergarten level through grade twelve. Unlike the Iowa Tests, a Stanford Achievement Test needs to be administered by an approved tester. Almost every group of homeschoolers has one; call your local support group or state homeschool organization for more information.

- **California Achievement Test:** This test spans grades two through twelve. You can administer the California Achievement Test to your own children without utilizing an approved tester, but not all states accept it as a proof of standardized testing. Christian Liberty Academy provides the test to homeschoolers for a fee.

How do I know what they're learning if I don't keep grades?

Some homeschooling parents who live in states that don't require grades still keep grades solely because they want to know what skills their children learn. Although these grade-keeping parents find grading a hassle, they continue to divide and percent because they think it's the only way to track Julia and Jose.

Actually, grades tell other people how your child is doing. If your child were in the public or private-school systems, her grades would provide a picture of her performance for you, the parent at home. As a homeschooler, the grades that you post show the local school district as well as any prospective homeschool satellite providers how your child measures up in the great scheme of things.

But if you're the one doing the teaching and you teach one-on-one, you know whether your child learns what you attempt to convey. Interested expressions, quick responses to questions and assignments, and the ability to repeat — in his own words — what you just said tells you that your child is learning. Correct math problems tell you that your child can add, subtract, or multiply without figuring a percentage for the top of the page.

On the other hand, that dazed is-it-time-for-lunch-yet expression tells you that maybe your child missed that last important announcement. An inability to complete the math problem that you just finished explaining tells you that your child was already out to lunch or you need to provide the same information in a different way. Try adding, subtracting, multiplying, and dividing with M&Ms or the counting rods.

If you keep an eye on your child's written work so you know whether she understands the concepts behind the chapter she read or the discussion you had together, you will be keenly aware of when she learns and when she doesn't. Because you know your child better than anyone else, you'll probably pick up on the signs that say she doesn't get it long before a teacher would. Every child is different — maybe you notice that arch to the eyebrow, a certain tilt of the head, or leaning forward or backward in the chair that alert you to a momentary lack of comprehension.

When you see these things that you know all too well, that's the time to stop and go over the concept again before your child becomes frustrated, angry, and begins to think he'll *never* get it. At our house, I try to watch for these signs. I don't always catch them because sometimes my mind wanders just as the children's do — wonder where they get it? I routinely ask them, "Do you understand what I'm trying to show you?" If they answer "No," that's acceptable.

I say this to them because somewhere along the line kids get the idea that "No" or "I don't understand" *isn't* an okay answer. Maybe we inadvertently teach it to them by the things we say and do. However they get this message, I want my children to know that "Huh?" is a perfectly acceptable response to a concept if they really don't get it. If there's a problem, I want to take the few moments that I need to grab the counting blocks and re-teach that concept right then and there. I don't want to wait three, five, or ten pages down the road until we have a certifiable problem on our hands. If you pay attention to what your children's nonverbals tell you, then catching the warning signs and being sure that they're learning as you go is easy.

Your state may require yearly or periodic standardized test scores. If your law requires standardized testing, you have the children tested and then send the scores to your state or district educational gurus (whoever's supposed to get them) by a particular deadline. Or your state may require the tests but ask that you file all the scores unless someone calls to ask for them. Check with your state homeschool organization if you aren't sure. Look for organizations by state in Appendix B. Even if your state doesn't require periodic testing, many homeschool families do it anyway so that they know how their children stack up against that mythical "average" student. A good standardized test score tells parents where students lag behind in particular subjects and gives them a general idea which topics may be good to review in the course of the next year.

Depending what information has been presented to him at what time, your child may or may not score well on every part of a standardized test. The tests are designed to measure students against what they *normally* learn within the course of a particular school year. If you vary from that at all, the test scores will use it. One good example is classical education. For the first several years, your student may not score well on standardized tests if you teach with a classical education emphasis — mostly because the test asks questions that you haven't covered yet. Your student may have no idea about Native American religious rites in third grade, for example, but she can wax poetic about the rise and fall of the ancient Egyptians. As with so many things, you need to take standardized testing with a grain of salt.

Another option is to use a nonstandardized test that tells you what your student does and does not know. One such test is the *Diagnostic Prescriptive Assessment* (DPS, P.O. Box 5098, Savannah, GA 31414; Internet: www. diagnosticprescriptive.com), which is available for kindergarten-through-fifth-grade students. Parents give *and score* the test themselves. It shows you what your child truly knows and has yet to master for a particular grade level so that you can tell what you need to review (if anything) and what grade level your child is actually performing at.

Chapter 22

Plugging in Your Schoolroom

*T*imes have changed. And it's a good thing! Students no longer work with slate and chalk, and they don't fret over inkblots that spoil an otherwise perfectly copied manuscript page. Although you may mourn the demise of beautiful Spencerian script, writing without having to dip your ink pen into an inkwell qualifies as a positive change in technology.

Students took another leap when they began writing college papers on computers instead of typewriters in the early 1980s. Now, computers serve up reference information, math drills, science topics, music theory, and much more. All you need is the machine, age-appropriate software, and time to use it.

More homeschoolers own and use computers than the general population. Perhaps it's because they understand that computer skills are a must for up-and-coming adults. Maybe they see the benefit that judicious computer use can bring to the home classroom. Whatever the reason, homeschoolers generally incorporate computer use and the Internet into their families.

If you don't have a computer, don't worry: It's certainly not a must for homeschooling. You may want to acquire one in the future, however, to teach basic typing and computing skills to your children who will be joining the computer-based work force or going to college in a few years.

Using the Mouse to Whip That PC into Shape

You bought the thing. Now, unloved and forlorn, it sits in the corner of your dining room while you homeschool. Incorporate your computer into your daily (or weekly) educational adventures. Your machine will love you for it — and so will your kids!

A computer is a welcome addition to the homeschool classroom, and most homeschoolers have computers these days. For one thing, the job market of the future will require basic keyboarding skills. Even kids who don't plan to grow up to be authors (and I know at least a few!) need to know basic computer operation, such as knowing how to open and save a word-processing file, typing letters and essays, and maybe even basic spreadsheet and database manipulation. Thankfully, you probably have almost everything that you need to teach these skills on your computer already.

Most computers come preloaded with software: a word processor like Microsoft Word or Works, financial software like Quicken or Money, and maybe a creativity program like Microsoft Publisher. If you purchase a new computer today, you'll find that the days of bundling your machine with ten or more software packages are long gone. But that's okay; selecting a few good programs for your homeschool yourself definitely beats the computer corporation's attempt to catch your attention by throwing software into the crate. You can read more about these topics in *Word 2002 For Dummies* by Dan Gookin, *Quicken 2001 For Dummies* by Stephen L. Nelson, CPA, *Microsoft Works 2000 For Dummies* by David Kay, *Microsoft Money 2000 For Dummies* by Peter Weverka, and *Microsoft Publisher 2000 For Dummies* by Jim McCarter (all published by Hungry Minds, Inc.).

Although you won't find as much truly educational software on the market as you can games and other packages, you can easily assemble enough programs to keep you busy for years. Besides the boxes clearly marked "educational," remember to include

- Basic-life-skills software (such as Microsoft Money)
- Business simulations (such as Sim City Classic or Sim Safari)
- Strategy games for logical thinking (such as a good chess program)

If the program teaches skills that you want your youngster to learn, then it counts as educational. If your learner has fun while learning, all the better!

I sit the kids down with a computer program when I need a sanity break. Especially during those weeks when I'm actually ahead of the plan book, the pace wears on me, and I need a day off every now and then. During extremely stressful seasons, such as the days that mark final-project deadlines, I alternate computer packages with hands-on subjects, such as art and handwriting. This way, the children can work outside my office door for two or three days at a time without having my constant and undivided attention.

Use the computer when

- ✔ **You need to accomplish something specific and it falls on a regular school day.** If you long to try the bulk-cooking-and-freezing routine, and your children are too old for naps yet too young to help, declare a school day with prolonged computer time. They happily chase Blasternaut through one of the Math Blaster programs and practice their math facts while you cook without too many interruptions — outside of "Hey! How much is nine times nine again?" (The answer, of course, is "Get the Cuisenaire Rods and figure it out yourself.")

- ✔ **You stand on the brink of burnout.** It hits all of us every now and then; take advantage of the computer on those days when you'd rather paint the living room black than spend time doing school again.

- ✔ **A child needs to practice concepts like math facts.** Turning a child loose with a drill program, such as Quarter Mile Math, lets them practice a particular math skill over, and over, and over . . . Long after you lose your patience and your voice, the computer patiently dishes up the same problem again and again and changes the numerals each time.

- ✔ **You want to teach a skill that you don't personally know.** Electricity and lasers fall into that category for me. Electricity is very nice, and I don't know what I'd do without it, but the whole idea of creating circuits with resistors, conductors, and voltage leaves me a little dizzy. My son, on the other hand, thinks electricity is way-cool. I load "Zap! Save the Show with Light, Electricity and Sound" from Edmark onto the computer, and the program takes him through elementary electricity, laser, and sound science. Whew! Thanks to the computer, I'm off the hook again.

- ✔ **Foreign languages find their way into your life.** Computers excel at working with foreign languages because you can actually hear a native speaker pronounce the words — over and over again, if you need them to. Chapter 25 talks more about foreign languages in your homeschool.

'Net-ting Resources

When one of your scholars needs to practice a particular math skill, when you want a unit study that teaches housekeeping to your little packrats (always a good idea!), or when the current history lesson calls for the

Articles of Confederation, then fire up your Internet connection and browse the Internet for the paperwork that you seek. Lesson plans for preschoolers through high school, unit studies galore, and science sites all await your mouse clicks. No matter what you want, the Internet probably offers a viable version, and you can usually unearth it for free!

Allowing some extra time is always a good idea if you need resources from the Internet. Just like redecorating the bathroom took longer the last time than you thought it would, unearthing wonderful Internet tidbits always takes more minutes than you think. If you get involved, it may actually take you hours — more because you find yourself interested in the sites that appear in your browser window than the actual time needed to find what you seek.

The easiest way to find sites on the Internet is to use a good search engine. Google (`www.google.com`), Yahoo (`www.yahoo.com`), and Excite (`www.excite.com`) all return a good number of sites, but Google ranks as my current favorite. Although I may need to wade through several more sites than the number of sites that another search engine may throw to the screen, Google does a great job of ferreting out the sites that I know are out there somewhere in cyberspace but difficult to find. After you locate what you want, remembering it is easy:

- ✔ E-mail the link (or Web address) to yourself by copying the Web address into a blank e-mail message and sending it to your e-mail box.
- ✔ Mark the site as one of your favorites or as a bookmark.

You can even use your favorites list to construct a lesson. If, for example, you want to cover space science as part of your day's lesson

1. **Use space science as a search term in your search engine.**

   When it returns a few thousand sites (they always suggest far more sites than the number that actually applies to the topic at hand), look at the first ten or twenty to see if they meet your specifications.

2. **Mark the sites that you really like as favorites.**

   Your lesson's already half done.

3. **When the time comes to teach your space-science lesson, open one site after another from the favorites list. Talk about what you see.**

It really is that easy. You may wish for a larger monitor screen as the group crowds around, but as with all computer skills, the person who controls the mouse controls the lesson. Open the sites that you want the children to see and watch video, read and discuss text, and utilize the "virtual textbook" for all it's worth. With a little advance planning, Internet sites open your children's eyes to the wonders of science, technology, wildlife, and more.

When you want something specific and the search engine doesn't seem to understand what you're asking for, try using **kids** or **homeschool** (one word) as part of the search term. Using the word **kids** in the search term returns only those sites designed for juveniles. If you're trying to locate educational sites on advanced topics, such as neurology or economics, try adding the word **kids** to the search term. Homeschool, on the other hand, gives you only those sites that were designed with homeschoolers in mind. (If you type **homeschool** as two words instead of one, the search engine gives you all the sites that contain references to both *home* and *school*, which takes you forever to wade through.)

Electrifying Your Frustration

Technology can be frustrating. With wires all over the floor and little boxes connected and supposedly talking to one another, something's bound to go wrong sometime. I'm neither a pessimist nor a Murphy's Law advocate, but when you really look at everything a computer goes through to complete a task or get onto the Internet, you have to marvel that it works at all. You can do some things, however, to keep frustration low as well as add to the overall fun factor.

If you don't have a computer yet or you're thinking of upgrading, buying an intermediate level computer gives you great functionality without a big purchase price. Although you can find a computer these days for a couple hundred dollars, your best bet is to purchase a system that falls somewhere in the middle of the technology curve. The latest-and-greatest computers often come with interesting glitches and features. Waiting a year or so gives the development team time to work through the hardware bugs so you don't have to. We buy the best of last year's technology.

Buying in the middle of the curve also gives you the bells and whistles that you're most likely to use in a homeschool. A CD-ROM drive is an absolute must because almost every educational software package out there comes on CD these days. If you purchase a new computer, a CD-ROM drive is in it automatically.

Which add-ons do you want to throw into your to-be-purchased stack for future holidays and gift opportunities? Some of the available gizmos actually help your homeschool, and others merely take up space and require an occasional dusting on Home Ec Day. Some of the available computer complements are

  ✔ **Scanners:** A scanner copies a page of text or graphics onto your hard drive. Unless you have a burning desire to turn all those heirloom photos into a huge scrapbook genealogy project, you don't really need a scanner specifically for your homeschool.

- **Little Fingers Keyboard:** This keyboard is 80 percent of the size of a regular computer keyboard, and it's actually designed for children's fingers. It includes a built-in trackball, works on both a Mac and PC, and you can connect an adult-size keyboard to the computer at the same time that you connect the Little Fingers Keyboard. If you plan to use the computer much with children under age 12 or so, keep this keyboard in mind. For more information, go online with the manufacturer, Datadesk Technologies, at www.data-desk.com or call 888-446-3222.

- **QX-3 Microscope:** A joint project between Intel and Mattel, this microscope attaches to your computer via a USB port (all new computers should have at least one). View objects on your computer monitor, take snapshots of what you see and arrange them into slide shows, or schedule the microscope to take pictures of melting snow or molding bread at regular intervals and then watch the progression. If you don't have a $300, high-school-quality microscope yet and your kids are interested in science, then the QX-3 is especially nice.

- **Color printer:** Although you can live without a color printer of some kind, a color inkjet printer is usually less expensive than a laser printer, which only prints black and gray tones. Printing out lesson plans, family newsletters, essays, pictures of King Tut, or whatever, a color printer will probably see plenty of use over the next few years.

- **LEGO Studios Movie-Making Kit:** Although definitely not a must-have, if your child is fascinated with the idea of motion pictures, you may want to take a look at this product. It's an inexpensive software-and-camera combination that was designed to introduce your child to stop-action photography, which is the art of making movies from things that don't move — as in LEGOs. Although LEGO obviously wants you to use the set with your own LEGO creations, you can also use it with clay figures that you create or even small, slow pets, such as turtles.

- **DVD drive:** This allows your computer to play movies on screen. It also functions as a CD-ROM drive, so it can run all your CDs, and it also runs some computer software specifically recorded on DVD disks. However, not as many programs have made the transition to DVD as you may think; for now, it's pretty much a luxury item that allows you to play movies on your computer. If your computer comes with one, enjoy it. But unless you're a movie buff, you probably don't need to run out and insist on a DVD drive this year or next.

- **Home copier:** Okay, so it's not actually a computer add-on. However, a home copier is possibly the best investment that we made in the past six years outside of the computer itself. It's small, sits on a table in the basement, and doesn't copy much at a time. It's also not very fast. But I need it for those reproducible-for-classroom-use pages that come in most unit-study books and other educational supplements these days. Having a little copier of my own means that I can copy off schoolwork, my planner pages, and even make a second copy of that unit study that I downloaded from the Internet without tying up our one printer for another 24 pages.

Connecting with Other Homeschoolers

Where do you turn if nobody who you know homeschools and you have questions? Who do you vent to when the Don't Wannas hit your homeschool? If you have Internet access or belong to an online service, such as America Online, community is as close as your computer and phone line. If you want to meet homeschoolers a little closer to home, see Chapter 23 for tips on finding them or see Appendix B for the large homeschool organizations in your state.

In years past, you almost had to belong to an online service to find other homeschoolers. Now, with the hundreds of homeschool sites and e-mail mailing lists available, that's no longer true. Web sites abound with opportunities for chatter with discussion boards, mailing lists, and interactive chat rooms.

Discussion or message boards

On discussion boards, you ask questions, assist other homeschoolers, and describe the latest way-cool widget that your daughter Susan built with blocks and twist ties. Look for homeschooling discussion boards in some of the most unlikely places! One of the busiest boards on the Internet resides at VegSource (`www.vegsource.com`), a wonderful, vegetarian site.

You can also find homeschool friendly discussion boards on America Online (keyword **Homeschooling**), CompuServe (**Go Homeschool**), and on many of the larger family and corporate homeschool Internet sites. Searching with the term **homeschool discussion** returns all sorts of possibilities.

Poke around the Internet until you find a site or two that answers the questions that you want answered or that seem to discuss about topics that interest you. Then introduce yourself, post a question or suggestion, and settle into the community. The vast majority of these groups are free for the congregating — all you need is your online membership (for AOL or CompuServe or another online service) or some type of Internet connection.

Mailing lists

Mailing lists gather Internet denizens together, they develop great conversations, and all the conversations appear in your e-mail box. So not only do you get to meet people and chat to your heart's content, you don't even have to search them out on the Web. After you sign up for a mailing list, all the talk comes to you.

E-mail to e-mail

For the first three or so years that I home-schooled, I knew very few people who home-schooled. My neighbors thought I was just a little odd, and because my children were little, I didn't really "click" with the couple of home-schoolers I knew who had junior high and high school children. In desperation, I turned to the Internet, and there I found other homeschoolers waiting to talk about their days, too.

Some of those people remain e-mail friends to this day. I've even met a few face to face. One family stopped by my home during a cross-country vacation, and we hooked up with another family for a weekend in Kansas City one year.

I get much of my information from various mailing lists. I subscribe to professional lists, personal lists, and hobby lists. Because I only subscribe to one or two in each area of my life, I don't become overwhelmed with messages. An active list can easily drop 30 to 50 messages into your box each day; multiply that by your five favorite lists and you quickly become engulfed in electronic messages.

When managing your mail becomes a chore rather than a task that you look forward to, it's time to take a hard look at the lists that you belong to and cut out a few. Better to end your e-mail relationship with a list than find yourself sending snippy replies because you're stressed to the max.

This is supposed to be fun and encouraging for you, not another "have to" on your list of duties.

Although you can find mailing lists scattered here and there throughout the Internet, one of the easiest ways to find a wealth of possibilities is to visit the Yahoo Groups Web site (www.groups.yahoo.com). Yahoo Groups offers over 1,000 homeschool mailing lists. Use the list name as a search term in the Yahoo Groups main window for more information. Here are a few of the lists available:

- ✔ **Chevra:** This list is for Jewish homeschoolers of all persuasions. Members discuss observance, homeschooling, and life in general.

- ✔ **Christianfocus:** A mailing list specifically for Christian homeschoolers. Members talk about curriculum, holidays, values, and living their faith.

- ✔ **Homeschoolzone:** One of the largest mailing lists on the Web, the Homeschool Zone list reaches over 3,000 members. Discussions consist of everything from curriculum choices to new homeschooler encouragement. Homeschoolers gather here regardless of religious affiliation or pet educational theory.

✔ **PHSU (Pagan Homeschoolers Unite):** Dedicated to supporting families who homeschool their children and teach them in the pagan traditions. Membership is limited to active pagans only.

✔ **Secularhomeschool:** Designed as a gathering place for homeschoolers who teach their children at home for other than religious reasons.

If you have trouble finding what you're looking for or you simply want to view more of the available lists without scrolling through 1,000 entries at a time, try one or more of these strategies:

✔ **Search under both *home school* and *homeschool*.** The two terms tend to reveal different homeschool mailing lists.

✔ **If you want a mailing list close to home, use your state name and the term *homeschool* when searching.** For example, **California home-school** gives you a selection of mailing lists that talk about homeschooling in California.

✔ **Find a list that speaks directly to your religious preference by typing its name and homeschool into the search text box.** So **Catholic home-school** returns a host of mailing lists specifically designed for Catholic homeschoolers.

When you join a mailing list, reading messages for a few days without posting gives you a feel for the flavor and flow of the list. Reading for weeks or months without announcing your presence, however, is called *lurking* in the computing world, and it's considered kind of rude. When you find a list that you like, gather up your courage and post a simple message that says you exist, you homeschool, and you're glad that you found the list. (If you aren't glad to find the list, you probably need to look for another one.)

Chat

Homeschool chat rooms flutter with excitement. Well, maybe not excitement, exactly. They exude enthusiasm. Most homeschoolers are excited to teach their kids at home (unless, of course, you catch them during the burnout days), and they love talking about what they do.

When you find a chat room (especially a scheduled chat with a defined topic) that you like, jot down its topic, day of the week, and the time so that you can find it again the next time that you want to chat. More than likely, the same group of cronies hangs out there week after week. If you show up for awhile and then miss the chat, you may get an e-mail message asking if everything's all right.

You can find chat rooms in the homeschool section of online services, as part of various homeschool Web sites, and at Talk City (www.talkcity.com). After you find a chat that you like and become part of the regular faces, don't be surprised if *you're* the one who answers a few questions. You may be surprised how much you know after you homeschool for a year.

For more information about connecting with others via online chats, see Chapter 23.

Enhancing Your Subjects with Multimedia

Let's face it: Textbooks can be dry — very dry. In fact, some texts that I've seen make Saltine crackers taste juicy. If you think the text contains good information and you feel you should go through it, how do you spice up the learning so everyone (including you) manages to stay awake?

Once again, your computer slides to the rescue. (It would run, but as everybody knows, computers don't have feet.) Today's CD-ROMs offer video, animation, and other eye candy to introduce and reinforce your youngster's skills. Of course, using some software does it better than others. But overall, using educational programs is a pretty good way for your student to work on a skill and keep his attention at the same time.

Some programs do it by framing the skills within a story, a challenge that must be met, or a puzzle to be solved. Others, such as Quarter Mile Math, allow your student to pit against himself over and over as he attempts to beat his previous scores. Using a few, like chess programs, your student can learn a skill if it interests him.

When you look for software for your home computer, keep in mind the subjects that you teach or want to teach. In addition to the standards that you already have, such as a word processor and financial software, you may want to consider these:

✔ **A reference title such as Microsoft's Encarta Reference Suite:** This package includes several video tours, such as a walk through the ruins of Pompeii, guides that help your student research a topic, and some very useful timelines.

When you purchase reference software, and you have three options, such as Adequate, Standard, and Deluxe, your best bet is to purchase the middle-to-top package. Although you may not see much difference between Standard and Deluxe, especially if Deluxe does little but add Web connectivity that you may or may not end up using, you usually see a huge chasm between Adequate and Standard. Adequate is just that: barely adequate, but Standard actually incorporates features that you can use as a homeschool family.

- ✔ **Typing programs like UltraKey 4.0 (Bytes of Learning), All The Right Type (Ingenuity Works), or Typing Tutor (Knowledge Adventure):** Your student can learn keyboarding skills while using these programs, and better than sitting your child down with a typewriter and typing book, these programs actually track progress and repeatedly stress fingering positions.

- ✔ **Simulation or strategy software:** If you've ever tried to teach a child the strategies behind a game like chess, you'll welcome the computer version. It patiently waits for your child's next move without anxiety. In much the same way, simulation software like Sim City Classic, Sim Safari, or Sim Park (or, actually, any of the other older Sim titles) give your child control over a simulated world. She spends money to create a park, for example, and then watches to see how it does.

If you find that you have several programs that you want your kids to work through this year or you want to teach computeresque skills, you may want to think about making one day a week Computer Day. We designate Computer Day as Friday, and the kids do their foreign language, science, language arts, typing instruction, and logic with computer programs that I set aside for that purpose.

Marking a day every week or two as Computer Day tends to cut down on the when-can-I-play-on-the-computer whines because you've already answered the question before anyone asked it. Are you together or what? Plus, it gets good use out of the programs that you bought, borrowed, or traded. Jot down the names of the programs the kids use under the appropriate subject headings, and you account for the day's school time.

Use computer time to concentrate on other students

Putting one student to work on the computer means that you have time for the other students in your life. While one child works with math drills, you can review science concepts with another one. This may not be incredibly important to you if your children are close enough in age that you teach everybody the same thing at the same time, but if your kids span a wide range of years, then you learn to cherish the quiet moments that you spend with one child concentrating on a particular skill.

With three or more children who are all at the beginning reading stage or above, one computer, and a bit of patience, you can schedule individual time with everyone in ten-to-twenty-minute intervals. Install one child in front of the computer with an appropriate program or task, work with a second, and assign reading to the others. When you're finished with the first student, you can rotate everybody by replacing the student (and perhaps the program as well) on the computer and working with another student.

This allows you to schedule drill or learning through the computer at the same time that you cover the regular class work. If you hold your normal classes five days a week yet you want to include computer skills too, this may be a viable option for you.

Chapter 23

Connecting with Likeminded Souls

. . . .

In This Chapter

▶ Attending homeschool conferences

▶ Joining an association

▶ Meeting online

▶ Scheduling a social day

. . . .

*H*ow do you find people who do what you do? I found one of my home-school buddies while I was walking across the cul de sac to the gray house at the end of the court. I'd just moved into the neighborhood and in neighborly conversation mentioned that I homeschool. My next-door neighbor announced that the family in the gray house homeschools their children, too. During the next thaw, we introduced ourselves in the middle of the street (you know how neighborhoods are) and a friendship was born.

Although situations like this do happen, more often than not you have to put a little more effort into finding other homeschool families than simply walking across the street. Locating a homeschool association, meeting people online, and attending organized homeschool events all help connect you with the homeschool community. Sometimes meeting one homeschooler introduces you to three more, and farther down the line, you *really* connect with a family that so-and-so introduced you to.

This chapter looks at some of your options for meeting other homeschool families. Although it certainly doesn't cover all available options, such as contacting your local parks department for scheduled homeschool activities, it does mention the most common methods of connecting with other homeschoolers.

Networking Isn't Just for Computer Geeks

You meet the most interesting people at homeschooling conferences. I see the same faces year after year. Some become more than faces as we exchange business cards or phone numbers, e-mail addresses, and curriculum ideas over a vendor's table or at the end of a presentation.

Each state or region conducts a yearly homeschool conference. (For a list of organizations in your area that may offer a yearly conference, see Appendix B). Although developing lifelong friendships probably isn't what you have in mind when you attend a conference, meeting another person that you click with is a possibility. If you find yourself sitting next to the same person presentation after presentation, you have a likely candidate on your hands. (Unless, of course, you're already friends and came to the conference together. That doesn't count.).

You'll find several things at a conference:

- ✔ **Speakers:** Conference organizers try hard to collect speakers who provide information and encouragement at the same time.

- ✔ **Vendors:** Many offer new curriculum or teaching ideas. This gives you the opportunity to see what you're buying before you send the money off to a publisher or homeschool catalog. You may even locate a local museum or field trip opportunity that you didn't know about if that organization appears as a vendor at your local homeschool conference. Contact your local organization or visit the organization's Web site for information on individual conferences, including fees, length of conference, and the like.

When you attend a homeschool conference, you're bound to find speakers you agree with and others you don't. As you look over the speaker schedule, if a particular speaker's topic interests you, give the talk a try. On the other hand, if you see a speaker and immediately chalk his topic up as sheer lunacy, you aren't going to get anything out of the talk. Don't waste your time or notebook paper listening to educational views that you know you don't agree with before you walk into the session. That hour is better spent attending another talk or visiting the vendor hall.

If you belong to a specific religious community that offers its own conference, your best bet is to attend that conference, even if it isn't as large as the state homeschooling conference. Within your own community, you will find curriculum and supplies specifically selected for their ability to mesh with your traditions, as well as active homeschoolers who already teach in your tradition who can offer advice and support. If you want to attend the state brouhaha as well, of course, you may pick up some wonderful ideas there, too. But don't overlook your own community when you search for information. Especially with a topic like homeschooling, homegrown community experts sometimes answer the questions no one else thinks to ask. Read more about finding those with similar religious beliefs in the "Praying for Guidance" section, coming up later in this chapter.

Associating and Consorting

Meeting people in your own community who homeschool gives you someone to call once in a while without incurring long distance charges. You suddenly know a family who may be interested in meeting you at the park for lunch without driving four hours. You could meet another homeschooler who wants to take swim lessons at the YM-YWCA when you do. Social outlets take on a local flair when you spend time with people in your own area.

Homeschool associations and support groups provide a great method of meeting others. You may need to poke around for a while before you actually locate them because homeschool groups tend to hide — after all, they know where they are. Why should they tell anyone else?

You may find information at your library, religious community, or state homeschool association. (For a listing of state associations, see Appendix B.)

Local associations, sometimes called *support groups,* can be big or small. They can incorporate hundreds of families throughout a region, meet once a year for a huge introductory meeting, and in turn spout smaller support groups that cater to the needs of teens, special-needs learners, or parents of preschoolers. On the other hand, some associations gather only a few families from a specific area together and offer monthly meetings and actual homeschooling *support:* They bring in veteran homeschoolers to talk about planning, organization, subject matter, and more. Sometimes your state organization can point you toward a local support group. Browse through the associations listings in Appendix B to get started, or if you have Internet access, visit the local support group area at the National Home Education Network Web site, at www.nhen.org. Which association proves to be better for you depends on what you need at any specific time. You may find that you don't need any of it. Or you may go through a period when belonging to several different groups actually meets your needs. Like everything else in the homeschool realm, your membership and attendance hinges most on your personal family needs.

Especially in the support group realm, stand your ground and resist the everybody-is-doing-it syndrome. Just because your three homeschool friends join a support group, you don't have to join, too — especially if the group doesn't give you something that you need. Few things are more frustrating than sitting through meeting after meeting, only to realize that you're wasting your time. If you think your time is better spent at home playing a game with your family, punt on the homeschool group and stay home.

You also may find that a support group that meets your needs today wanes in significance next year. That's okay — as you spend time teaching your kids at home your needs will change. Go with the flow, and seek out the support you need *today*. Next year's needs may be different.

Praying for Guidance

Don't overlook your own religious community when you search for possible homeschool friends. Even if your community operates its own private school (which your children don't attend because you teach them at home), you may still find a homeschooling family or two nestled somewhere in the community membership rolls. After all, you decided to homeschool your children. What stops another family in your tradition from choosing the same thing?

Connecting with another homeschool family in your own religious tradition offers you some distinct advantages:

- ✔ **You don't have to explain anything.** If your holidays differ from the national norm in some way, you're saved the problem of describing — one more time — why and how they differ.

- ✔ **This gives you someone to celebrate those holidays with.** Arranging daytime holiday parties for your children is plenty of fun, and these gatherings teach tradition and values at the same time. These events give your children great memories of homeschooling, childhood friendships, *and* religious tradition.

- ✔ **Gathering with homeschoolers whose values match yours actually removes a good deal of stress.** You don't have to wonder what comments you'll have to explain to your children on the way home. You can refer to things important to you without defining them. And — perhaps most importantly — if you enjoy your religious tradition, you're going to find it enjoyable to spend time with another family that shares the same values.

Dancing and homeschooling in unison

Almost half of my religious community homeschools. My daughter belongs to a community dance troupe, and nearly every girl in the group (if not *every* girl) was homeschooled at one time or currently homeschools. Did we plan it that way? Of course not.

I happen to live in an area where homeschooling thrives, and many parents choose it as an option for their children. The girls interested in dance have the free time for lessons, practices, and performances. And these girls also homeschool, which gives them yet another connecting point — plus offering an additional topic of conversation to the patient parents while they watch their children twirl.

Chatting It Up

Homeschooling can get lonely for the adults in the family. You may be especially lonely if a recent career change leaves you home all day with the kids for the first time in awhile. For the first year or so, the lack of adult conversation can get to you if you let it. Thankfully, your Internet connection offers a chatty relief.

Online chats give you a social outlet much like the corporate cooler. You meet with other homeschoolers or potential homeschoolers in an online chat room and discuss, banter, vent, and tend the virtual soda bar. After awhile these people become part of your (virtual) life, and you find yourself looking forward to the chat rooms that you haunt.

You may need to poke around the Internet for a few weeks until you find a chat room that truly meets your needs. The Internet has plenty of chat rooms, but finding one just for you can be a bit tricky. To begin with, you may want to seek out a general we're-all-glad-it's-Friday (or Thursday, or whatever) chat. These tend to offer the most corporate-cooler talk.

Some online chatters meet with a particular focus in mind. For example, you may find yourself dropping into a chat room that discusses one particular curriculum at a time when your schedule is set, and it doesn't include the curriculum at hand. Or you locate an unschooling chat room and arrive with some particular curriculum questions that the others in the room can't answer.

This doesn't mean the people in the room with you lack knowledge; it's simply a result of their educational methodology. (Isn't that a great term? It means *the way they think things oughta be taught*.) An unschooler gets exactly the same response if she visits a curriculum-focused chat room and asks how to track her child's exploratory days on planner pages. You can practically hear the "Huhs?" reverberate through the room.

Online chats combined with e-mail give you a truly great opportunity to connect with homeschoolers all over the world. (Most homeschoolers reside in North America but by no means all of them.) The chat room excels for sharing experiences, asking and answering questions, and generally building a sense of community. And if you're the only person who you know who does this, community becomes extremely important in your part of the universe.

Some options for online chats follow:

- ✓ **Various online services, such as America Online and CompuServe, regularly schedule homeschool chats.** Dive into your service's homeschool area and check it out.

- ✓ **About.com's Homeschooling site offers a chat room and scheduled chats.** The chat room (Internet: www.homeschooling.about.com) is available all the time if you want to meet a friend online, or mark your calendar and attend one of the regular, weekly chats.

✔ **Load AIM (AOL Instant Messenger) on your system for one-on-one chatting.** AIM gives anyone on the Internet the ability to talk any time using the Instant Messenger window. I load my AIM window with the screen names (AIM nicknames) of homeschool buddies all over the States and chatter the hour away when I find both of us online at the same time. One limitation is that AIM only works for one-on-one discussions, not group sharing.

✔ **Join a homeschool interest group at ICQ Inc.** This site (Internet: `www.icq.com/icqchat`) offers several different homeschool chat groups that you may want to visit.

✔ **Search for homeschool chat on the Web.** Although the search may return bunches of chats that don't interest you, it may be worth combing through the lists to find a golden opportunity.

You can literally spend hours in a chat room, especially if people come and go throughout the day. If you tend to lose track of time, and you really need to get other things done throughout a day, you may want to pick homeschool chats that fit in between activities that are even more important to you, such as dinner and your favorite television show.

Getting Together for Socialization

Sometimes you just need to socialize. These are the days that you call your favorite homeschool family and schedule an afternoon together in the near future. Meeting for lunch and a play day (or games if your students are older) gives your children a chance to hang out with other homeschoolers at the same time that the adults relax with some well-deserved iced tea.

Now, if you've known any diehard homeschoolers for long, you may wonder why you need to schedule free time with all the scout meetings, ballet lessons, go-kart racing, roller skating, music lessons, and group bike riding that generally goes on. Fitting a free social afternoon in among all those other homeschool activities can be tough, I agree. But once you do it, you may place this activity on your monthly to-do list. (On the other hand, my socialization excursions led me to teaching a homeschool art class each Friday for a year, so maybe you want to rethink that.)

Actually, hanging out with another homeschool family once in a while, even if it's to send the kids outside to play or share games and videos on a rainy day, helps to sharpen your perspective. Watching all these kids together, taking note of their likes and differences, and enjoying their company reminds you why you're doing this in the first place. When you get together with others on a regular basis, you watch other children develop in a way that you sometimes overlook with your own because you're with them every day. Then, when a friend says something like, "Wow. Your Madison's attitude really changed over the past few months," you realize that it's true.

For more information about socialization and homeschooling, flip over to Chapter 3.

Curling up with a friend in print

If you find a homeschool magazine that you like, discovering it in the mailbox each month or two gives you an educational shot in the arm. These magazines feature articles on organization, teaching methods, and making it through the school year. This is definitely not a one-publication-fits-all world; different magazines focus their efforts on reaching various portions of the homeschooling world.

Some magazines present homeschooling information with a religious flair: Christian, Catholic, Jewish, and Muslim homeschoolers can all find periodicals written especially for them. Other magazines cater to a particular learning style:

Parents who prefer the unschooling approach can find a magazine or two designed to meet their needs, and others who rely on curriculum or use a classical approach also find appropriate periodicals.

The trick is finding the magazine that fits your family best. A trip to the local bookstore may help you decide. Or perhaps your public library contains an issue or two of various titles (mine does). To help your search, the Cheat Sheet in the front of this book lists several of the magazines available to homeschoolers, and gives you some basic information about each of them.

Chapter 24

Opting for a Cooperative

· ·

In This Chapter

▶ Sharing the load with others

▶ Learning and discovering as part of a team

▶ Joining a large, structured cooperative

· ·

Creating your own cooperative Homeschooling doesn't have to happen in a vacuum. For most families with a couple years' teaching under their belts, staying home and concentrating on the books is much harder than joining together with other families for times of learning, fun, and frolic. One of the most instructive and enjoyable ways to gather with other families is to share in *cooperative learning,* also known as a *co-op.* A co-op introduces some very different dynamics into your homeschool.

Co-ops by nature incorporate other homeschool families, so you can mark off the week's socialization requirement when your classes meet. They also give you an opportunity to teach children other than your own because many co-ops require you to take your turn teaching one or two sessions of a course, assist the head instructor in a course, or teach an entire course of your own while your children attend someone else's class.

TEAM: Together, Everyone Achieves More

We all can't be experts at everything. If we were, the sheer amount of stuff required to organize our vast information vaults would overwhelm us and overfill our homes. Perhaps specializing is good for homeschool parents.

When you find another homeschool family that you click with, joining together for various educational activities means that you can both pursue the same topic with twice the fun. You may schedule a trip to the local zoo, an excursion outdoors to look at trees and their leaves, or even a trip to the local library to decipher the Dewey Decimal System as a combined adventure. You've just entered the world of cooperative learning.

These informal experiences eventually bridge into the healthiest co-ops. If you find yourself scheduling these outings on a semi-regular basis, you actually have the beginning of a small co-op without a huge amount of effort. Add another family here, one there, and before you know it a certified group forms. Although this is the most informal method of cooperative learning, it's definitely a good start if you want to share the excitement with another family once in a while. Joining with other families also gives you the energy to pursue a topic more deeply than you may otherwise. Building a working volcano may seem like a great effort for your own brood alone. If you add another parent and a few more children, the audience gets bigger and you suddenly have an extra pair of hands to form the volcano base and keep track of the vinegar.

Holidays make a great time to join together cooperatively because holiday celebrations are always more fun with a small crowd. One year, I created a piñata for our Christmas celebration, and we still giggle over the photos and memories that day produced. Pictures of small children diving after the candy as it flew through the air come to mind to this day as we recall that celebration, and gathering the co-op group together certainly made the experience memorable. Plus, my children alone could never eat all the candy in the piñata, and it took all fourteen kids' efforts to break the thing!

Gathering Informally

Most homeschool co-ops, if you count the number of members, consist of a few homeschool families who gather together for a particular purpose. These groups usually meet in someone's home once a week (or once every other week) and concentrate on the subjects that homeschoolers generally don't enjoy teaching themselves. They may last only a semester or a year, or they may continue for several years until the members grow beyond whatever subjects the co-op was designed to teach.

Art, music, drama, speech, science, history, and (in some cases) religion all make good co-op subjects. If you plan to teach religion, it's a good idea if all your co-op members come from your own community. Otherwise, tempers tend to flare after a few weeks when the resident adults find they don't exactly agree with the instructor at hand.

Although you can find out about these small (usually private) groups through a friend of a friend, generally you learn about them because you're one of the homeschoolers who wants the children to learn such-and-such. You gather with a group of likeminded parents, designate one of them the resident teacher for a particular course (or perhaps join together and hire a tutor to teach the group as a whole) and a co-op is begun. You can find ideas on finding these folks in Chapter 23.

Even the small co-ops periodically have openings, as families drop out due to scheduling conflicts or changes in interests. If you want to try a learning experience like this, joining an existing group gives you a taste of cooperative education without the hassles of beginning and managing a group on your own. The best way to find an opening is to mention to other homeschoolers that you're looking for a co-op to join. You may follow a few false leads at first, but sooner or later, you'll land a group that fits your needs.

Because these co-ops are small and unadvertised, you may hang out with homeschoolers for quite awhile before you find out a co-op exists in your area. Your friends aren't trying to exclude you; the group meets once a week or so for a few hours so it probably doesn't warrant much conversation time away from planning sessions or the co-op itself. They get together, do their thing for two or three hours, and then adjourn for another week of school-work, soccer games, and the myriad details of life.

When I first started homeschooling, I spent some time looking for a large area co-op. Well-meaning homeschoolers gave me phone number after phone number, and looking for a group that I knew existed (and later actually joined), I called them all. The phone calls generally ended with the person on the other end of the phone saying something like, "Our co-op is full. We're not accepting any new families at this time." If you get someone like this on the other end of the line, be assured that they're not actually trying to be rude. What they're *trying* to say is "Our co-op is a private group of five or so families who meet for a specific purpose. We met as friends, and we'd really like to keep it only among ourselves. Good luck forming a co-op of your own." They just may not be able to articulate it well.

Formalizing Your Group

Imagine a school away from school, and you get close to the picture of a large co-op. These groups may incorporate as many as fifty or more families at a time, or as few as ten. The classes often resemble college courses more than the small, intimate cooperative classes mentioned earlier. You may fill out a registration form for the classes that you want your children to take, pay a course fee to the co-op treasurer, and follow the co-op rules (which usually include statements such as "Keep your children under control. Please don't run in the building," and so on).

Finding a large co-op

The easiest way to find a place in a co-op like this, of course, is to offer to teach a class to other homeschool children. However, the best co-ops are designed to incorporate nonteaching options as well. That way, those who need a course in introductory biology, for instance, can find one without hiring an individual tutor.

Sometimes locating a large co-op can be tough, but during other seasons, co-ops may seem to appear out of nowhere. When you want to find a large, formal co-op, your best bet is to contact someone who may know where it meets. Try one or more of these options:

- ✔ The homeschoolers you know who have taught their kids the longest.

- ✔ Your state homeschool association (run independently of your state department of education).

- ✔ Any area or county representatives for the state organization who may know what's available in your area.

- ✔ Other homeschoolers you run into at baseball practice, tennis lessons, or other hobbies about town.

- ✔ An area- or citywide homeschooling support group that may sponsor or provide a co-op like this. Asking around eventually points you to large support groups.

Dissecting a large co-op

Because these learning opportunities occur on a grander scale, they tend to take on a life of their own. Group physical education classes may last years after the founding homeschool family graduates the last progeny. Co-ops that offer several different courses at one time simply change the course offerings as the students grow older and require different information. Instructors who move in and out of the system also determine the courses offered.

A large co-op usually meets once per week for a semester or a school term at a time and can offer courses in anything from high school nutrition to first-grade art. Most of the time, because these groups cater to families with several children, you see a large range of classes. Sometimes the courses offered span the preschool through the middle school grades, and others may go all the way to high school.

These organizations usually require registration paperwork that helps keep track of everyone. Parents volunteer to teach the classes a semester or two at a time, and the co-op places their children into appropriate courses taught by other parents. Then the co-op often opens its doors to anyone else who wants to register, attend, and pay the course fee. Some of these groups charge materials fees for particular classes, and others actually charge enough to give the volunteer instructor a little spending money for his efforts.

Home(school) -made

Several years ago, I sat around a table with three other homeschool parents. We all wanted to join a co-op, but couldn't find one that met our needs. We shared bagels and cream cheese while the assorted collection of children (who had already scarfed their bagels down) played outside. A plan formed in our minds.

Why not start our own small co-op, and see how it went? Between us, we had a financial wiz who loved everything to do with science, a former speech and drama teacher, a mom fluent in French, and someone experienced in teaching art (and arts and crafts) classes. We decided to teach art, drama with music, science experiments, and French. A cooperative was born.

We divided the fourteen children into four roughly equal groups (it took a couple different divisions before we found the groupings that helped the children work together the best), and each of us taught our little classes four times at the various age levels. Sometimes, for example, the art class presented the same lesson to everyone. During other sessions, the 5- and 6-year-olds learned a different skill than the 12-year-olds.

That co-op lasted over a year, and we all learned plenty from it. We learned about each other (some of the families didn't know each other well when we began), we learned about working together (kids and adults, too) and we learned a little about art, drama, French, and science. Sometimes thinking up a new weekly project for the kids was a bit of a pain, but overall, we had a great time.

That's my co-op story. If you decide to start a co-op of your own, your story will be different. You can teach any classes you want, and meet for any reason you like. Some groups meet once a month only for field trips. Others concentrate on the "extras": physical education, music, and art. Many co-ops contain only three to seven families because that's a manageable number of children when you attempt to do something as a group. Other co-ops contain hundreds of families, and they all sign up for twenty or more different courses as they need them.

No matter what you decide to teach and how you want to teach it, the important thing is that you give it a try. If you really want to join together with other families, then gather them together for a brainstorming session and see what comes of it. The kids may have some decided ideas about what they want to learn. Or maybe you'll find that you all want to cover one subject, such as physical education, but you aren't really sure how to go about it as an isolated family. Discussions like these were made for birthing co-ops.

Part V
Making Your Year Sing with Extras

The 5th Wave   By Rich Tennant

In this part . . .

Music soothes the savage beast. Do you doubt the truth of this statement? How many irate tigers do you meet at your front door when you put on your favorite CD? See? It works.

Venture into the realm of music and art or other extraordinary learning experiences, such as using building blocks, visiting museums, and watching videos, and calm the savage beasts at your house. When you incorporate some unusual educational experiences as part of the school week, it gives your students something to look forward to (and bug you endlessly about).

This part introduces you to learning outside the box of traditional education. Choose a technique that interests you or one that you already have all the parts for lying around the house and give it a try. Your kids will be glad you did, and you will, too — even if your vacuum sucks up nuts and bolts from the toy construction set for weeks afterwards. (You may want to remind the little darlings to make sure that they get all the parts off the floor when they're done.)

Chapter 25

Adding Spice with Special Classes

. . . .

In This Chapter

▶ Fitting the extras into the schedule

▶ Delving into art and music

▶ Speaking and debating

▶ Practicing bunts and runs

▶ Following a foreign language

▶ Teaching life skills is home economics

. . . .

*E*nglish. Math. Science. History . . . English. Math. Science. History . . . Hey! There's more to life than the core four subjects. Isn't that great? I'm glad, too — without a break every now and then, the core four get pretty boring. Besides, with a little inventiveness, you can use carefully scheduled additional courses to liven up even the English, math, history, and science classes.

How about investigating art and music from a particular time period as part of your history class? That way, it counts as two courses: You fit the artists within the framework of their times, and you cover both art and history. Or you may want your students to look at music through the eyes of math, and study musical notation as an exercise in fractions. How about studying the connections between music, math, and science? That takes care of three subjects with one topic.

This chapter looks at the various elective classes that schools sometimes offer and gives you tips for including them in your homeschool if you choose. Although you probably won't want to include all these subjects (at least at the beginning), they all do double duty in that they give you a break from the normal routine, and they enlarge your children's repertoire of knowledge and skills at the same time.

Making Time for the Extras

At the very time that school administrators are busily eliminating the electives that they commonly term *the extras,* homeschoolers embrace the opportunity to include them in the school year. Generally, *the extras* refer to physical education, art, and music. Some of the other subjects covered in this chapter, such as foreign language and speech, are so far outside the range of most public school systems (especially at the elementary level) that they only find a place in specialized magnet or international schools.

The fact that the extras are sometimes absent from the public school curriculum actually makes them prime targets as homeschool subjects. Without the benefit of home education, these subjects would be available to only a select few. In this case, homeschooling helps to level the playing field because, in most cases, you can choose (or at least add on) any subjects that you want to teach.

Before you decide that you, too, are too busy teaching the core four to incorporate any of the extra classes into your schedule, let me suggest a few reasons for including any of them in your homeschool:

- ✔ **Additional classes mean well-rounded students.** Although I'm certainly not an advocate of *doing the circuit,* which is a term meaning filling every available extra hour with lessons or extracurricular activities, there is something to be said for a variety of experiences.

- ✔ **Varied courses give you a break.** You can structure many of these classes so that you don't need to hold your children's hands so much as guide them along the way. For example, you don't have to sit with your children and help with art class. At least, after they reach an age when they can follow simple directions, work from a model project, and hold a pencil without poking their little sisters, your children should be able to work on their own. This takes less mental energy on your part.

- ✔ **The extras round out resumes and portfolios.** Although not every part-time employer or educational system portfolio reviewer looks for a student who can translate Spanish into Latin or present a ten-minute speech without hiding under the desk, incorporating subjects such as these into your curriculum gives your student an edge. It proves that he's willing to move beyond the core four and pursue some knowledge and skills for their own sake. That always looks good on a resume.

- ✔ **The more you learn, the more you can learn.** If your student is exposed to baseball and soccer, she learns the basics of working with a team. Likewise, if she takes art now and picks up photography later, she already knows the basics of viewing an object with an eye toward its surroundings. These courses give your students a foundation that they may need for later learning.

✔ **You may rouse a latent interest or talent.** Many students begin a subject reluctantly, only to learn that they have an interest or a real talent at it. If I hadn't incorporated art early as a subject in our homeschool, I wouldn't know that my daughter, at age four, could take red, yellow, and blue paint and effortlessly mix mauve and lavender for painting. She liked mauve and lavender, you see, but wasn't too crazy about red, yellow, or blue. Seeing this made me focus more on art than I may have otherwise.

When you fit an elective subject into your curriculum, that doesn't mean that you need to include it every day. In fact, incorporating some of these options into your week more than once or twice may be a great recipe for parent-child burnout. If your student does high-school-level work, then creating a daily class or two from this chapter is reasonable; however, trying to incorporate speech, art, music, physical education each day leaves little room for the math and English that you need to teach. The thought makes me tired, and I'm not even part of your homeschool!

Select one or two additional courses to begin with, and delve into them once or twice a week where you need them most. If you find that Thursday is a low-energy day all around, for example, perhaps adding a fun class like art or music can spice up the day. When your students have a hard time getting started on Monday, maybe that's the time to include physical education.

In much the same way, if lunchtime drags and energy levels feel low for the next half hour or so, you could incorporate a few minutes of foreign language listening to build skills. While you are adding one of the extras each day in this case, you can limit the class to twenty minutes or less (depending on your children's ages) and still cover the same amount of material that you would if you declared a special class twice a week.

Remember that this is your school and your program. If the very sound of these subjects makes you think, "Oh, no! More work!" then shelve this chapter for a while until you have the emotional energy to tackle the idea of adding more into your school day. These courses are all available to homeschoolers; this doesn't, however, mean that any of them are right for you and your school right now (or in some cases, ever!). Keep your own needs foremost as you read. Take what sounds good to you and throw out the rest.

Bringing Out Their Inner Artists

Culture and education go hand in hand. Without some kind of culture you really don't have a civilization: If you look at any civilization in any time period (including our own), you see that its people pursued some type of art and music. Although you may not consider Industrial Grunge an actual music form, this new musical style does speak to a particular portion of the population.

Which brings me to an important point: As a homeschooler, you can focus on whatever art and music forms speak to you. If, as far as you are concerned, *music* means baroque chamber pieces, then introduce your children to them by all means. If, on the other hand, the term *music* conjures up memories of folk music and campfires, teach them those folk tunes instead. As you share your musical loves, you pass on your culture to your children — a precious reason for homeschooling in itself.

Music

Many homeschoolers use outside music lessons to fulfill their music requirement, but you don't have to. Music instruction actually comes in two flavors: music appreciation and music performance. Although music performance (as in learning to play an instrument) is nice, it certainly isn't necessary for you to enjoy music. Children without a lick of musical talent can learn to enjoy music in other ways.

Music appreciation

All you need for music appreciation is a set of ears. Other components, such as a radio or CD player, may help, but all you really *need* are ears. At its most basic, the goal of music appreciation is to expose your children to music that they may otherwise overlook and hope that their musical understanding will be broadened as a result. Music comes in so many different forms that you could appreciate music for years and never hear the end of it. Generally, *music appreciation* means classical music, but it doesn't have to. I know several classical musicians who don't know a thing about blues, calypso, or zydeco. Yet my children love all these — in addition to Beethoven, Mozart, Gershwin, and light opera.

You can find books on true music appreciation, but if your children are still little (in other words, you don't actually need a high school credit in this), simply exposing them to different types of music works wonders. In your quest for listening materials, in case you don't already own at least one CD of every music type ever produced, you may try

- ✓ **Library lending:** The library music departments usually lend folk music, classical, opera, musicals, jazz, blues, and sometimes calypso. Rummage through your library's stacks and see what you can find. (You also may want to look in the video section for ballets, operas, and composer biographical documentaries.)

- ✓ **Classical Kids Series:** Follow a mysterious violin around Venice as you learn about Vivaldi and his music, listen to the observations of a young boy who lives below Beethoven, or meet Handel just as he finishes the *Messiah*. These CDs, audio- and videotapes introduce children to one composer's music while unfolding a radio drama that teaches them about the man's life and works. Look for titles like *Beethoven Lives*

Upstairs, Vivaldi's Ring of Mystery, or *Hallelujah! Handel,* and you can find them on the Internet at www.childrensgroup.com, or through your favorite homeschool catalog (Rainbow Resource Center's catalog and Web site at www.rainbowresource.com carries them, as an example).

✔ **Free community concerts:** Many towns and cities offer free spring and summer concerts that feature local musicians. Check into your parks' department schedule and see if your community may be one of them — they usually offer an entertaining evening. Some of these groups are really good!

Music performance

Not everybody grows up to be Chopin. Perhaps this is a good thing. In the same way that not every child desires to play on the football team (some are perfectly happy to sit in the stands and cheer), every child does *not* desire to learn to play an instrument. I know this may be hard for some of you to comprehend, but it's true. And of those who do want to play something, they may find certain objections to your instrument of choice.

For example, maybe your progeny wants to learn a portable instrument, yet the piano provides your only vision of musical performance. These two goals do not mix. Who ever heard of slinging a baby grand into your backpack for that next long hike? Music performance can mean playing as part of a homeschool or community orchestra. It can also mean solo performance on a piano, violin, or flute.

But if you want your child to learn notes and timing, and not specifically orchestral arrangements, why not introduce the recorder? Or even the Irish tin penny whistle? An instrument doesn't have to be expensive to make music or provide sheet music that your child can learn to read. Music is music.

Here are some ideas for incorporating music instruction into your homeschool:

✔ **Sign the children up for piano or violin lessons.** If you don't feel comfortable enough teaching music, note reading, and theory on your own, you can probably find someone in your area who will do it for a fee. If you select one of the smaller instruments, you can often rent one instead of purchasing it outright.

✔ **Introduce the recorder, flutophone, or tonette.** These little flutes have been used to teach basic music classes for years. All are relatively inexpensive, and they give you an idea whether your child is even interested in music before you swing for a piano or violin. If you can read music, you can teach the tonette or recorder.

✔ **Use a computerized music theory program, such as Music Ace or Music Ace 2.** These programs teach note reading, chords, basic harmony, and much more. Students can write their own compositions on screen and then listen to them, or select from a large number of prerecorded classical and nonclassical pieces.

I realize that outside piano lessons are the normal homeschool way to teach music, but we don't do it at our house. My husband plays piano more than adequately — after taking piano lessons for thirteen years as a child — so I purchased the introductory volumes of a standard piano curriculum that you can find in any good music store and now we teach them ourselves.

Art

Like music, art also falls into two categories: appreciation and creation. A trip to the nearest art museum immerses you in art appreciation, and you may go to every art museum in the country and still not be able to draw a tree that looks like a tree. That's okay. In this case, you put much effort into appreciation, but not much into performance so to speak.

Art appreciation

To appreciate art, you need to look at art. Much like music appreciation, art classes assume that you want to appreciate the great artists: the Van Goghs, Rembrandts, Vermeers, and Titians of the world. If you want to explore the world of art one artist at a time, take a trip to the library and see what it offers. You'll probably find biographies as well as bound reproductions of the artists' most famous works.

Another way to investigate art is by time period. Each time you cover a period in history, look up the artists that lived during that time. What did they paint, sculpt, or draw? Why? Which artists and works were the most popular within a particular time period? Have they become more or less popular throughout the years? You can answer these questions and more that you'll undoubtedly come up with on your own at the library — the place to start you and yours off on a pretty healthy pursuit of art.

A third way to look at art is by type of work and the influences on the artist. For example, your daughter shows an interest in impressionism from a calendar page she sees. From there, you and yours investigate impressionism as an art form. When did it occur? Who created using this style? How was it received by the culture of the time? The library can also guide you here.

Don't overlook the more unconventional art forms in your pursuit of art appreciation. If your children don't embrace the great artists and their works, then you may want to make a special effort to find out-of-the-mainstream art forms that your children can relate to. Cartoon animation qualifies as art, as does the lowly cereal box (usually referred to as graphics, but still art). Use your imagination and see what turns up.

Art creation

Finger paints. Water colors. Pencil drawings. Cut-and-paste. Creating art yourself encompasses everything from construction paper and glue to oil pastels on canvas. You can delve as much or as little into art creation as you like. Let your students' interests be your guide more than any external must-do list.

Although watching a tremendous artist develop through the art classes that you teach your children may be nice, what you really want to aim for is a release of creativity. When they begin to see beauty in ordinary objects, they think like artists. When they want to capture the lines of a leaf with a pencil on paper because they love it, they think like artists.

While participating in art classes, your children also learn project creation and completion, especially if your students are at the crayon-and-scissors stage. Through beginning an art project, creating the project, and finishing the project, your students learn that even something fun has a beginning, a middle, and an end. If they leave the art project unfinished on the school table for a week and a half instead of finishing it and taping it to the side of the bookshelf (which is where all our great art projects end up), they soon learn what happens. They find themselves resurrecting a crumpled piece of paper from underneath a pile of books and paperwork. Poor, sad art project.

If you want to incorporate art class into your homeschool:

- ✔ **Look for a homeschool parent who can teach art.** Someone out there either had art training in school or actually works as a graphics artist or the like. Maybe he would enjoy (or at least be willing) to teach art basics to a group of homeschool students.

- ✔ **Purchase and work through an art curriculum.** Walter Foster art books teach one technique at a time, and you can use as many or as few of them as you like for your art curriculum. Christian homeschoolers may be interested in How Great Thou Art materials. These books encompass three years of art instruction per volume, and teach pencil drawing, color theory, colored-pencil drawing, marker art, and acrylic paint mixing and painting. The top portion of each page introduces the day's skill, while the student practices in the bottom portion. Call 1-800-982-3729 for more information, or check out the Web site: www.howgreatthouart.com.

- ✔ **Check out books from the library on pencil, watercolor, pen-and-ink drawing.** Unless your library staff just finished purging art books, your library may stock some pretty good options in art books. If you like, you can even check out books with famous works of art in them and attempt to copy them on your own paper. This teaches you plenty about the artists and their sense of perspective.

- ✔ **Please, please, please buy decent materials.** Nothing is more frustrating than spending hours on one picture only to find out that it looks awful when you're finished because you used the same pencil that you usually use for math problems. A good drawing pencil costs about $1.00, and I'm still using the ones I purchased in college . . . um . . . *several* years ago. They really do work better for drawing.

✔ **Take a look at online art lessons:** Several Web sites offer lesson plans for art if you want to create your own curriculum from scratch. WannaLearn (Internet: `www.wannalearn.com/Fine_Arts/Visual_Art`), offers over 23 online links for drawing lessons alone.

✔ **Have your materials sent to you:** This is one place that you really do save time shopping online or through catalogs, primarily because art supply stores are so hard to find these days. MisterArt.com (Internet: `www.misterart.com`) sells all kinds of art supplies over the web. KidsArt (Internet: `www.kidsart.com`; Phone: 530-926-5076) specializes in children's art, art supplies, and art curriculum. The Nasco Arts & Crafts catalog (Internet: `www.nasco.com`; Phone: 800-558-9595) offers over 450 pages of art materials.

Go ahead — Be Dramatic

Maybe the whole idea of standing in front of a group of people and expounding on some deep thought makes you queasy. Before your audience arrives, you wonder whether you can fit into the hall closet. Or perhaps you love speaking in front of people and can't imagine why your child declines the offer. After all, that last mime routine that someone talked you into remains a gratifying memory.

No matter which way you personally see it, giving a speech, participating in a debate, and developing drama skills help to round out your homeschool curriculum. Your child will find herself called on to deliver a short explanation, detailed analysis, or rousing wedding toast sooner or later. Because you know that situations involving public speaking are going to come up, your best bet is to prepare your students for them before they descend on your life and wreck your kids' nervous systems.

Speech and debate

Speech can be formal or informal, funny or serious, planned or impromptu. What you say and how you say it depends on your audience and the occasion — not the speaker's current whim (much as we wish that could be true). Learning to gauge what speech would be most appropriate for a particular occasion is part of formal speech training.

Debate, on the other hand, is a particular form of speaking that takes a particular topic and argues for or against it (depending on your assigned side). It incorporates two participants and one topic, often called a Lincoln-Douglas debate, or four participants and one topic. With four debaters, you speak with a partner instead of going it alone.

As you explore the various topics included in speech and debate, you find that you absolutely love some forms though you may loathe others. Personally, I always hated giving impromptu speeches, but my husband loves it. So our kids are slated for training in both prepared and impromptu speaking. Introducing your children to as many of the forms as possible in their twelve to sixteen years of school gives them the experience to say they enjoy public speaking or they don't.

For basic information on speech and debate from a homeschool (and classical school) perspective, you may want to visit Trivium Pursuit's Homeschool Speech and Debate Web site, `www.triviumpursuit.com/speech_debate`. This page gives you an introduction to speech and debate, and points you to links that may prove helpful.

Institute for Excellence in Writing

Although *Teaching Writing: Structure and Style* from the Institute for Excellence in Writing is actually a writing program, a major part of the curriculum includes drafting an outline for every paper before writing it, and presenting the outline orally — which is actually public speaking. (I know that I shouldn't let the cat out of the bag that way.)

Toastmasters International

Originally designed to teach business people how to speak in public in the 1920s, Toastmasters now happily takes anyone interested in improving their public-speaking skills. According to the charters, a member must be 18 years old before she joins, but I've known clubs to informally "adopt" younger students who showed an interest in the club's activities. My husband, for example, began attending a very patient club with his member father at the tender age of 8, and then returned to become an informal groupie at age 16.

The Toastmasters well-written manuals cover basic public speaking, gestures, humor, speaking to inform, after-dinner speeches, and a whole collection of other speaking topics. Although they prefer that you enroll in the clubs to purchase the manuals, Toastmasters sell their speech manuals online (along with the other forms and essentials necessary for club members) at `www.toastmasters.org`.

If you (or a homeschool parent you know) is interested in learning about speaking skills and intrigued with the idea of teaching a homeschool speech class, the interested party could always join Toastmasters International and then pass along what he learns to the children.

Reader's Theater

Also known as *choral reading,* reader's theater gathers a group of willing students together, and they read (in parts or together) some literature form. Reader's theater can be a blast, especially if you work with kids who enjoy doing this type of thing. The selections usually last no more than fifteen to twenty minutes at the most, and they incorporate up to fifteen or so students at a time. This actually counts as a form of speech and drama because the kids usually end up performing this in front of someone sooner or later (besides you), and they learn to incorporate inflection and suspense into their words as they read.

To pull off a reader's theater selection, you first get a copy of something everyone will enjoy reading. Children's books and poetry both make excellent selections because the language used to tell the tale is descriptive as well as easily understood. Possible selections for reader's theater include

- **Dr. Seuss books,** including *Yertle the Turtle* and *The Cat in the Hat*. Stick to the Seuss books that use the most words in your native language at first, and reserve the books with phonetic nonsense for your more advanced performers.

- **Shel Silverstein poetry:** Imagine a group of 10- to 12-year-olds performing a poem like "Someone Ate the Baby." What a scream!

- **Nursery rhymes and poems:** Although "Jack and Jill" may prove to be uninspiring, other lesser-known nursery rhymes, such as "Wee Willie Winkie" could work well as a reader's theater selection.

After you have a copy of the story or poem that you want to use, here's how to do it:

1. **Make a copy for each child.** Every child needs her own copy so she isn't trying to read over someone else's shoulder and still speak at the appropriate time.

2. **Give each child a part.** Some lines a student can read individually, and other lines work better if read in unison.

3. **Highlight each child's "lines" with marker.** This tells him when to jump into the story.

4. **Keep a master copy for yourself with initials or names next to each line.** Now you know who speaks when, and silences don't leave you asking who has the next line.

5. **Read the selection with inflection.** You may need to go over it several times before the children "get it."

Drama

There's much more to drama than full-scale plays, and you can do plenty with drama in your homeschool without 41 students milling around your living room waiting for their lines. Drama is, at its most basic, the ability to pretend you're something or someone else for a short time. When your 4-year-old crawls around the house with the baby's bottle in his mouth, that's drama. Likewise, when your 6-year-old creates some fantastic scenario for her doll collection to act out, that's drama, too.

You should be able to find books on all these drama forms at your local library.

Puppetry

Most children learn about puppetry instinctively as they wave their dolls in the air and screech some earth-shattering cry. If you want to formalize the learning a bit, you can always make puppets out of paper, cloth, wood and string, clay, or whatever else you may have handy. Then enact a childhood story that your little ones know well.

A table or chair turned on its side becomes an easy puppet stage. Watching a beginning puppet show, it's hard for the audience to stifle their giggles when they hear the muffled laughter coming from the other side of the table. Puppetry teaches vocal inflection, story development and ending, and general stick-to-itiveness.

Mime

Think of mime as drama without words. Mime artists enact emotions, movement, and a story's entire lines without uttering a sound. For some reason, mime intrigues some small children, and they take to it easily. By the age of 3 or 4, my little one enjoyed some of the basic mime moves: climbing in a window, picking up things and setting them back down, and so on.

You can act out the words to songs, nursery tales, parts of fairy tales, and more with mime. Perhaps your area offers a mime troupe sponsored by a local arts school or church. Taking your children to see a mime (or watching a Marcel Marceau video) may be all it takes to inspire them. Street mimes seem to sprout from the very sidewalks of larger cities, especially in the summertime.

Theater games

These are popular with the kindergarten-through-sixth-grade crowd. Playing theater games basically can teach one, tiny portion of drama in a fun way. Although your children won't make it to Broadway doing nothing but theater games, these pastimes certainly introduce the rudiments of drama and you can use them with as large or as small a group as you like.

Some theater game ideas are

✔ **Mirror:** Stand two children facing one another. One is the *person* and the other the *mirror*. The mirror's job is to copy, as identically as possible, the movements of the person facing it.

✔ **Emotions:** Pair up the children, or place them in groups of three (if you have at least six), and have everybody make a sad face, a happy face, and a puzzled face.

✔ **Mime:** Act out reading a book or pouring a drink without words or props.

ThinkQuest (`http://tqjunior.thinkquest.org/5291/games.html`), a Web site devoted to kids and thinking, supplies an excellent list of even more theater game ideas.

Skits

These short, usually humorous, acted-out stories give your students a chance to memorize dialogue (which mime, theater games, and even reader's theater do not) and learn about actual acting and stage business. (Stage business is the term for nonspeaking actions that the cast pursues while on stage — picking up the hairbrush, gazing out the window, and tugging at a sweater are all stage business).

Usually ten to fifteen minutes in length, sometimes containing a moral of some sort, and relatively easy to pull off, skits require far less planning than a large-scale play. You limit costumes to what you have on hand, sets consist of a chair or two and maybe a table with flowers, and you memorize a few pages of dialogue and actions. That's it.

And they're fun. They give the director in you a chance to direct, the actors in your children a chance to act, and you don't spend months preparing for three performances. If you find that you love doing skits, you could easily do several a month and perfect your skit skill.

Look for prewritten skits in the drama section of your library, the language-arts section of your local educational store, or online using **drama skit** or **children drama skit** as the search term.

Formal plays

The big brother to all these other drama forms, a play incorporates sets, costumes, numerous people, lights, and a huge amount of time. Now that I've given you all the downers, let me also say that a play is loads of fun to do, both from the acting and backstage perspectives, and it provides some great memories if your children enjoy doing something like this.

A big advantage of a formal play is that everybody can become involved, even if they're not terribly inclined to act or dance on stage. My particular specialty in the theater world, for example, is costuming. I love designing, creating, or assembling the costumes that help tell the story. A relatively large-scale production gives me, and homeschool students like me, the opportunity to create sets, lighting assemblies, and more. The stage crew can feel as though they are part of the action without needing to experience the warmth of the footlights.

Check into community theater in your area if the footlights call your name. These are volunteers who routinely put on plays because they love theater, and they enjoy working together on a large project. Sometimes a scheduled play calls for young players as well as adults, and the community groups always appreciate a hand with sets, costumes, and props.

Homeschool groups

Almost every local high school sports a speech-and-debate team and drama class. Taking their lead, many area homeschool groups are starting to offer classes in speech or debate. Homeschoolers may also get together to produce a play each semester. Joining together with a large local homeschool group gives your children hands-on drama training — the opportunity to speak before others and refine their skills.

Check with your state organization or area support groups if you're interested in group speech or drama classes. They may be able to point you in the right direction.

Taking Some Laps

Physical education (PE) has long been a bane to homeschoolers unless one parent specialized in recreational sports in high school or college. Most homeschoolers understand that their kids need some type of PE, but they aren't sure how to get it. If you count yourself as one of the most, don't worry — you're in good company.

Fourteen states currently specifically list physical education as a required course for resident homeschoolers. If your state's requirements say "equivalent to the public schools" and your state requires PE for school children, then that means you, too — in addition to the listed fourteen states. Most homeschoolers incorporate some type of individualized physical training (such as ongoing dance or gymnastics classes) or summer team sports into their schedule, and call it done.

Is that enough? Well, it depends on what your state law says and whether you are bound by it. Using your state guidelines as an example, you can always devise a complete homeschool PE program on your own. You can find links to physical education standards for all the states at the Putnam Valley Schools Web site, putnamvalleyschools.org/StSu/PE.html.

Another option is to do what many homeschool families across the country do: Enroll your children in ongoing physical education classes that meet in various places throughout your community. If the ultimate goal is to guide children into a love of physical movement, then here are some ideas for reaching that goal:

- Enroll in a gymnastics class.
- Explore Little League baseball or team soccer.
- Join the local parks' department tennis class.
- Learn to juggle.
- Sign up for skating lessons.
- Take courses at the local YM-YWCA in swimming, basketball, and so on. (Some Ys even offer a Homeschool Physical Education class.)
- Take horseback riding lessons.
- Take ongoing dance classes, such as ballet, tap, jazz, modern, or interpretive dance.

Although these may not *seem* like a well-rounded curriculum individually, if your student explores several of them over a multiyear period, she can amass all the skills necessary to play with a team, refine gross motor skills, and demonstrate proficiency at a sport. This is actually the heart of the national physical education standards that guide the local and state standards.

Many homeschoolers annually complete the President's Challenge Youth Physical Fitness Program (Internet: www.indiana.edu/~preschal; Phone: 800-258-8146). This program awards students who meet certain minimum standards in five events: curl-ups, shuttle run, one-mile walk/run, pull-ups, and the V-sit reach. The Web site contains a section for homeschoolers that explains how to participate in the program.

Finally, you can purchase a physical education book specifically written for homeschools. Practicing and degreed physical education specialists who homeschool their own children usually author these books, which outline a complete physical education program for kindergarten through grade twelve. You may want to try *Homeschool Family Fitness: A Complete Curriculum Guide* by Dr. Bruce Whitney (H.S.F.F.I. 159 Oakwood Dr., New Brighton, MN 55112; Internet: www.tc.umn.edu/~whitn003).

Before you and your children jump into a full-scale physical education program, checking with your family's physician is always a good idea. Your doctor may offer recommendations or cautions specific to your family situation.

Parlez-vous Greek?

If you decide to include a foreign language or two in your subject mix, then your children's education (at least this part of it) resembles European schooling much more than it does that of the United States. English-speaking children abroad learn at least French from the time they are little, and often they pick up Latin and another language or two (German, for example) along the way.

One of the reasons they learn so many languages, of course, is that the countries are so close that it makes living together much easier on everybody if most people share a language in common. Around the world, in fact, it is unusual for people to only know their native tongue. Many cultures in Africa and Asia know several languages: One language is spoken in the home community, but residents use another language for trade and business dealings and sometimes even a third to communicate with people in the towns and villages not all that far away.

Speaking in the lingua franca

We began our foreign language journey with French, mostly because that's the language I took in high school and I could translate some words and phrases for my children on the fly. Plus, French is the first additional language that's usually taught in England. The English have much more experience teaching children than I do, so I adopted their practice.

We recently moved to a city that functions as a gateway to the nations — I still haven't quite figured out why it's so attractive. Not many French-speaking people stroll along our streets, but we regularly hear Spanish, Chinese, Russian, and a whole collection of languages that I can't begin to identify. Even though we aren't fluent French speakers yet, French recently took a backseat to Spanish.

After our children met other children who were bilingual (or beginning to be bilingual), the impetus to learn the language that these children speak became much stronger. Talking with 3- and 4-year-olds in their own language thrilled my kids — even though their foreign language vocabulary may be limited to, "Hi. How ya doing?" and "See you later." *Now* the reason for learning a new language isn't just so they cram more knowledge into their brains. They understand that the reason for you learn a new language is so that you can talk to new kids. Eureka! It was a blinding flash moment in their lives. (After Spanish, we want to tackle Russian so that our vocabulary extends beyond *"Yes,"* *"No,"* and enthusiastic nods and smiles.)

By my experience alone, you can see there are a couple different ways to pick your target foreign language. First, I chose a language that I had some experience with. That made introducing it to my children all the easier. Next, I selected a language that I didn't know at all, but one that people around me spoke fluently. Even if I don't engage the Spanish speakers (who are *very* patient with those of us trying to learn the language) in long, drawn-out discussions, I can listen to the flow of the language as they talk together.

If you decide that you want your children to learn an additional language or two, you aren't weird (even though your neighbors may find the idea a little odd). Think of yourself as global, trans-metropolitan, and culture current.

We've found that one way to learn the cadence of a language like Spanish is to attend lectures or sermons delivered in the target language. Will you understand everything spoken? Almost certainly not. However, you may be surprised at the words that you pick up from extended listening. And unlike a preprogrammed, foreign-language curriculum, a live speaker uses real language spontaneously, so you actually hear a much wider variety of spoken words during a lecture than you would following a program.

So which language do you learn first?

- ✔ **Start with a language that means something to you.** Does the kids' great grandmother speak Croatian? Then teach them rudimentary Croatian so they can talk to Grandma. She'll love it, and so will the children. In a situation like this, you're actually meeting two homeschooling goals: You're teaching a new language, and you're doing it in a way that brings your family closer together.

- ✔ **Start with a language you like.** Has Greek always fascinated you? Then learn Greek. It means learning a new alphabet, sure — but I taught the Greek alphabet to a 5- and 6-year-old. If they can learn it, you can! (And if you try hard, I bet you can also imagine the looks I got in restaurants with two bored kids chanting alpha, beta, gamma, delta, epsilon.)

- ✔ **Select from the languages that have good instructional materials available.** Several companies produce language curriculums in various formats, and of course each company thinks their method is the best. (If they didn't, they wouldn't be in business long.) Today you can learn a language through video, CD/cassette and books, or computer CD-ROMs. The choice is up to you.

Some of the best foreign-language packages available are

- ✔ **Muzzy:** (Internet: www.early-advantage.com; Phone: 888-999-4670) This animated video program from the BBC teaches a target language to children ages 2 through 12. The Muzzy videos use complete immersion, which means that the videos feature dialogue in only the target language. Each Muzzy kit does include identical videos in English to use if your children don't understand the words from the animation sequences. Languages include French, Spanish, German, Italian, Gaelic, and Japanese. How can anyone resist a green, clock-eating monster?

- ✔ **Power-Glide:** (Internet: www.power-glide.com; Phone: 800-596-0910) These programs use cassettes or audio CDs along with workbooks.

Beginning in English, the program weaves more and more target language words into an adventure story until you find yourself reading and understanding the language. The main programs, available in Spanish, French, German, Latin, Japanese, and Russian are designed for sixth grade through adults. Recently, Power-Glide created children's versions of Spanish, German, French, and Latin for kindergarten through fifth grade. Simpler in approach and vocabulary, the children's versions also tell an adventure story as the child listens and follows along in the children's book.

✔ **The Rosetta Stone:** (Internet: www.rosettastone.com; Phone: 800-788-0822) This computer CD-ROM method has been tested through use. Both the U.S. State Department and the Peace Corps have used Rosetta Stone languages to teach their workers. The CD covers 92 lessons in one of 24 different languages. Many of the languages also have a second instructional level available if you finish the first course and want to continue. What makes this unique is that you set up the program to teach however you learn. If you learn best through hearing, you set up the program to talk to you. If you learn best by sight, set the program to show you text with pictures or text, sound, and pictures all at the same time.

Cleaning the House and Calling It Schoolwork

If one of your goals in homeschooling is to turn out a productive, useful member of society, then somewhere along the line you want to incorporate life skills into the educational mix. An ace student, who spouts philosophical theories yet appears clueless in front of a washing machine, missed something along the way. These students manage to finally function in the real world — I know several of them — but learning rudimentary skills, such as clothes-dryer manipulation, soup-can opening, and button sewing takes much more time and effort than it needs to if you begin early. (Okay. You're right. Some of them never get to button sewing.)

Some life skills, such as tooth brushing and face washing, fall into the normal preschool routine of your day. Unless these skills need to be actively taught (as with a special-needs student) they probably don't qualify as homeschool subject material. Cleaning, cooking, and mending or sewing, on the other hand, definitely count as school-worthy subjects. Schools call these topics Home Education and award a credit or more to students who pursue this information in high school.

Teaching home skills as part of your homeschool offers a couple of distinct advantages.

- ✔ **If you set aside specific time during your week to accomplish something, it's more likely to get done than the projects you plan to get around to sooner or later.** At our house, "sooner or later" never comes, and the pile of laundry continues to sit in the corner unsorted and unloved.

- ✔ **If you set aside a particular portion of your day or week to tackle certain tasks, you can teach them in a somewhat organized manner.** Showing your 5-year-old how to wipe down the baseboards with a warm moist cloth takes a bit more time than demonstrating to a 12-year-old, but 5 year olds think wiping baseboards is fun, and they're closer to the ground than 12 year olds to begin with.

You can teach an abundance of skills as Home Economics. A few ideas to get you started are

- ✔ **House cleaning basics:** Making the bed, picking up clothes, sorting and shelving toys in the children's bedrooms. Also includes dusting and vacuuming.

- ✔ **House cleaning advanced:** Closet organization, baseboard dusting, bathroom and kitchen cleansing.

- ✔ **Cooking skills:** Measuring ingredients (also math), oven and microwave use, dish washing.

- ✔ **Cooking skills advanced:** Meal preparation, meal planning, nutrition, gourmet holiday dishes.

- ✔ **Sewing skills:** Sewing on buttons, mending holes, cutting off pants to make shorts, and so on.

- ✔ **Sewing advanced:** Creating a garment from a pattern, making household items, such as placemats, napkins, and simple curtains.

- ✔ **Needle arts:** Crochet, rug hooking, knitting, needlepoint projects to decorate the house. These projects count as home ec and recreation at the same time.

We use Friday afternoon as Home Ec day. From the time after lunch to whenever the cookies come out of the oven, I focus on wet and dry measurements, food preparation, table settings, nutrition, kitchen organization, meal planning, and other aspects of cooking. Currently we concentrate on making fun foods, such as crisp rice treats, peanut butter cookies, and snack mix because I want my children to enjoy their time in the kitchen before they begin creating vegetarian meals or meat extravaganzas.

Arrange your week around an arts day

One way to incorporate the arts into your schedule is to set aside an entire day or afternoon to pursue art, music, physical education, or drama. Art, music, speech, and drama fit together into a nice four-subject package that fills an afternoon. PE can take up an entire afternoon on its own if you let it.

Too much creativity at one time tends to fry your learners, so select your classes with care. Scheduling all the extras on one day may be a little bit of arts overload, but you can certainly incorporate two or more — depending on the classes you choose — without much brain strain. And the change in course work gives your children a break from the endless round of math, English, social studies, and science.

If you know a parent who specializes in one of the areas who you want to teach, ask her if she'd like to join with you and teach the class. Her children then become part of your arts day classes, and the kids have someone to share the day with. If you like, you can teach the classes on your own and keep the learning within your own family.

Whichever way you choose to go, everyone benefits from a day spent away from the daily grind. In much the same way that a field trip revives low spirits, an arts day keeps creative juices running. Who knows? Your children may even think of this as a "free day" each week because the subjects differ so much from the daily routine.

Saturday morning, although not officially a school day, functions as Home Ec day number two: We spend a couple hours picking up the house and doing the cleaning jobs that don't get done during the week. The vacuum, carpet cleaner, dust rags, and other implements of organization make their appearance and do their duty. Then we sit down to lunch in a much cleaner atmosphere than the one that greeted us over breakfast.

Chapter 26

Making It Adventurous

Homeschooling doesn't have to take place at home each and every day. Perhaps you want to augment this week's art class, so you load up the kids and take them to the nearest art museum. You and yours have spent some time studying pointillism, and your scholars want to see an actual specimen or two. Or maybe your child shows an interest in machines. Instead of working through a textbook on machines and how they go, your students take a few afternoons to build a model engine that demonstrates how engines actually work.

Homeschool gives you the flexibility to add the not-so-typical educational opportunities into your family's week. These adventures may last an afternoon, a week, or a whole semester. If you and yours find them extremely worthwhile, they may even take a permanent place in your planning.

This chapter delves into the excitement of outside-the-box learning, those times that you pursue information for its own sake. These experiences create both memories and knowledge. Your students remember what they *do* more than the words they read every time. Give one or more of these ideas a try and create memories at the same time.

Dirtying Your Hands with a Project

I know, I know. Projects take time. They take space. And they're messy.

But what provides a greater sense of "I did it myself" than a good project? Whether you choose a relatively clean plastic model or definitely messy papier mâché, projects get your students involved in doing rather than reading. They experience instead of passively watching. And you hope they have fun in the process.

Not all these ideas appeal to every student. Go with your family's likes and dislikes; in fact, you'll probably come up with a possible project list on your own that includes a few of the options that I describe in the following sections. After you discover a worthwhile project, schedule it and give it a try.

Dissecting an owl pellet

People feel strongly about owl pellets. You are in the this-is-truly-cool camp or the how-gross-can-you-get camp. There seems to be no neutral ground.

Owl pellets are inexpensive, they usually come two or more to a package, and they're . . . um . . . well, I guess you could call them owl hairballs. The idea is that the owl eats something, such as a small mammal, and then regurgitates the animal's bones, which the owl's digestive system has already wrapped into a neat bundle. A helpful science company locates these pellets, disinfects them (I have no idea how), and then sells them to willing students.

If your child shows an interest in skeletons, bones, or the insides of living things, then she may enjoy disassembling one of these and finding out what the owl ate. Most owl-pellet companies give you a chart along with the pellets that help you identify the skeleton.

If you want to see how this is done before you attempt it at home, you can undertake a virtual owl-pellet dissection online at www.borg.com/~svcselem/kirkland/owlpellets. Any science supply company or good teacher education store should sell owl pellets. Online, Genesis Inc. sells an Owl Pellet Investigation kit (Internet: www.pellet.com; Phone: 800-473-5538), and Mountain Home Biological (Internet: www.pelletlab.com; Phone: 800-958-9629) sells individual pellets.

Playing amateur archaeologist

Short of a local 2,000-year-old-burial pit, amateur archaeology is actually as close as your local toy or educational store that sell "artifacts" actually embedded into blocks of hard clay that your child can spend the next several weeks uncovering. Those toy people are helpful. Aren't they?

You may shudder inwardly at the mess that such a project makes. (And it does make quite a mess. Think dust. Little piles of dust. Layers of dust. Now you get the picture.) However, if you can get past the dust, these kits leave your children with much more than the stones or trinkets they uncover.

One of my children is currently recycling an archaeology kit. The first child, the actual recipient, was excited about the idea of archaeology until he realized that this particular scientist spends much more time with a toothbrush and pocketknife than in front of the press announcing amazing discoveries. A few weeks with the tool and paintbrush, and he was happy to pass the kit to his little sister. I rejoice to think of the thousands of dollars and extra years in college this little kit may save me. Now, you see, archaeology longer appears on my son's list of possible college majors. (Good thing he found out *before* taking advanced courses.)

The child that the kit was passed down to, by the way, loves the process as well as the promised booty. So I prepare myself for several more weeks of red dust.

Creating a garden

What better way to explore botany than by planting, managing, and harvesting a small garden? Daily trips to your garden involves as little time or as much time as you like, yet through those visits your child watches as seeds sprout (or fail to), leaves appear, stalks grow, and finally fruit and seeds make an appearance. She also learns firsthand that plants need water and sunlight, zucchini grow as big as you let them, and spearmint smells great but takes over the entire yard unless you hem it in.

Gardening doesn't require a huge space of land. A couple small pots on the windowsill with herb seeds in them make a great garden! That way, you don't even have to go outside to watch the plants grow; checking their progress becomes as easy as walking by the kitchen window. And if you're not into gardening personally, the smaller the garden, the fewer plants you . . . er . . . your children need to care for.

Building a train layout

What's educational about a train layout? In addition to being just plain fun and a great way to pull family talents together, train buffs learn some basic electricity skills, physics, and spatial skills. With loose track pieces, for example, the current ceases to flow and the train goes nowhere. A home-built trestle that doesn't take load into account will *not* defy the laws of physics. Instead, it will crash. And the layout enhances your child's spatial skills because the whole design needs to take building size, terrain features, such as mountains and track flow, into account.

Train and track size, optional model building kits, and sculpting terrain all add interest and skills to the hobby. Trains sizes range from the tiny Z scale that fits into the palm of your hand to the G scale that you may see wandering around Christmas trees or outdoor gardens. Learning to create scenery and buildings opens yet another fascinating hobby for your child at the same time that it trims the overall railroading costs. You also save when you purchase model car kits that your railroad lover can assemble himself rather than buying the ready-made variety.

This is a hobby that easily includes the entire family or anyone who happens to be interested in it. Train cars and layouts fail to thrill me, for example, but I thoroughly enjoy creating the buildings that complete the scene. And the train lovers at my house are happy to let me do it because that way Mom's involved in a hobby they love, and they don't have to mess with the small plastic house parts. They much prefer messing with track pieces than assembling buildings with glue.

If you decide to pursue model railroading in earnest, keep in mind that the most important (and most expensive) part of the train should be the engine. Because the engine does all the work, you're better off to purchase all your cars separately and pay a little more for the engine than to buy a train in a box that contains all the parts the manufacturer thinks you need.

Burying yourself in papier mâché

Although papier mâché may not be your medium of choice, your children can still create an amazing number of things with wet, soggy paper. Bowls, platters, piñatas, masks, volcano forms, model train layouts, draped decorative figures, and much more emerge under their hands with the help of paper and watered-down glue (if they're doing it the second grader's way, watered-down flour).

Although incredibly messy during the creation process, papier mâché generally cleans up with warm soapy water — as do mâché-covered children. An excellent opportunity for getting your children's hands into your work if the children enjoy that type of thing, papier mâché tends to be a multiday project. Your children assemble a layer of wet paper strips over a form, let it dry, and repeat the process. After it's dry, it can be painted, decoupaged, decorated with strips of tissue paper, or whatever.

Assembling a model

Putting a paper, plastic, and/or wood model together can teach your kids project completion and attention to detail at the same time that it reinforces history or science. Your children learn much more about the *Titanic,* for example, when they take the time to assemble and paint a scale model of the *Titanic* than they will learn from browsing through pictures of the ship on the Web. There's something to be said for involving your hands in the process.

You can find most models of animals (with or without visible internal parts), boats, planes, vehicles, historical armies, the brain, buildings, and much more at your local hobby store. For anatomical models, if you can't find them locally, you may try Efston Science (Internet: www.e-sci.com; Phone: 888-777-5255). A Canadian company, they carry all sorts of child-friendly science items.

Taming the Boob Tube

Subscribe to cable, turn on your television, and explore the universe. With a programmable VCR or one of the new recorders, such as TiVo, you don't even have to be there when the original show airs — simply pick the shows that correlate with your current interests or curriculum track and tape them.

Tons of great educational channels exist:

- A&E
- Animal Planet
- Black Entertainment Television
- Bravo
- CSPAN
- CSPAN-2
- Discovery Channel
- The History Channel
- Lifetime
- Ovation
- The Weather Channel

As part of the Discovery family channels alone, optional add-on channels include Science, Civilization, Home & Leisure, and Wings. With all these selections, plus your personal favorite channels, which run educational shows from time to time, you can actually use the television as an educational tool without resorting to the stock ticker at the bottom of the screen.

With your VCR, you can even catch programs specifically designed for education as part of an effort called Cable in the Classroom. The Weather Channel, for example, offers educational programming from 4:00 to 4:30 a.m. Eastern Time Mondays (and repeated Thursdays). Topics include discussions on weather-related occupations, atmosphere, geography, and other weather-oriented science subjects. When you tape the episode, look online for a free downloadable lesson plan at The Weather Channel Web site, www.weather.com. It's under Interact; then Learn About Weather.

The Discovery Channel presents daily educational programming — *Assignment Discovery.* Each program appears four times in the year's rotation, usually at 9 a.m. ET/PT, and the Web site www.discovery.com also offers free lesson plans to go along with the episodes. This past year's topics included plants, structures, and scientific investigations, among others.

The Arts and Entertainment Channel (A&E) offers an hourly show much like Discovery, except that A&E features historical figures, culture (such as art and music), and peeks into issues such as crime and investigation. Look for lesson plans to accompany the presentations at A&E's Web site, www.aande.com. Because *Biography* is one of A&E's flagship shows, you find many biographical lesson plans here.

Visit Cable in the Classroom online at www.ciconline.org for monthly listings that encompass all participating stations. One two-month span alone returned 588 options for educational programming. While you're there, you may want to download the monthly programming calendar (the Taping Highlights Calendar) to quickly view several daily options over a month's time.

Pretending It's Le Louvre

Whether you go to an art museum, natural history museum, science museum, or children's museum, or even if you include a truly unusual museum during your vacation travels (such as the Hallmark Card Visitors Center in Kansas City), your children come away with new knowledge. Even if the museum becomes a monthly event, you can concentrate on a specific part each time you visit.

If you find yourself visiting museums much, you may want to look into a membership. Many museums offer a membership exchange that automatically grants you entrance to museums across the country. For example, the passes we received when we joined our local science museum got us into Chicago's Museum of Science and Industry. This little perk turns into quite a deal if you enjoy road trips *and* museums.

You can incorporate several museum-going strategies that enhance the educational benefit that your children receive from museum visits.

> ✔ **Equip each child with a sketchbook and pencil.** Sketching an exhibit or two in a museum is popular among students in England. My children thoroughly enjoy carrying their sketchbooks with them when they travel. They return home with illustrations of Charlie Chaplin's hat and cane and dinosaur feet. Do they actually look like hats and canes and feet? Don't ask. The kids had fun.

✔ **Study the exhibit before you get there.** Many museums these days offer educational supplements online that you can use to bone up on the exhibit contents before you arrive. This way, you do some of the investigation beforehand, and your children arrive prepared.

✔ **Study the exhibit after you get home.** Carry a flyer home with you or download an online educational guide to increase your student's knowledge after the trip has ended. Look up the exhibit topic in the library or in reference books. This turns a one-day trip into a memorable knowledge-gathering adventure.

✔ **Ask your student to write you a short synopsis of the exhibit(s) she enjoyed the most.** Why were these the favorites? What did she learn that she didn't know before? What would she like to know next about the exhibit if she continued studying it? Questions like these help your student process new information, and they give you an insight into what your child truly enjoyed about the trip.

Getting Past Bugs Bunny

Give history class a new twist when you fire up the video or DVD player. Sometimes the best way to explain a concept is to show it. Thankfully, movie reels exist from before 1915 to the present, and some of them (transferred to video or DVDs) provide excellent, dated footage that allows you to use the films for their cultural content — not necessarily their movie magic.

Old movies and cartoons do a great job of presenting the views of their times. This, in addition to the great historical information that you can glean from costuming and sets, makes them a treasure trove. You do, however, need to sit close so you can explain what the children see and how views change through the years.

Every now and then, you may run across a video that takes one subject and treats its use throughout the years. We have, for example, a video that shows the development of movie special effects while incorporating several early film snippets to tell the story. When the video mentioned the 1902 movie, *A Trip to the Moon* as a landmark in early special effects, we dug up a copy of the 1902 classic and showed it to the kids. Thus, our children received a good introduction to the topic as well as an in-depth look at historical footage.

Cartoons also provide a great look at the development of color and animation in addition to cultural history. Watching the cartoons of the early 30s, when animation studios were only allowed to use music that they already owned, gives your students a great peek into a different time. If you have the opportunity to see some done with early Technicolor, it shows you how inventive the artists could be with only shades of red and green.

You may want to look at

- ✔ **Cartoons from the '30s and '40s:** Watching cartoons from this time period gives the viewer an understanding of the development of color in animation. Watch a few of these to see how many movies reflect American culture during the Depression and World War II years. You can also use them as examples of social propaganda.

- ✔ **Silent movies from the 1920s:** These take you back to the time when cars were new and the ice truck still plodded down the streets. *Metropolis, The Black Pirate,* and *The General* are examples of classic silent movies. The best-known actors and actresses of the era included Charlie Chaplin, Mary Pickford, and Douglas Fairbanks.

- ✔ **Musicals from the '40s and '50s:** Musicals specialize in the art of escapism, and the gems of the '40s and '50s weren't any different. In the 1940s, the film industry, combining escapism with patriotism, gave us *Holiday Inn, Blue Skies,* and *Yankee Doodle Dandy*. The 1950s tried to keep the ball rolling with *Oklahoma, The King and I,* and *Pajama Game*. By the end of the 1950s, the heyday of the screen musical was mostly over.

- ✔ **Movies created from books:** Because most books take place during a specific identifiable time period, either present, past, or future, they make good launching points for cultural studies. And although a movie made from a book may not remain letter true, it does add a visual component that the pages sometimes lack. For books-made-into-movies that provide historical chewiness, you may want to look at *Rebecca* (still considered one of the best suspense novels ever written), *To Kill A Mockingbird* (set in the south during the Depression) or the 1951 version of *A Christmas Carol,* starring Alastair Sim.

Volunteering Builds Compassion

Compassion happens in your children when they reach out and help someone or something else. If you want your kids to care about those around them, introduce them to volunteering. Although they can probably volunteer at the local museum after a certain age, museum work won't enlarge their ability to care quite as much as some of the other available options.

If you want to know if an organization or institution would be interested in working with your children, give them a call. Some organizations, such as nursing homes, welcome weekly or semi-weekly visitors as long as a parent comes with the children to keep them on track. Other groups prefer to work with the students directly without parental help.

Some organizations love to work with homeschoolers because they're available during the day when other helpers aren't. This is definitely a mark in your favor because many groups keep business hours and would prefer help in the 9-to-5 range rather than the 5-to-9-time period when most students are actually available.

To jumpstart the volunteering bandwagon, you may want to contact

- ✔ **The local animal shelter or Humane Society:** Especially if you have an animal lover at your house, the Humane Society and its kin provide a great place for helping out. It may quell the protective instinct in your child without you giving every stray turtle, snake, and puppy dog a home. (Be aware, however, that shelters routinely euthanize many of the sick, dangerous, or unadoptable animals that they take in. If visiting Fufu's cage the next week and finding it empty will upset your child, then you may want to choose another volunteer option.)

- ✔ **A nursing home or retirement center:** Sometimes the administrators and staff at these institutions enjoy providing small programs or ongoing companions for residents who may appreciate someone to talk to.

- ✔ **Assist with a local food drive:** The folks at food pantries need help unpacking crates, checking off products, shelving products, and sometimes even packing baskets that go to families or groups.

- ✔ **Afterschool programs:** Students who are willing to tutor or help younger children are often welcome.

Although this isn't an exhaustive list, you can see from the variety presented that many opportunities exist. You may find a few of them in your own local community. Grab your phone book, look up a few nonprofit organizations, and see what you can find.

If volunteering doesn't fit neatly into any other subject category, then record it under Volunteer Experience. Portfolio reviewers, college admissions staff, and potential employers appreciate students who spend time helping others.

Packing Up the Minivan

Schedule the family vacation to do double duty as school time. Of course, if you want to teach on the road, you have to schedule an educational destination of some sort or pack schoolbooks for the hotel room. Simply piling everybody into the car and announcing the trip as official school time doesn't really count.

AT OUR HOUSE

Viva Las Vegas

Part of the reason we travel is to teach the children about the world around them. Therefore, each time the kids pack their bags, we consider it schooling on the road. We always take math and spelling because they're ongoing subjects whose lessons we never seem to finish. I also pack their flight bags with books (usually biographical histories that they love) that I want them to read on the way. If we travel more than six hours by car or plane, most of the week's reading is done before we ever reach our destination!

Usually we try to work at least one learning destination into the trip because others tend to pop up along the way. A trip to the Orlando Mouse House probably counts only as walking exercise, but visiting the reproduction of Tutankhamen's tomb in the King Tut Museum (at the Luxor hotel) counts as history. (And it's much less expensive.)

Last spring, we descended on Las Vegas with the sole intent of exploring the city's educational attractions. Believe it or not, Las Vegas offers plenty of educational content. In the three days we were there, we racked up about eight hours of purely educational adventures each day. (The other four hours probably counted as play.)

To use Las Vegas and its environs as an example of an educational romp (perhaps not one of the cities that you thought about taking your children to), you can:

- **Visit the reproduction King Tutankhamen's tomb in the Luxor Hotel.** We recently finished a study of ancient Egypt, and the children thought this was absolutely fascinating.

- **Visit the Hoover Dam and its Depression-era exhibits.** We talked quite a bit about the 1930s as we toured the exhibit and discussed the various stories and memories passed down to the children through each family line.

- **Identify desert plants on the way from Las Vegas to the Hoover Dam.** Although my children have read about deserts, my children had never seen one. So the trip through the Mojave Desert provided for lively conversation.

- **Tour the dolphin exhibit at the Mirage hotel.** This tour includes several small dolphin tanks as well as an optional (albeit free) tour through the tank water purification systems and science rooms. Great for budding engineers.

- **See the white tigers and lions at the Mirage hotel.** In back of the dolphin exhibit, you can tour a garden full of exotic animals used in the Siegfried and Roy animal show.

✔ **Visit the Venetian Hotel and discuss Venetian and Renaissance life.**
Though they think a city with canals would be grand, my children have
never seen Venice. We wandered through the hotel and discussed true
Venetian architecture, culture, and civilization.

And that's only the beginning. With this partial list alone, you spend time in
history with Tut's tomb and the Hoover Dam, science with the Hoover Dam,
the desert, and the animals, and culture with the Venetian hotel. Add the conversations (this counts as social studies) that your children inevitably get
into with various residents, such as store clerks, and you have a full week's
work. Set aside some math time each morning before you set out, and you're
there!

TIP

Avoid textbook boredom

If you ever went to school, you probably remember how boring textbooks could be — page after page, chapter after chapter, problem after problem. That shiny new book that looked so inviting in September lost its appeal sometime around January (sometimes even before). Some books are well written, but even the best texts drag in spots. I always thought they were *supposed* to read that way.

If your child feels the way I do, then you begin to see that unmistakable "Oh, no! Not again!" look in her eyes when you present The Textbook for school day number 153. Can you blame her?

When you schedule a little break now and then, it revives interest in the text when it reappears. Breaks can be just as educational as textbook learning, even if they don't exactly match the material covered on page 688 of said book. (Some homeschool families avoid what they consider the textbook problem altogether by reading almost exclusively from library books and what they term *real books*.)

Look at learning through a wider lens than grade-level textbooks, and you begin to see a big, useful world out there. Did anyone give you a parenting handbook when you began the journey? Probably not. You learned about baths and bedtimes the hard way, maybe with the help of a more experienced person at your elbow — or on the other end of the phone.

Likewise, learning encompasses much more than the narrow fields assembled in most textbooks. The books have their place, but there's something to be said for real-life learning as well. What constitutes real-life learning? If you take a break for a few days, you could

Take a hike and learn about the trees and plants around you.

Fly a kite and notice when and why it flies — as well as when it doesn't.

Visit a museum and learn something new.

Bring home a video from the library about a topic that you always wanted to explore.

Design and plant an outdoor or container garden.

If you use textbooks, walking away from them for a few days won't kill you or your student. And, if you use the time to embark on other educational adventures, you both return to the book routine with new information as well as refreshed.

Of course, some destinations start out more learning-oriented than others. If you look at things creatively, however, you can find education in many places:

✔ A trip to the coast counts as ocean science (or oceanography if your students are beyond third grade).

✔ A trip to the Northeast counts as history when you spend time in Boston, Philadelphia, and a number of other cities that played a part in the founding of the United States.

✔ If you leave the house to visit a different culture or part of the country, it counts as social studies and geography, no matter what else the area may offer in historical or scientific worth.

Chapter 27

Throothing Open the Toy Box

Dig into the toy box and drag out some fun! Whether you play a good board game, spend some time building robots at the computer, or build the greatest K'NEX contraption known to man, you're actually learning as you go. And so is your child — unless you "help" by building or playing while your child looks on. Be a good parent and buy your own building set if you find yourself "helping" for hours on end. Or at least play with the toys after your child goes to bed in the evenings. (That's what I do.)

Educational mavens and even some homeschoolers eschew games because they're not *educational* enough — these people have a problem with fun in education. They believe that if it's fun, it can't be educational. But think about it: Which do you remember more? That science chapter you read in sixth grade that discussed the ins and outs of force and planes? Or the last track that you built for your small, metal racing cars that started with a magnificent hill?

The point is that you learn more when you enjoy it. Although playing with a game or toy actually takes more time than simply reading a page of information and checking the topic off your list, your child probably won't remember it tomorrow. Let her spend an entire afternoon building with (or without) some general parameters, however, and you may be surprised what she learns by trying things out.

This chapter takes you into the toy box and gives you some ideas about how to use the games and gizmos you already have lying around the house. If you have children, you probably have more toys than you know what to do with. Now you can drag them out without guilt during the day because they're educational.

Thinking about Playing or Playing to Think?

How do you learn logic and strategy? Well, you could work through an introductory logic book. (If you use a classical curriculum and you want to teach formal logic skills, you'll probably do that anyway. Classical curriculum is described in Chapter 12.) Another option is to learn to play chess, the game of Go, or even checkers.

To play these games, one player is pitted against another player with playing pieces in the middle. Strategy games come to us from all corners of the earth and all time periods. The ancient Chinese and the Vikings played strategy games to sharpen thinking skills and while away extra hours, as did the English knights and Japanese strategists. Participation in strategy games can help your child

- ✔ **Build his math skills.**

- ✔ **Learn to think ahead.** Strategy games rely on logical progression; if you want to win, you need to move your pieces in the right way while always keeping your final goal in mind.

- ✔ **Learn to be patient.** You can't sit down to a game of chess and finish in ten minutes, unless you play a variant of chess, such as Tic-Tac-Check, where the board is only sixteen spaces square and your goal is to move your pieces into four spaces vertically or horizontally. Your pieces, however, move the way they do on a regular chessboard. (The last time I played this game, I got slaughtered by a 12-year-old, but I digress.)

If you don't know how to play strategy games on your own but you want your children to play, you have several options. You can

- ✔ **Learn to play the game together.** This adds another game to your arsenal of knowledge, and it ensures that you both have someone to play with. Midnite Snack Magnetics, on the Internet at www.magneticgames. com, offers a stunning selection of strategy games from around the world, in addition to chess and checkers. The neat thing about these games is that they're small and easy to store, they come with clear plastic pouches for travel, and they're completely magnetic. This means that you can stick the board (as well as the pieces) to your refrigerator or filing cabinet and keep a game going in the kitchen or school area. Look for them at your local specialty game store or order them directly from Midnite Snack Magnetics.

- ✔ **Join a local chess or Go club.** These clubs often offer tournament play for members of all ages, so a strategy club membership may be an option if your child enjoys competition.

✔ **Purchase and use a computerized instructional program.** Although chess is the big winner here, you can find computer versions of many strategy games. Edmark produces two different packages that they call Strategy Challenges 1 and Strategy Challenges 2. The first package includes Go-Maku, Nine Men's Morris, and Mancala, and package number two has Jungle Chess, Surakarta, and Tablut. Both software packages are designed for third grade on up.

Ante Up

There's more to board games these days than Monopoly and Clue. For the past thirty years or so, game manufacturers have produced games that actually have learning value, and they're not the ones stamped "Educational Game" on the side. Who wants to play an Educational Game? No one at my house, and probably no one at yours!

Games come in all different price ranges and complexities. The one thing they have in common is that you aren't going to find them at your local Target or Toys "R" Us. These games are produced for the specialty game market, and they're sold exclusively through stores that specialize in games.

They also take a varying amount of time to play. You can pick up a German game that plays out in 40 minutes to an hour because almost all German games do. Or you can assemble a group of your favorite cronies and spend three days building ancient civilizations (minus time to run home for sleep and a shower). It's entirely up to you.

Just to whet your appetite, here is a smattering of available games and what your children can learn from playing them:

✔ **American Adventure Games:** These inexpensive cut-and-fold-paper games all feature a particular snapshot of history. Build Model-A cars in Henry Ford's River Rouge, and learn about assembly-line production at the same time. Play The Redcoats Are Coming, and recreate Paul Revere and William Dawes' ride. Game publisher Chatham Hill offers 18 different games that enhance your study of the colonial period from the Underground Railroad to (and beyond) the industrialized nation. Each game retails at about $8, and they all come with a page of notes for educators.

✔ **Authors and kin:** Popular in drawing rooms during the nineteenth century, an Authors deck gives you 13 different authors. Each featured author appears on four different cards that highlight one of four works by that author. You proceed to play a Go Fish type of game with the deck, learning about the authors as you go. The company that makes these cards also offers decks that feature inventors, musicians, presidents, nursery rhymes, Black history, scientists, and more.

✔ **CatchPenny:** You're an eighteenth-century businessperson, and your goal is to become the CatchPenny — "King of the beggars, Vagabonds, and Street Pedlars." The game comes with rules designed like an eighteenth-century London newspaper. The board spaces, characters, and other tidbits of life at the time are all defined for you. Playing CatchPenny can help your child broaden his understanding of history or social studies as well as business.

✔ **Empire Builder and kin:** Learn about the expansion of the nineteenth-century railroads as you build rails and pick up and drop off goods to complete contracts. The goal of the game is to complete your contracts and amass the most money; actually, what you learn by playing the game is what various areas of the country produced (or needed from other states) as well as *why* the railroad barons designed the rails the way they did. The designer also created a children's version — Uncle Happy's Train Game.

✔ **1-2-3 Oy!:** I have no idea why this game is so named. It contains a stack of number cards with directions for several different number games. We use 1-2-3 Oy! to solidify addition, subtraction, multiplication, and division facts through game play.

✔ **Pick Two:** No matter what language you're learning, you can probably find a version of Pick Two that contains the vowels you need. This game comes in English, French, German, Latin, and Spanish versions. Pick Two is like Scrabble — only without a board and with a twist. Your goal is to build words with your sturdy, plastic-letter tiles. If you get rid of all your tiles first, you yell "Pick Two!" Then everybody grabs two more tiles from the pile, and play continues. Pick Two is useful for building up your child's vocabulary, his understanding of a foreign language, and language arts.

If you can't find a game store in your area, a few vendors sell these games online. One of the benefits of finding a local game store is that you meet other people who play the same games you do. Another perk (if the staff is worth its salt) is that the game store personnel can point you to new or additional games that are similar to your current favorite.

Most game-store owners don't know a whit about the educational content of games. I know because I talk to many of them. If you want to do business with a company that understands both games and homeschooling, take a look at Jumping Dragon Games (Internet: www.jumpingdragongames.com), a game store that specializes in games for homeschoolers. This company carries most of what I'd recommend to you, and they even offer a list of games by subject. You can also check Linguaplay Games on the Internet at www.linguaplay.com. They're threatening to open an online store, and they promise to carry everything that I recommend to you (mostly because my husband runs it).

Plugging In for Fun

If you select useful computer games, you can pop a CD-ROM into the PC or Mac and take an educational break while your children pursue a worthwhile activity. What constitutes a useful computer game? Determining what is *not* a useful computer game is easier: Playing the first person shoot 'em ups, for example, do nothing but enhance your child's hand-eye coordination. A sling-shot, soft foam ball, and a tree or a rousing game of marbles may do as well without fear of eyestrain. (See Chapter 22 for more computer-in-the-class-room reading.)

Computer games fall into a few basic, broad categories: Adventure, grade-level review, simulations, creativity, and programming are most of the biggies. Within each category you can find programs to fit nearly every age level. (Productivity is also a booming computer-software category, but I have yet to see a home-school child who thrills at the thought of spending time with his faithful word processor.)

As the parent, you're the one who needs to exercise judgment when buying computer games. If you object to witchcraft and other occult themes, for example, and the computer program in your hand is titled something like "Sad Sam Visits the Haunted House," don't buy it. If you object to violence of any kind, and the ESRB rating on the box says "Mild Violence," then you may not want that title in your home. For more about the Entertainment Software Rating Board and its determinations, see www.esrb.com on the Internet.

Here are a few examples of available software by category. The software industry shifts more than the sand of the Sahara, so don't be surprised if a few of these titles are out of print by the time you pick up this book:

- ✔ **Adventure:** Solve the puzzle, finish the race, and learn something along the way. From titles like Pajama Sam 2: Thunder and Lightning Aren't So Frightening to the Physicus that caters to older tastes, adventure programs teach logic and reasoning skills, which makes them a math topic. Humongous Entertainment produces several of these titles for adventurers 3 to 10 years of age; for older learners, look for software manufacturers such as Tivola, Interplay, Electronic Arts, or Sierra Studios. The Myst cycle: Myst, Riven, and Myst3: Exile, propels players into a puzzle-filled world without violence.

- ✔ **Creativity:** Design greeting cards, bookmarks, banners, and even paper toys with one of the many creativity programs available. Print Shop, Print Artist, and American Greetings are a few of the names to look for.

- **Grade Level Review:** When you want to ensure that your child masters the basics of kindergarten, third grade, or any other grade through high school, the grade-level-review programs allow them to refresh skills without your personal input. The JumpStart series from Knowledge Adventure and ClueFinders from The Learning Company both incorporate grade-level-skill games into their titles. For grade ranges without specific identifying levels, you may want to look at Encore Software's Advantage line: Each box in Elementary Advantage, Middle School Advantage and High School Advantage includes ten different subjects for the specific grade ranges.

- **Programming:** Some students thrill at the idea of making the computer do what *they* want it to. Although you can purchase a compiler to program in C++ or a host of other languages, you can also tackle the problem creatively and download the Logo computer language from the Logo Foundation Web site (`http://el.www.media.mit.edu/groups/logo-foundation`). If your student uses Compton's Learning Programming Made Easy from The Learning Company, he may discover an introduction to C, BASIC, and Java. Once in a while, a software company releases a programming CD-ROM for BASIC or another language; if you're interested, you may want to pick it up when you see it; they don't tend to stay on the market for too many years.

- **Simulations:** Build simulated towns, theme parks, roller coasters, or take a virtual trip back through time. Participation in these programs may strengthen business and money management skills because players need to pretend pay for whatever they build or purchase and still make money at the end of the simulation. Depending on the scenario, playing a simulation game can also build knowledge about the past if you choose a historical simulation or build knowledge of the world if you select a program such as Sim Safari for your young social studies lover. Titles such as Sim City Classic, Sim Town, and SimCoaster are available from Electronic Arts, (Internet: `www.ea.com`). Microsoft Train Simulator appeals to older students, where players build a train line and run the train as an engineer (among other options). Or delve into history with titles such as Caesar III, Pharaoh, or Cleopatra, all available from Impressions Games (Internet: `www.impressionsgames.com`).

Thrilling the Engineer's Heart

What way-cool thing can I build today? If your child thinks along these lines, then you may want to decide on a building system and accumulate a set from here and there. One of the nice things about the various building systems is that after you select one, the individual components intermix so your child's only boundary is the realm of the imagination.

Viewing the world through creative eyes

When you walk down the streets of New York City, do you see the trash on the sidewalks and the pollution in the air? Or do you see the beauty of the skyline, the busyness of the sidewalks, and catch the excitement in the air? Two people who trot down the same street in New York can see two entirely different scenes. It all depends on your perspective.

Looking at the world through eyes that see potential is much more fun than being a fuddy-duddy. Believe me, I know a few of each, and the creative people enjoy life more. They can always think of something to do, whether that means dragging out the tissue paper to decorate the main room in paper flowers or using every piece of green construction paper in the house to design a piecemeal landscape for the model train layout. It may even mean gathering up a few of your best quilts to create a tent

outdoors. Whatever they're up to, they're always busy.

Using games and toys as educational tools helps to foster that kind of thinking. Basically, it shows your children how to think outside the box without ever stating that today they must think outside the box. They figure out that learning is much more than completing workbook pages; that learning has more to do with living life and working with what you're given than writing the correct answer on a blank line.

Your job is to walk with them, praise their progress, and quietly determine where the activities fit into your planner. If you do it this way, it may be years before they realize that they're really learning. By the time they figure it out, your children will probably be so used to having fun that they keep on doing it — one game at a time.

 Although science toys certainly aren't limited to building sets, playing with science toys provides an excellent means of instilling creativity and learning about simple machines and some physics. Chemistry sets, microscopes, and weather stations are also available, but they're more educational in scope and this chapter focuses on learning while you play rather than buying a box marked "Educational Toy" and expecting the children to play with it for hours on end.

 Several companies produce a few science toys and building systems:

- ✔ **Architecture blocks:** Whether your child builds with a simple set of wooden blocks or a reproduction of a nineteenth-century stone set, she learns about arches, support, and structures as she goes. Building some fantastic structure counts as science; telling you about it in lavish detail is language arts.

- ✔ **Capsela:** Maybe you remember playing with Capsela kits as a child. They're still around, but not as plentiful as they used to be. These clear plastic capsules allow children to see motors run, fans move, and gears rotate as they build moving models. You can also find a Capsela weather station that children build themselves to learn about weather science. All Capsela pieces fit together, regardless of the kit, just like LEGOs.

✔ **K'NEX:** This building system makes everything from moving vehicles to roller coasters. Like LEGO Dacta, K'NEX offers both a consumer division and an educational division. If your child already fell in love with K'NEX, you can add simple machines and robotics to the collection that you already have. K'NEX even has a primary math line that shows you how to use your collection as math manipulatives. For more information, see their Web site: www.knex.com.

✔ **LEGO:** Who doesn't have enough LEGO bricks to build a life-size shed behind the house? If you have a LEGO lover at your house, then you already have the makings of great science learning. Write down what they do as they do it and count it as school time. If they build a bridge, that's engineering and physics. Playing with moving robots becomes a part of small machines class. Taking small parts and building larger objects out of them is math because your student then works with parts to make a whole.

✔ **LEGO Dacta:** The educational arm of LEGO, the Dacta division specializes in creating LEGO pieces that your child can put together in such a way as to learn about science. Your child can learn a special set of science skills — the workings of simple machines, industrial machines, and so on — from putting together individual sets that are science-specific. Although not sold as a toy (and certainly not priced like one) if your child already learns through LEGOs and you want to add a motor and specific scientific parts to your collection, this may be a good next step. Although we have a few problems keeping the Dacta pieces in their educational box (so I can find them the next time that I want to teach a lesson on simple machines during school time), my pre-engineer loves these sets and has learned enough through them to be well worth my money. For more information, go on the Internet: www.pitsco-legodacta.com or call 800-362-4308.

✔ **LEGO Mindstorms:** Using this computerized system, your child can learn the basics of robotic theory and programming. Your child programs the robot using a PC, downloads the program into the robot, and watches it go. The Robotics Invention System (the flagship product) comes with LEGO pieces and sensors that your child can use to build his own robot as well as the CD-ROM he needs to program the robot to follow a trail, act as a burglar alarm, and much more. LEGO Mindstorms (Internet: www.mindstorms.lego.com) is available at many toy stores.

✔ **Switch On:** Components snap together like LEGO pieces to form circuits. Designed for children age 8 on up, the child places a clear plastic base plate over a full-size schematic and builds the models right over the schematic. Working with this set, your child can learn about the principles of electricity, schematic reading, and develop creatively as he builds door-bells, burglar alarms, fans, lighting, and more. If you would like to know more about Switch On, go to the Internet: www.homeschoolscience. com or call 800-694-7225.

✔ **Zome Tools:** Scientists designed this building system. Watch your children create DNA strands, molecular structures, or giraffes with the Zome System. My husband stumbled across this set years ago while on a business trip, and my children have used it for a long time. Now the Zome Tools people even provide lesson plans that you can download for free from the Internet at www.zometool.com or purchase as a printed set. Most science museums and upscale toy stores carry these; the Web site offers a retail store finder by state.

Part VI
The Part of Tens

In this part . . .

Browse through the lists in Chapters 28 and 29 for ideas, resources, or encouragement. Also, turn to the celebrated *For Dummies* Part of Tens when you need responses to the questions that inquisitive neighbors invariably ask. No need to copy them onto sticky notes and plaster them around your school area; simply read and enjoy.

Chapter 28

Ten Educational Games That Enhance Your School Day

*W*hat do you pull out when you want to play school rather than actually teach? Why, one of these games, of course! The games in this chapter offer you much more than Monopoly or Connect Four; in fact, you can substitute any one of these for a subject lesson once in a while with no regrets. From electrical circuits to business conglomerates and from food chains to famous battles, these games cover math, science, social studies, and language arts in the finest tradition of play. Although playing these games may take longer than it would to present a ten-to-twenty-minute lesson in whatever, there's something to be said for variety in the home schoolroom.

TIP

You should be able to find all (or most) of these games at your local specialty game retailer. If your city manages to exist without a game store, you can try the following Web sites, the second site special orders whatever you need:

✔ The Jumping Dragon; Internet: www.jumpingdragongames.com

✔ LinguaPlay Games; Internet: www.linguaplaygames.com

AC/DC

Immerse yourself in electric circuits with the card game AC/DC. You lay your cards down to complete 6- or 110-volt circuits. But watch out for the short or shock cards! They affect your circuit in some not-so-fun ways. Play AC/DC and count the time as science; you don't need a never-ending battery supply when the circuit exists on cards. Appropriate for two through six players, ages 8 on up.

Acquire

Buy and sell stocks. Build an empire. Go bankrupt — um, that's not exactly the goal. Acquire is a classic business game from way back. You create a hotel chain and learn about business along the way — how and why companies merge, how they acquire one another, and how stock prices effect profitability. Appropriate for two through six players, ages 12 and up; Avalon Hill/Hasbro.

Apples to Apples

Apples to Apples is a game of comparisons. The dealer draws a green topic card, and you frantically look through your hand to see which card or cards match the best. So, for example, if the topic is Fragrant, and the cards in your hand read George Washington, Toenails, Paint, and Bubbles, which one is the most fragrant? Well, none of them, actually, and that's where the fun comes in. Perfume is the best match, but somebody else probably has that one in his hand.

You choose the card that you think matches the topic the best and lay it on the table face down. Move fast, because the number of cards allowable on the table equals the number of players, and you can lay one or two cards at a time — which means the slowpokes don't get a turn that round. When the maximum number of cards appear on the table, the dealer turns them face up and you begin to negotiate for your choice to be awarded The Closest Match. The card that matches the topic more closely than any of the others gets the point. Enough points and you win the game.

Apples to Apples is fast moving, hilarious, and thought-provoking. (George Washington and Candy Apples both qualify as Unique? Who'd have thought?) The game comes in a regular version for ages 10 and up, as well as a junior version for ages seven (able to read) and up. The game accommodates four to ten players; Out of the Box Publishing.

Blue vs. Gray

Every general, every flag, every major battle, every battle site. That's what you get when you open the two card boxes of Blue vs. Gray, subtitled "The Civil War Game." Designed by a history professor who swears that you can play the game in 45 minutes (I stood and watched him play with an opponent for two to three hours), you build the map and battle campaigns as you go.

Your goal is to play out the entire war strategically. The outcome depends on your decisions and strategy. Each card shows a picture of the person or flag, plus a good paragraph of biographical or historical information. While you don't need to know the facts to play, Civil War buffs love the career notes and other minute details. Definitely count this one for history and geography. For two players, ages 12 and up; Q.E.D. Games.

Chrononauts

What would happen if the *Titanic* stayed afloat? How would history be altered if John F. Kennedy recovered from his bullet wound? Chrononauts is a card game of time travel and alternate realities. First you build a timeline from 1865 to 1999 with 32 cards; then you spend the rest of the game attempting to complete a secret goal that you glean from your Mission card. You also draw a Time Traveler Identity card that tells who you are. You have three ways to win: Complete your mission, get your time traveler back to his or her version of reality, or have exactly ten cards in your hand at the end of your turn.

If the idea of discussing "what ifs" and tragedy makes you uneasy, then you probably won't like this game. A few of the cards highlight relatively recent disasters, such as Columbine and the Oklahoma City bombing.

An interesting activity for history class, playing this game makes your children consider how events effect one another. Taking the *Titanic* for an example, how might intercontinental voyages be different today if the largest pleasure palace in 1912 had stayed afloat and set a new standard in travel? One through six players, ages 11 and up, can learn from playing this game. Looney Labs.

The Garden Game

What do you get when you cross seeds, pollinators, predators, and the weather? Well, if you do it outside, you may get a garden out of it. If you do it inside, you'll probably find yourself in the middle of The Garden Game.

Your goal is to plant and pollinate your seeds before the predators or nasty weather gets the better of you. At the same time, you move around the board through the seasons. This game includes a nice, multipage discussion on plant pollination and gardening, and it definitely fits within an upper elementary or middle school science curriculum. For two through six players, ages 8 and up; Ampersand Press (Internet: www.ampersandpress.com), sells it for $27.

Into the Forest

This card game explores the food chains of the forest. From the animal and plant cards in your hand, you pit one portion of the food chain against another, much like the game of war. So if you lay down a Grass card, and your opponent places Millipedes on the table, your opponent gets your Grass card because Millipedes eat decaying grass.

Rather than win by point accumulation, players compete against a timer to simulate the never-ending cycle of life in the forest. List this game under science. (If your students really enjoy the game and its concepts, this company also produces the game "Onto the Desert," which focuses on survival in the desert climate.) For two to six players, 7-years-old on up; Ampersand Press produces this game that sells for $16.

Keep Quiet

Learn the manual sign language alphabet in a fun and inventive way or practice the skill you already have with Keep Quiet. In the box, you find a set of wooden cubes; each side features an alphabet letter — pictured in sign. Roll the dice and create as many words as you can from the letters crossword style; if you misspell a word, your opponent can challenge you; if she then spells the word correctly (using sign language, of course), that word's score is subtracted instead of added to your total.

The game comes with two copies of an Interpreter Card that shows each letter of the manual alphabet along with its letter in case you're not already up on the signs. Play this game in foreign language class, language arts class, or both. One or more players, ages 7 and up can participate; Kopptronix (Internet: www.kopptronix.com), manufactures Keep Quiet, which sells for $16.

Krypto

Krypto is one of those classic card games that people muse over. "Oh yes, I remember Krypto . . . " and they lapse into silence, wondering if it's still available. Although kind of difficult to locate, the game is still around.

Each player gets five numerical cards, ranging anywhere from one to twenty five. Then a target card is turned face up; this is your goal card. Using all five cards, you need to somehow equal the target number through addition, subtraction, multiplication, or division.

Krypto also comes in a primary version as well as a fractions supplement (fraction cards that you add to the regular Krypto game). Kryto accommodates one to ten players of any age; MPH Games manufactures the game, which sells for $8.

Oh, Scrud!

This fast-paced spelling game leaves us laughing more often than not. With Oh, Scrud! the dealer deals several cards for your hand. Hopefully you get a combination of consonants and vowels because your goal is to create two three-letter words and a four-letter word before your opponents do.(Parents playing with children can add to the challenge by making the parental words longer, if they like.)

Of course, that's assuming nobody throws down a Lose All Vowels card that leaves you with only consonants or a Lose Your Hand card that makes you draw all over again. This game uses no turns, so from the first "Go!" the play is a flurry of activity. This card game counts as language arts, spelling, and vocabulary. (Playing Oh, Scrud! with their dad, our children learn more new words: "Ambivalence? What's that mean?"). Oh, Scrud!, manufactured by M&A, is for three to ten players, ages 7-years-old and up and sells for $8.

Chapter 29

Ten Common Homeschool Fears

. . . .

In This Chapter

▶ Making friends as a homeschooler

▶ Purchasing the right curriculum

▶ Free time as a homeschooling parent

. . . .

*E*very homeschooler has fears that nag and whisper in the night. Maybe going with the flow would be better. Whether you're contemplating taking the leap into homeschooling, you're a first-year homeschooler, or you've been doing this for ages, one or more of the fears that I discuss in this chapter is bound to hit you sooner or later.

The good news is that they're only fears and nothing more. When the sun shines again and you look into those bright eyes that live at your house, you reach for the math book and know you're doing the right thing. For the benefit of your middle-of-the-night uneasiness, this chapter contains the answers to classic homeschool fears.

My child will never make friends if I homeschool.

Actually, the truth is that it's harder to stay at home and actually do the work than it is to pile everybody into the car and trek across town to another homeschooler's house for the day. When I began teaching my children at home, I had it easy: Another homeschooler lived four houses down. However, keeping everybody inside until the day's work was done was still hard. Play sets longed for company, bikes sat idle, and five pairs of inline skates (belonging to the other children as well as to mine) cried for attention.

As long as you involve your child in activities with other homeschoolers or in the community and let him out of the house once in a while, your child will make friends. Due to the nonsegregated nature of homeschooling, your child's friends may surprise you: Some will probably be a bit older, others younger, and she may even take a liking to the grandma down the street. (Who wouldn't like a woman who cultivates gorgeous flowerbeds and serves great cookies?)

One of the easiest ways to meet other homeschoolers is to hang out where they hang out. Join a homeschool co-op. Participate in the local library home-school activities. Call your YMCA, YWCA, or other athletic club and ask about daytime classes for homeschoolers. Sooner or later, you're bound to meet another family or two like yours.

I don't know enough to teach my child.

If you took it, you can teach it. Did you make it through second grade? Then you can teach second-grade math and reading.

Remember that I'm not talking about lecturing to a thirty-member class. Picture yourself with your second grader reading words and sentences while snuggled on your lap. Perhaps you sit next to your fourth grader and talk about fractions while you cut an extra-large, chocolate-chip cookie into sixths for a tasty math lesson.

After awhile, when your child brings questions to you that you can't answer off the top of your head, you learn together. Hand in hand with your child, you read through the textbook or research at the library or on the Internet. You'll want to stay a bit ahead of your student in some classes, and you can pursue other subjects together. If you have high-school-age students, they can do the legwork and bring you the answers.

I already find myself relearning or reading ahead a bit to cover lessons in our homeschool. For some subjects, such as Greek, I actually keep a text ahead of the children so that I can answer questions as they arise. (I also happen to enjoy Greek, and I work through the lessons myself to keep my mind sharp.) In other subjects, such as world history, I wing it as we go, and I look up infor-mation that I've forgotten as the need arises.

My child will miss out on socialization.

That depends. What kind of socialization do you want your child to have? If you're talking about being herded into a room with twenty or more other chil-dren and told not to talk all day, then your child's probably going to miss that experience. If you mean the socialization that your child receives during ten-minute lunches in an impersonal school cafeteria where a monitor walks around the room constantly so that children remain silent while they eat, then your child probably won't experience that at home, either.

If you mean the kind of socialization that arises from the opportunity to interact with other humans in a natural environment, then homeschooling provides a sterling chance to gain the social skills that can prepare your child for a well-adjusted adulthood. Homeschooling gives your child the chance to experience life as it is lived, rather than institutionalization for six hours each day. Your child gets to socialize with people of all different ages and various walks of life throughout the day as he accompanies you to the post office, greets the FedEx-delivery person at the door, and participates in co-op classes across town.

Homeschool children don't feel threatened when they come into contact with younger or older children because, in their world, people come in all shapes, sizes, and ages. A 12-year-old homeschooler can interact just as easily with a 5-year-old as she can with a 16-year-old because, in her eyes, age doesn't segregate people. Isn't this the kind of socialization that you want your kids to experience?

I will buy the wrong curriculum.

Take a deep breath. Homeschoolers buy the wrong curriculum sooner or later. It happens. It happened to me, it happened to nearly every homeschooler I know, and it's part of life.

The problem only occurs if you *keep* buying the wrong curriculum even after you know it doesn't fit your child. Because every child is different, some books, approaches, and projects work better with one child than they do another. Often you have the extremes right in your own household, like I do. I purchase the curriculums for a few subjects with both children in mind, but I need to buy other curriculums from separate publishers because my children learn differently.

If you have more than one child, and you buy the "wrong" curriculum for the oldest one or two, you can always keep it around in the hopes that a younger child may use the curriculum. When I purchase something for one child and it doesn't work, I try it with the other one awhile to see if it clicks. With children only one grade level apart, I can do that, and it minimizes my off purchases.

Purchasing one year's books at a time also helps to minimize the damage. If you buy a language-arts curriculum that does *not* click with your child this year, you can always struggle through (maybe with some homegrown modifications) and try another publisher next year. Deciding that a new curriculum is the best thing since sliced zucchini and purchasing all eight years' worth without testing it out first may be a waste of money if your little darling doesn't like it or if the new curriculum presents information in a way that your child doesn't comprehend.

If you find yourself with a stack of unusable books after the beginning of a school year, you can always pass them along to a homeschooler who needs them, donate them to your local homeschool lending library, or sell them used through your area vendor or an online swap shop, such as VegSource (Internet: www.vegsource.com). Although the curriculum doesn't fit your child, someone will be delighted to get it because it matches that child's needs.

My child will learn less at home than he does at school.

If you took your child out of school because he wasn't learning, then you already know how little information your child amassed at school. You also know that with a little effort you can match or exceed that level at home. Good for you!

Most parents who worry about a child's learning levels are the ones who never sent their children to school in the first place. They somehow think that those hours spent poring over math books, learning parts of speech, and dissecting tulips this past spring count for less because they were done at home. Or maybe they believe that the schools teach something that they can't duplicate at home.

Relax. As long as you select a grade-level book for the year and follow it, your child can learn at least as much as her school-aged peers. Because you don't have to keep pace with the slowest child in the class, you actually have the freedom to work at your child's pace. In some courses, that may mean taking a year-and-a-half to finish a textbook, but when you're done you know that your child understands the material. He didn't simply read the words and move on.

In other classes, you may stay right on target or even do a book and a half within a year's time. If your child assimilates science quickly, and you find yourself moving through the science book faster than you thought, you can always take the extra time to incorporate experiments into the class instead of moving to the next book.

One way to keep tabs on your child's grade levels, even if your state doesn't require it, is to give your child a standardized test each year. That gives you a general idea how your child regurgitates information and applies knowledge based on the current national norms. If your child scores above 50 percent on a standardized test, that means that he performed as well as or better than half the students who took the test. Not a very minute way of measuring progress, but it may ease your mind.

I'll never have free time again.

Oh, sure you will. And it may even happen before they graduate!

Actually, one of the best things you can do for your kids — as well as for yourself — is to carve out a niche of time each week especially for you. Maybe that means watching a movie *you* want to see one evening after the kids go to bed. Perhaps you leave all the darlings in the care of your spouse and go shopping for a couple hours.

 Because I rarely get away during the daylight hours, I tend to do my shopping at stores that remain open all night or at least until ten. Thus, I find myself wandering the scrapbook aisle at Wal-Mart more often than not, picking new colors and gathering ideas for my next *pièce de résistance* the next time I drag out the paper and scalloped scissors. Wouldn't it be nice if other stores catered to nocturnal shoppers?

When you take a couple hours to do whatever you want to do (within reason, of course), you return to the job-at-hand refreshed and ready to go. You don't have to take a really long break. Sometimes soaking for an hour with your favorite novel does the trick. The very fact that you thought enough of *you* to schedule some alone time does your heart good.

My child may not be learning at the right pace.

As long as your child is learning, adding new skills to the ones already mastered, then you're doing fine. After all, what is the "right" pace for learning? That depends on whom you talk to.

If you want your child to actually learn the material, it may take a bit longer than breezing through the pages and marking them with checks to show you read them. The best learning involves active participation. Instead of reading through the sample math problem, your child needs to complete a couple problems on his own so he really knows how it's done.

The parent of a special-needs scholar takes learning at the child's own pace. This student covers material one concept at a time until it's all mastered. Sometimes it moves quickly; on other days, it goes pretty slow. As a tutor, you can do the same with your child. If she catches onto a concept quickly and gives you that bored I've-got-it-already look, you can safely move on. If she struggles to master another concept, then you can take as long as you need to master it before you continue. If you stick with it day after day, you'll probably still get through the book before the end of the year or close to it.

I won't be able to do it all.

Of course you won't be able to do it all. Nobody does it *all* and stays sane. It's impossible to homeschool every day, cook a six-course meal each evening, mow the lawn twice a week, clean the house till it's spotless on the weekend, wax the dog on Saturdays, and hand buff the car every other week while running a home business and decorating the house to look like a million bucks.

Lives like this only happen with A-squared personalities or in the movies. A-squared personalities have way too much stress in their lives to be healthy, and the movies don't happen in real life. In real life, you find yourself cleaning up the spilled cereal milk while engaging in a futile effort to catch the dog — futile because you waxed him yesterday. I can't tell you the last time I went out to dinner with a Hollywood star (well, I could tell you but you wouldn't believe me). However, I do recall the day that I homeschooled for four hours, mopped the kitchen floor, and made a dinner that was more than a casserole with a side salad.

So rest in the knowledge that nobody real gets it all done every day. Pick your priorities and go with those. If a spotless house is high on your list, make that a priority and encourage everybody to pitch in to make it happen. On the other hand, if you'd rather wax the dog and run a home business while you homeschool, the house will probably look lived in most of the time. (Is that so bad, if you truly live there?) The dog, however, consistently shines.

After I start, I have to do this forever.

Nope. Not so. You don't even *have* to finish the year out although sticking with homeschooling one year at a time is probably the wisest thing you can do. Giving up on a three-month-old experiment doesn't tell you much except that you quit before the end of the year. Sticking it out until spring tells you more — you have an idea where your strengths lie, what your weaknesses may be (in curriculum, planning, or even other areas), and the facets of your homeschool that you may change next year — if there is a next year.

Most homeschoolers teach one year at a time. Very few start out in preschool declaring that they plan to do this through college. Your child may only need to be home for a year or two before you send her back to school. Or you may decide to teach for the first eight years at home and send him to high school.

What is the best plan for your family? No matter what the plan looks like, that is the plan you should follow. If it means taking it one year at a time until you look up one day and your oldest is nearing the end of her senior year, then that's great! But if you teach your child at home for the first three years and then decide he has enough of a head start to move into the school system, then that's just as good.

As long as your decision strengthens your family and meets your needs as a family unit, then it's the right decision and you homeschooled just long enough.

I'm not keeping the right (or enough) records on my child's progress.

If you're tracking whatever your state asks you to track, then you're probably doing all right. Your state may require attendance records and immunization records only — keep those up to date and nobody can argue with you. On the other hand, if you live in a state that wants you to keep track of each book that you use, to keep a file for a portion of your child's worksheets and creative writing, and you do it, you're fine.

Most of us struggle with the paper concept: More is better — the more records, worksheets, poems, coloring pages, and construction-paper creations that are kept on file, the better. Actually, as long as you keep the *right* snippets of paper, you can happily throw the rest of the stuff away with a clear conscience.

If you have a high schooler, then you need to track individual courses, textbooks (with authors), grades, and sometimes hours of instruction, depending on your state law. This is the information that you use to create the high-school transcript for colleges and other post-secondary schools.

Part VII

Appendixes

The 5th Wave   By Rich Tennant

"Okay - mommy's going off now to build a Boeing B-29 Superfortress. You kids behave or I'll bring my rivet gun home with me."

In this part . . .

*E*ver search through a chest and look for the doodad that you're sure that you squirreled away back in 1984? You empty the contents of that extra-special box in the closet. Even blanket chests only hold so much; after they're full, you need to look at other options.

The appendixes in this part, like the extra-special box, hold the information that didn't logically fit anywhere else. Look for educational and homeschooling terms in the glossary — if you want a term that you can't locate there, you'll probably find it as the topic of one of the individual chapters. (A sneaky way to get you to read the rest of the book, eh?)

Also turn to the Appendix B when you need to find a homeschool organization for your state. (Or to find state-specific homeschool organization.) Additional curriculum providers and resources are also listed in this part.

Appendix A
Homeschooling Curriculum and Resources

*L*ook at the following descriptions and contact information for those organizations and resources that I couldn't fit anywhere else in this book: national homeschooling organizations, homeschool book publishers, religious-specific curriculum, and gadgets to make your day easier.

A Beka

One of the classic Christian publishers and a division of Pensacola Christian College, A Beka sells student books, workbooks, and teacher's texts to interested homeschool families. These books cover a full curriculum from kindergarten through twelfth grade. You can purchase as many or as few books as you like; their *Nation Notebook* and *My State Notebook* volumes have pre-planned scrapbook pages to help fourth graders on up construct a multipage report about a country or state. For more information, call 877-223-5226 or visit their Web site: www.abeka.com.

Artes Latinae

Artes Latinae gives students two full years of high school Latin and plenty of reading practice. An audiotape with a book is available, or you can get a CD/CD-ROM with book combination. Two levels are available, and you can purchase them together or separately. Contact Bolchazy-Carducci Publishers (also the producers of *The Cat in the Hat* and *How The Grinch Stole Christmas* in Latin) by calling 800-392-6453 or visit their Web site at www.bolchazy.com/alindex.html.

Behrman House

Look to Behrman House for Hebrew textbooks on Jewish religious studies and for books to help you teach Jewish tradition to your children, 5 years of age on up. The New Siddur Program offers a Hebrew prayer book primer that has excerpts of those prayers translated into English to help your child's comprehension. To teach your third or fourth grader how to speak modern Hebrew, get *Shalom Uvrachah,* a new Hebrew primer. Companion flashcards and posters are also available. For more information, call 800-221-2755 or go online at www.behrmanhouse.com.

Brother Backster Lx570

If you make your own flashcards, crafts, or teaching games for your kids, you may want to know about this product. It uses no electricity, no batteries, and you can buy cartridges that turn this little machine into a laminator, sticker maker, magnet creator, or sticker with laminated front. The laminating and sticker film is only five inches wide, so your creations need to be that size or smaller, but it saves you multiple trips to the local educational store to have your latest creation laminated. Call 877-552-MALL to place your order or visit their Web site: www.brother.com.

California Homeschool Network Companion CD

California homeschoolers may want to check into this CD-ROM, which contains all the forms you need to file as a private school under California educational law. The CD also includes planning forms to help you keep your homeschool on track. Go to the California Homeschool Network Web site: www.cahomeschoolnet.org.

Critical Thinking Books and Software

Interested in teaching your children problem solving skills? Then take a look at the books from Critical Thinking. They offer logic, word problems, and other books that teach creative thinking. To order, call 800-458-4849 or go to the Internet: www.criticalthinking.com.

Great Books Academy

The Great Books Academy online store is a great place to unearth Harcourt and Glencoe (public school) science texts for various grade levels, if you want a nonreligious science curriculum. You can also find some good classic reading material, divided by grade level, as well as the *Developmental Math* curriculum, books to develop map skills, and much more. This site gives you a one-stop-shop alternative for many of the books usually sold directly to schools; this way you skip the potential hassles that come with educational publishers who aren't used to individual sales. Contact Harcourt and Glencoe's online store at www.greatbooksacademy.org.

Greenleaf Press

In addition to a great history curriculum, the folks at Greenleaf Press also offer a great stock of reading material on history available at practically every reading level. Whether you study the Trojan horse in the third grade or the eighth, Greenleaf Press carries a book to meet your needs — the Childhood of Famous Americans books, Landmark history series, plus many other options for filling out your history curriculum. Some of the books contain Christian content; the Christian books are usually identifiable through the book descriptions. To find out more or to order, call 800-311-1508 or visit on the Internet: www.greenleafpress.com.

Hebrew Home School

Kitah Babayit Hebrew Home School provides a curriculum so that parents can teach Hebrew and Judaism as part of homeschool. The curriculum includes Hebrew instruction, lessons on Judaism, and instruction required for Bar/Bat Mitzvah. The curriculum is customized for individual learners. To learn more about their curriculums, call 952-473-1201 or visit their Web site: www.creativesoftwareinc.com/hhs.

Home School Legal Defense Association (HSLDA)

The Home School Legal Defense Association (HSLDA) is a Christian legal group that defends member homeschool families in court if necessary. The association staff also lobbies extensively and sends out periodic legislative updates. Visit their Web site at www.hslda.com.

Home Science Adventures

These folks send you a kit that lets your kids conduct once-a-week science experiments for a year. If the idea of hands-on science intrigues you and your children are in grades one through eight, this science company may intrigue you. To place your order, visit on the Internet: www.homeschoolscience.com.

The Learnables Foreign Language

The Learnables uses audiocassettes and companion books to teach foreign language. Students listen to words and sentences spoken by a native speaker and look at a corresponding picture that describes the action or event. Available for nine different languages, these were designed with the auditory learner in mind. Call 800-237-1830 to place your order, or take a look at the Web site: www.learnables.com.

LessonPlanz.com

This is one of many lesson plan sites that link you to free unit studies, lesson worksheets, and more. This particular site links you to unit studies for practically every event you could think of, from voting to Thanksgiving. Plus it also lets you browse for lesson plans by grade level. Because this site was created with classroom teachers in mind, you may need to scale down some of the ideas, but this Web site gives you a place to start: www.lessonplanz.com.

To find other lesson sites online, search the Web with the term "free lesson plan." You're guaranteed to unearth more ideas than you have time to use!

Mary Frances Books

You probably won't find these listed in any curriculum catalog. Originally written between 1912 and 1918, these little volumes taught girls about home arts: cooking, gardening, housekeeping, knitting and crocheting, and sewing. Each book covers one topic, and it does it in a story format. So, for example, Mary Frances learns about sewing as she enters into an adventure with the Thimble People; Sewing Bird and all her friends teach little Mary Frances to sew by hand and make clothes for her doll along the way. Because these books are complete reprints, they're good tools to teach your students about the attitudes and customs of the time as well as giving you hands-on volumes to help with those home economics skills. After looking at everything currently available, I bought these for my daughter. To find out more, go to the publisher's Web site: www.lacis.com.

MindWare

Interested in purchasing a parachute for your support group's physical education class? How about a handbook on theater games to stimulate creativity and movement? Maybe brain-stretching books on logic or a manual about teaching tessellations interests you more. MindWare carries all kinds of thought-provoking games and toys that add zing to your homeschool. Call 800-999-0398 or go on the Internet: www.mindwareonline.com.

National Black Home Educators Resource Association

This national organization helps new homeschoolers locate their state laws. In addition, the association's staff answers questions about homeschooling and points families towards the resources they need to teach their children at home. The National Black Home Educators Resource Association is located at 6943 Stoneview Avenue in Baker, LA 70714; Phone: 225-778-0169; E-mail: nbhera@internet8.net.

National Curriculum

If you're interested in some unique ideas to spark your students' interest in learning, you may try the United Kingdom's National Curriculum Web site. You can find lesson plans, suggestions for covering the subjects, and Web sites that discuss physical education, music, art, religious studies, and much more. Spend a day or two investigating the Romans, Britain, or the Victorians. When I'm out of ideas, I turn to this Web site for inspiration: www.nc.uk.net.

National Home Education Network

If your family is part of the military, the National Home Education Network compiled a whole list of useful resources on their Web site. Visit the site to determine whose state or country laws you follow, how to locate support groups on the installation, and an overview of the military regulations as they apply to homeschooling. To find some very useful information, go online to www.nhen.org/nhen/pov/military.

Native American Homeschool Association

Parents who want to teach their children Native American traditions may be interested in the Native American Homeschool Association. This national group wants to design a homeschool curriculum that contains the subjects necessary to meet state guidelines along with subject matter on Native American traditions. To find out more, write to P.O. Box 979, Fries, Virginia 24330, or visit the association's Web site: http://expage.com/page/nahomeschool.

Rainbow Resource Center

This catalog is a biggie: almost 400 pages of homeschool appropriate curriculum, toys, and add-ons. The book includes curriculum for everybody: While much of the first section (called Homeschool Helps) includes primarily Christian homeschooling information, regardless of your reasons for homeschooling, you can find an abundance that you can use after you get into the subject matter (the other 375 pages). From science kits to math books and beyond, this catalog carries a huge cross section of what's available and almost all at discounted prices. Rainbow Resource is definitely a catalog for your homeschool stack. Call 888-841-3456 or visit the Rainbow Web site: www.rainbowresource.com.

Robinson Curriculum

This much-advertised curriculum says that you can spend about $200 and use the 22 CD-ROMs in this set to teach your children through grade twelve. Basically, the CDs contain out-of-print science textbooks, a 1911 encyclopedia, plus a couple hundred out-of-print children's books and classic texts. You need to provide your own math curriculum. The author suggests that you print out and bind each book on CD — this will cost you in the four-figure range for printer cartridges, paper, and bindings if you print it all. I know many homeschoolers who bought this curriculum and very, very few who actually use it as it is intended. Most of them keep the CDs as a resource to print out occasional reading material for their children. Check out the curriculum's Web site at www.robinsoncurriculum.com.

Science Weekly

Think of it as a weekly science newsletter. Published 16 times a year, *Science Weekly* arrives at your house every other week or so. Each issue focuses on a different topic. One week you may study the history and science of the circus, and then a few weeks later, you take an in-depth look at chocolate. Individual issues for grades pre-K through eight include games, experiments, puzzles, and information. My children absolutely loved this newsletter. Steck-Vaughn publishes *Science Weekly*. To subscribe, call 800-531-5015 or go on the Web at www.scienceweekly.com.

Sing 'n Learn

Do you not know where to turn because your children memorize best through song lyrics? Sing 'n Learn is a company that sells materials created for the auditory learner. Sing songs about history, geography, or grammar. The Geography Songs kit, for example, puts the name of every country to music. You learn to sing the songs while you identify the countries on a map. To learn more about Sing 'n Learn products, call 800-460-1973 or visit their Web site at www.singnlearn.com.

Appendix B

State by State Homeschool Associations

● ●

*T*he associations in this Appendix usually offer support, tips, a monthly or bi-monthly newsletter, and can act as a clearinghouse for field trip organization. Sometimes they organize statewide homeschool conventions each spring or summer. If you need a copy of your state homeschool law, one of these groups is likely to have one.

As you read the listings (in alphabetical order by state) in the following Table B-1, you'll see the word *inclusive*, which means that the homeschooling association delights in diversity — you are not required to follow a specific religion, teaching style, or dress code to join. In those instances where the association's affiliation is left blank, however, the association claims none.

Table B-1	Homeschool Associations	
Name of Organization	*Affiliation*	*Contact Information*
Central **Alabama** Resource for Home Educators	Inclusive	Internet: www.geocities.com/ Athens/Agora/7633/cafsg. html.
Home Educators of **Alabama** Round Table (HEART)	Inclusive	P.O. Box 55182, Birmingham, AL 35255; Internet: www. educationalfreedom. com/heart.
Alaska Private and Home Educators Association	Christian	P.O. Box 141764, Anchorage, AK 99514; Internet: www.aphea.org.
Apache Junction Unschoolers (**AZ**)	Unschooling	P.O. Box 2880, Apache Junction, AZ 85217; Internet: http:// members.aol.com/ ajunschl/index.htm.

(continued)

Table B-1 *(continued)*

Name of Organization	Affiliation	Contact Information
Arizona Families for Home Education	Christian	P.O. Box 2035, Chandler, AZ 85244-2035; Internet: www.afhe.org.
Home Educators of **Arkansas**		P.O. Box 192455, Little Rock, AR 72219; Internet: www.geocities.com/Heartland/Garden/4555.
Live and Learn (**AR**)	Inclusive	Internet: www.geocities.com/live-and-learn.geo.
California Homeschool Network	Inclusive	P.O. Box 55485, Hayward, CA 94545, call 800-327-5339 in California; Internet: www.cahomeschoolnet.org.
CHEA (Christian Home Educators Association) (**CA**)	Christian	P.O. Box 2009, Norwalk, CA 90651-2009, call 800-564-CHEA; Internet: www.cheaofca.org.
Home School Association of **California**	Inclusive	P.O. Box 868, Davis, CA 95617; Internet: www.hsc.org.
Christian Home Educators of **Colorado**	Christian	10431 South Parker Road, Parker, CO 80134; Internet: www.chec.org.
Secular Homeschool Support Group (**CO**)	Inclusive	Call 719-749-9126; Internet: http://shssg.home.mindspring.com/Support.htm.
Connecticut Home Educator's Association	Inclusive	Call 203-781-8569; Internet: www.cthomeschoolers.com.
The Education Association of Christian Homeschoolers of **Connecticut** (TEACH)	Christian	Call 860-793-9968; Internet: www.teachct.org.
Delaware Home Education Association	Christian	500 N. Dual Highway, PMB 415, Seaford, DE 19973; Call 302-337-0990.
Tri-State Homeschool Network (**DE**)		P.O. Box 7193, Newark, DE 19714; Call 302-234-0516.
Florida Inclusive Home Education Network	Inclusive	Internet: http://fihen.org/fihen.

Name of Organization	Affiliation	Contact Information
Florida Parent-Educator's Association		P.O. Box 50685, Jacksonville Beach, FL 32240-0685; Call 877-ASK-FPEA; Internet: www.fpea.com.
Georgia Home Education Association	Christian	245 Buckeye Lane, Fayetteville, GA 30214; Internet: www.ghea.org.
Home Education Information Resource (**GA**)	Inclusive	P.O. Box 2111, Roswell, GA 30077-2111; Internet: www.heir.org.
Hawaii Homeschool Association	Inclusive	P.O. Box 893476, Mililani, HI 96789; Internet: www.geocities.com/Heartland/Hollow/4239.
Christian Homeschoolers of **Idaho** State	Christian	P.O. Box 45062, Boise, ID 83711-5062; Internet: www.chois.org.
Idaho Coalition of Home Educators		5415 Kendall Street, Boise, ID 83706; Internet: www.homeschoolwatch.com/id/iche.htm.
Christian Home Educators Coalition (**IL**)	Christian	P.O. Box 47322, Chicago, IL 60647-0322; Call 773-278-0673; Internet: www.chec.cc.
Illinois H.O.U.S.E. (Home Oriented Unique Schooling Experience)	Inclusive	E-mail: Illinois_house@hotmail.com; Internet: www.geocities.com/Athens/Acropolis/7804.
Indiana Home Educators Association	Christian	8106 Madison Avenue, Indianapolis, IN 46227; Call 317-859-1202; Internet: www.inhomeeducators.org.
Michiana L.I.F.E. (Learning in Family Environment) Homeschooling Support (**IN**)	Inclusive	Internet: www.geocities.com/Heartland/Trail/3405.
Iowans Dedicated to Educational Alternatives	Inclusive	P.O. Box 17, Teeds Grove, IA 52771; Internet: http://home.plutonium.net/~pdiltz/idea.
NICHE (The Network of **Iowa** Christian Home Educators)	Christian	Box 158, Dexter, IA 50070; Internet: www.the-niche.org.

(continued)

Table B-1 (continued)

Name of Organization	Affiliation	Contact Information
Christian Home Educators Confederation of **Kansas**	Christian	Internet: www.kansashomeschool.org.
Christian Home Educators of **Kentucky**	Christian	Internet: www.chek.org.
Kentucky Home Education Association	Inclusive	P.O. BOX 81, Winchester, KY 40392-0081; Internet: ww4.choice.net/~buglet/KHEApage/KHEAhome.html.
CHEF of **Louisiana**	Christian	Call 888-876-CHEF; Internet: www.chefofla.org.
Louisiana Home Education Network	Inclusive	PMB 700, 602 W. Prien Lake Rd, Lake Charles, LA 70601; Internet: www.la-home-education.com.
Home Schoolers of **Maine**	Christian	337 Hatchet Mountain Road, Hope, ME 04847; Internet: www.homeschool-maine.org.
Maine Home Education Association	Inclusive	56 Long Hill Road, Gray, ME 04039, or call 207-657-6018; Internet: www.geocities.com/mainehomeed.
Christian Home Educators Network (**MD**)	Christian	1153 Circle Drive, Baltimore, MD 21227; Internet: www.chenmd.org.
Maryland Home Education Association	Inclusive	9085 Flamepool Way, Columbia, MD 21045; Call 410-730-0073; Internet: www.mhea.com.
Massachusetts Home Learning Association	Inclusive	P.O. Box 1558, Marston's Mills, MA 02648; Internet: www.mhla.org.
Massachusetts Homeschool Organization of Parent Educators	Christian	5 Atwood Road, Cherry Valley, MA 01611; Call 508-755-4467; Internet: www.masshope.org.
Michigan Homeschoolers	Inclusive	Internet: www.michiganhomeschoolers.homestead.com.

Name of Organization	Affiliation	Contact Information
Cultural Home Educators Association (**MN**)	Inclusive	2324 University Avenue #103, St. Paul, MN 55104; Call 651-408-1810 or 612-282-8032; Internet: www.happyhomeschoolers.com.
Minnesota Association of Christian Home Educators	Christian	Call 952-717-9070; Internet: www.mache.org.
Home Educators of Central **Mississippi**		1500 Beverly Drive, Clinton, MS 39056-3507; Internet: www2.netdoor.com/~nfgcgrb/home_educators_of_central_ms.html.
Missouri Association of Teaching Christian Homes	Christian	Call 417-255-2824; Internet: www.match-inc.org.
Montana Coalition of Home Educators	Inclusive	Box 43, Gallatin Gateway, MT 59730; Internet: www.mtche.org.
Nebraska Christian Home Educators Association	Christian	P.O. Box 57041, Lincoln, Nebraska 68505-7041; Internet: www.nchea.org.
Homeschool Melting Pot (**NV**)	Inclusive	1000 N. Green Valley Pkwy. #440-231, Henderson, NV 89014; Call 702-320-4840; Internet: www.angelfire.com/nv/homeschoolmeltingpot/index.html.
Northern **Nevada** Home Schools	Christian	P.O. Box 21323, Reno, NV 89515; Call 775-852-NNHS; Internet: www.angelfire.com/nv/NNHS.
Christian Home Educators of **New Hampshire**	Christian	P.O. Box 961, Manchester, NH 03105; Internet: www.mv.com/ipusers/chenh.
New Hampshire Home Schooling Coalition	Inclusive	P.O. Box 2224, Concord, NH 03302; Internet: www.nhhomeschooling.org.
Education Network of Christian Home-schoolers of **New Jersey**	Christian	P.O. Box 308, Atlantic Highlands, NJ 07716; Call 732-291-7800; Internet: www.enochnj.org.
New Jersey Homeschool Association	Inclusive	P.O. Box 1386, Medford, NJ 08055; Internet: www.geocities.com/Athens/Agora/3009.

(continued)

Table B-1 *(continued)*

Name of Organization	Affiliation	Contact Information
Christian Association of Parent Educators – **New Mexico**	Christian	P.O. Box 25046, Albuquerque, NM 87125; Internet: www.cape-nm.org.
Apple Family and Homeschooling Group **(NY)**		P.O. Box 2036, No. Babylon, NY 11703; Internet: www.geocities.com/applefamilygroup/apple.html.
Loving Education at Home (LEAH) **(NY)**	Christian	Internet: www.leah.org.
North Carolinians for Home Education		419 N Boylan Avenue, Raleigh, NC 27603-1211; Call 919-834-6243; Internet: www.nche.org.
North Dakota Home School Association		Box 7400, Bismarck, ND 58507-7400.
Christian Home Educators of **Ohio**	Christian	117 W. Main Street, Ste. #103 Lancaster, OH 43130; Call 740-654-3331; Internet: www.cheohome.org.
Ohio Home Educators Network	Inclusive	P.O. Box 38132, Olmsted Falls, OH 44138-8132; Internet: http://grafixbynix.com/ohen.
Eclectic Home Educators **(OK)**	Inclusive	Internet: http://eclectichomeeducators.faithweb.com.
Oklahoma Christian Home Educators' Consociation	Christian	3801 NW 63rd Street, Building 3, Suite 236, Oklahoma City, OK 73116; Call 405-810-0386; Internet: www.telepath.com/ochec.
Oregon Christian Home Education Association Network	Christian	17985 Falls City Road, Dallas, OR 97338; Internet: www.teleport.com/~oceanet.
Oregon Home Education Network	Inclusive	OHEN, P.O. Box 218, Beaverton, OR 97075-0218; Call 503-321-5166; Internet: www.teleport.com/~ohen.

Name of Organization	Affiliation	Contact Information
Christian Home School Association of **Pennsylvania**	Christian	P.O. Box 115, Mount Joy, PA 17552-0115; Internet: www. chapboard.org.
Pennsylvania Home Education Network	Inclusive	285 Allegheny Street, Meadville, PA 16335; Internet: www.pgh. net/~ctellis/pahs/ groups/phen.html.
Rhode Island Guild of Home Teachers		P.O. Box 11, Hope, RI 02831; Internet: http://members. tripod.com/righthome.
Homeward Education Association (**SC**)		4940 Dubose Siding Rd., Sumter, SC 29153; Call 803-469-4511; Internet: www.homewarded.com.
South Carolina Association of Independent Home Schools		930 Knox Abbott Drive, Cayce, SC 29033; Call 803-454-0427; Internet: www.scaihs.org.
South Dakota Home School Association		P.O. Box 882, Sioux Falls, SD 57101.
Eclectic Homeschoolers of **Tennessee**	Inclusive	Call 615-889-4938.
Middle **Tennessee** Home Education Association	Christian	Box 1382, Franklin, TN 37065; Internet: www.mthea.org.
Texas Home Educators		Internet: www. texashomeeducators.com.
Texas Home School Coalition	Christian	P.O. Box 6747, Lubbock, TX 79493, call 806-744-4441; Internet: www. thsc.org.
Utah Christian Home School Association (U-TeaCH)	Christian	P.O. Box 3942, Salt Lake City, UT 84110-3942; Call 801-296-7198; Internet: www.utch.org.
Utah Home Education Association	Inclusive	P.O. Box 1492 Riverton, UT 84065-1492; Internet: www. utah-uhea.org.
Christian Home Educators of **Vermont**	Christian	146 Sherwood Circle, Brattleboro, VT 05301; Internet: www. christianity.com/chev.

(continued)

Table B-1 *(continued)*

Name of Organization	Affiliation	Contact Information
Vermont Association of Home Educators	Inclusive	RR 1, Box 847, Bethel, VT 05032.
Home Educators Association of **Virginia**	Christian	Call 804-288-1608; Internet: www.heav.org.
Virginia Home Educators Association	Inclusive	P.O. Box 5131, Charlottesville, VA 22905; call 540-832-3578; Internet: www.vhea.org.
Washington Association of Teaching Christian Homes	Christian	1026 224th Avenue N.E., Sammamish, WA 98074; Call 206-729-4804; Internet: www.watchhome.org.
Washington Homeschool Association	Inclusive	6632 S. 191st Place, Suite E-100, Kent, WA 98032-211; Internet: www.washhomeschool.org.
Christian Home Educators of **West Virginia**	Christian	Internet: www.geocities.com/Athens/Forum/8045.
West Virginia Home Education Association	Inclusive	Call 800-736-WVHEA; Internet: www.wvheahome.homestead.com.
Wisconsin Christian Home Educators Association	Christian	2307 Carmel Avenue, Racine, WI 53405; Call 262-637-5127; Internet: www.wisconsinchea.com.
Wisconsin Parents Association	Inclusive	Call 608-283-3131; Internet: www.homeschooling-wpa.org.
Homeschoolers of **Wyoming**		P.O. Box 3151, Jackson, WY 83001; Call 307-733-2834.
Wyoming Homeschoolers		P.O. Box 1386, Lyman, WY 82937.

Appendix C

Speaking the Language: Glossary of Educational and Homeschooling Terms

. . . .

*O*nce in a while, you stumble across a term that may as well be written in a foreign language. Like any group of people who concentrate on one thing, both education and homeschooling have a vocabulary of their own. (It happens everywhere: Have you been to an engineering conference recently?) This is where you turn when you come across a word or concept that you hear thrown about in homeschooling (or educational) circles. If you're looking for a word that you can't find here, see the index.

accelerated learning

Accelerated learning means to run through a certain set of materials faster than normal. Sometimes this happens almost by accident. Perhaps you have an 8-year-old child who is already learning high school algebra because she assimilates the information so quickly. Most of the time, however, accelerated learning is structured. One way to structure accelerated learning is to teach year-round without taking a summer break. Teaching year-round gives you about three school years for each two calendar years.

auditory learner

An *auditory learner* (someone who learns best by listening) parrots song lyrics, memorizes radio shows, and relates movie dialog effortlessly. If you have an auditory learner at your house, you'll find that music, tapes, videos, and computer programs — anything the child can hear rather than see — work best for teaching your child.

consumable

If a book is *consumable* the author expects you to write in it as you use it. Consumable books do *not* carry a permission-to-reproduce statement because the publisher wants you to purchase one for each child who uses the book. In fact, most consumables contain two or four color pages, which makes photocopying less than satisfactory if you do attempt it. Take the plunge. If you plan to use the book this year, buy it and use it as it was intended. Or find a nonconsumable book that offers the same information.

correlated to state standards

Big phrase, eh? If a book is *correlated to state standards*, it means that the content of that book matches what an individual state (or group of states) determined should be taught at a specific grade level. You also may see *correlated to national and state standards*. For example, "This book on dog grooming is correlated to state standards." It meets or exceeds the requirements for your state's mandatory fourth-grade course on pets.

distance learning

If you physically take classes somewhere other than the school that offers them, it's called *distance learning*. Basically, distance learning is the new term for correspondence course, but it also can incorporate much more, such as interactive Web tutorials, videos, and so on. Usually, organizations that cater to homeschools use the term *satellite school* or *umbrella school* rather than distance education or distance learning to describe their programs. You see the term distance learning sometimes at the high school level, and definitely beyond. For example, "My distance learning course takes place in a Web chat room this semester."

educational game

Educational games are teaching tools poorly disguised as entertainment. Some companies produce games specifically for the educational establishment, and these are the games no one wants to play. An educational game designed to teach geography, for example, takes geography terms and facts and incorporates them into game pieces that shove the details down the player's throat — *not* to be confused with a game, such as Empire Builder, where the student learns geography almost as a side issue while playing a great game. As a general guideline, if the box says, "An Educational Game" along the side, avoid it like the plague unless someone you trust recommends it to you.

inclusive

Just as you may surmise, this means that everybody's invited. The term *inclusive* arose from the frustrations homeschoolers felt at being excluded from this support group or that organization due to religious or educational beliefs. The inclusive groups try to welcome everyone as long as they homeschool. Inclusive groups state no religious, ethnic, or educational methodology stipulations on would-be members.

intent to homeschool

This is a simple letter or form that you send to your educational officials, usually the superintendent of your local schools. It explains that you plan to remove your child and teach them at home. Not all states require an *intent-to-homeschool* letter; so be sure to check your state law or call your state homeschool association before you send anything.

ISP (Independent Study Program)

Students enrolled in an ISP contract with a private school that provides oversight to a homeschooling family. This option is popular in California because it allows families to escape the paperwork headaches of forming their own private school. ISPs may provide curriculum along with the oversight, or they may simply keep paperwork and offer their accredited credentials to anyone who asks for an enrolled family's homeschool verification.

kinesthetic learner

The *kinesthetic* (also *kinetic*) *learner* understands best when he does it himself. This is a hands-on child who learns by doing. If your child gives you a blank look when you talk about fractions, for example, but understands after you hand him construction paper halves and help him to fit them together into a whole, then you have an example of kinesthetic learning. A child who responds well with hands-on exercises time after time, subject after subject, probably qualifies as a kinesthetic learner.

The educational establishment really isn't equipped to deal with kinesthetic learners because school education is basically a book-and-lecture experience. Teaching a kinesthetic learner requires creativity as you devise physical explanations for the subject matter that you need to teach. But it can be plenty of fun — fractions become particularly tasty when you apply them to cooking class.

lesson plan

Basically, a *lesson plan* is a list of what you plan to do today for a particular subject. If your state requires lesson plans (this would occur if you're assigned to an oversight teacher from the local school district as part of state regulations), then you jot down what you do during class time.

Lesson plans can be formal or informal; the most informal lesson plan is abbreviated, such as Sci pg 5–6; q. 1–4. Translated, that means you open the science book to pages five and six and cover those, and then complete questions one through four as a review.

More formal lesson plans include a title (the name of the lesson plan), an objective (what you plan to teach), and a procedure (how you plan to get there). The procedure is the longest part and usually consists of several steps. I know very few people who go to this level of detail when they plan their day. If you want this kind of planning, enroll as a satellite school and let the school send you completed lesson plans.

Raymond Moore

Raymond Moore, one of home education's pioneers, advocates allowing children to learn in a supportive family environment at their own pace. Thousands of homeschoolers have read Moore's books, *Home Style Teaching* and *Successful Homeschool Family Handbook*.

real books

This term refers to subject books as opposed to textbooks. A textbook on science, for example, may contain chapters on clouds, weather, planets, and trees. *Real books* for the same subjects would include an introductory volume on clouds, a book that discusses weather, a guide to the solar system, and a book about plants and trees. Also known as *trade books*.

reproducible black line masters

Simply put, these are pages (usually in books) that you can photocopy and use as worksheets in your homeschool. If the book says *reproducible black line masters* on the front cover or title page, that means you have free permission to copy the pages as many times as you like to teach your children. Black line means that the pages are black print on white paper.

RU-4

The *RU-4* is a form that California requires from its homeschoolers each year. If California residents enroll with an ISP, the independent study program organization usually files the RU-4 for them.

standardized test

A test has been standardized when it's given to enough children across the country that similar test scores appear no matter where the test is administered. A *standardized test* tells you how your child performs on *this test* compared to children throughout the nation. When you receive a percentile rank score, it does not mean that your child got such-and-so percentage correct. What it means is that your child scored better on this test than the percentage number of students who took the test. Basically, it tells you that on the national average, your child scored at a certain point.

visual learner

The *visual learner* predominately understands what he sees. You can tell a visual learner what you want him to do all day long and get little response, but if you write a little sticky note and post it to the bathroom mirror, he responds. What visual learners hear may pass through their ears without even slowing down, but they remember what they read. Visual learners respond well to videos, computer programs, and books, because all have visual components — but if you try to teach a visual learner through an audio series that has no accompanying book, you ask for a fiasco.

Waldorf

You may hear the term *Waldorf education* bantered about in homeschool circles. The Waldorf system attempts to teach the whole child — the physical and emotional aspects of the child's personality as well as the academic. In a Waldorf school, a teacher may move up with the students from grade to grade to continue their education personally. This is probably one reason it appeals to homeschoolers so much because that's what they do by teaching at home. Creativity in the classroom becomes a reality as Waldorf advocates attempt to encourage learning in all avenues of a child's life. For more information, see the Web site for Association of Waldorf Schools of North America: www.awsna.org, or search the Web for Waldorf homeschool.

Index